A Dictionary Guide to American Visas*

Joseph I. Monye, Ph.D.

ISBN:

Reviews

Ms. C. Bell (USA)

A Dictionary Guide to American Visas by Dr. Joseph I. Monye is based on 45 years of involvement with immigration and weaves personal experience with critically important details to support readers' understanding of American citizenship. Complex information is organized in a clear, conversational tone, and examples enhance the text's lucidity. This is an important read for any American citizen hoping to better understand the immigrant experience.

Mr. J. McFadden (Ghana)

Personal Financial Planner

A Dictionary Guide to American Visas by Joseph I. Monye, Ph.D., is an invaluable resource for anyone seeking to understand the complexities of U.S. visas. What sets this book apart is the expertise of its author, who presents essential visa information in clear, straightforward language. This well-organized guide distills intricate legal details into an accessible format, potentially saving readers countless hours of research. Whether you are a student, traveler, or professional navigating the visa process, this book is an indispensable tool for gaining clarity and confidence in your journey.

Dr. J. Muti (Tanzania)

A Dictionary Guide to American Visas by Joseph I. Monye, Ph.D., is an outstanding resource that explicitly explains an immigrant's journey to the United States. The book is structured into sections that build on the core concept of immigration. The author incorporates research-based data and information to support his message, providing valuable insights into the immigration process while addressing common misconceptions. For potential or actual immigrants, this book offers detailed guidance on different visa categories and issuance policies. Additionally, the author highlights the role of legal representation in the immigration process, demonstrating a genuine commitment to presenting the realities of the journey with honesty and accuracy.

Ayandiji Daniel Aina, Ph.D. (Nigeria)

University Administrator and Youth Counsellor

March 19, 2025

A Dictionary Guide to American Visas is an excellent and timely book that offers fresh insight into the quest of millions of potential immigrants and non-immigrants seeking a legitimate understanding of the American visa system. Drawing from 45 years of experience as an African American immigrant, Dr. Joseph I. Monye provides a holistic perspective on the key factors influencing U.S. visa issuance and rejection. His background as a scholar and educator makes this book not only detailed and highly informative but also a vital consular advisory tool from a non-legal perspective. It serves as an encyclopedia of practical knowledge, exploring American culture, consular officers' expectations, and what to anticipate during visa interviews—without making unrealistic promises. Candid. Thorough. Expository. Didactic. Informative.

Dr. I. Dangleben (F.P.H.S. IEP Chief)

A Dictionary Guide to American Visas by Dr. Joseph I. Monye is a highly beneficial resource for anyone seeking to better understand the U.S. visa process and procedures. With his extensive knowledge of immigration policies, Dr. Monye presents clear and candid explanations that make complex legal concepts accessible. This well-structured guide simplifies intricate legal facts, providing readers with a solid foundation for navigating the immigration system with confidence.

Contents

Acknowledgements

This book has been forty-five years in the making. As soon as I arrived in the US, I immediately noticed my naivety. I had read the adventure fiction novel, Treasure Island by Robert L. Stevenson, and had imagined the San Francisco Golden Gate Bridge to be curated in gold! It was all a lie.
One summer afternoon, I had driven my newly purchased Honda Civic from Corpus Christi Texas on a cross-country drive into California and headed directly into San-Francisco. Bay area. My purpose? I wanted to see the Golden Gate Bridge up close. To my surprise, the bridge was not made of gold. Disappointed? Yes. But I remained in California and never went back to Texas. I continued to observe, learn, and read all that I could read about my new homeland, the United States of America.

Sometimes, I would recline and go into hiatus from writing, only to begin writing again after three to five years' subsequent summer breaks. As I near the completion of this book and its' eventual publication, I can't help but think about all those who have helped me along the way-either directly or tangentially. This section of the book is about acknowledging those who have been of help to me from the time of writing this book till the end. Almost all staff members of Forest Park High School, Baltimore, Maryland encouraged my development. They blurred the distinction between being born great teachers and being made great teachers and especially Ms C. Bell of the English department. I appropriated much of her instructional competencies and ideas to inform my practice. In the Math department, thanks to you, Ms. D. Zavela, Mr. Davis, Ms. Perez, Ms. Arana, and Ms. Womack. I have learned a lot from you guys, and especially, from the never-ending creative, ingenuity and innovative mind of school Principal N. Mouzone. I extend my sincere thanks and gratitude to the publishers at Xlibris in-house specialists. Although I have decided to self-publish this guidebook, and I have received much-needed help to enhance the readability of my manuscript and the quality of work, beginning with formatting, typesetting, and core design elements to publication packages and marketing advise.

I have been on this journey with you since the publication of my first book, exploring the Evolution of Special Education Practices: A Systems Approach (2013), to my most recent book, Purpose Driven Teacher: College and Career Readiness Mathematics Skills (2023). The American society has immensely benefited from its immigrant population. But, today, with immigration topics being at the forefront of the Presidential election, many new immigrants find themselves at the crosshairs of the never-ending anti-immigrant sentiment in the country. Should there occur massive deportation as proposed by some political leaders, American economy will undoubtedly face a nose-dive. Although, acknowledging this fact, many of the political leaders tend to remain silent thinking the worse may never come to pass.

Some, however, while secretly acknowledge that immigrants remain the backbone of the American economy, they however, appear unwilling or incapable of publicly voicing their opinions or disapproval to the die-hard anti-immigrants. In the end, according to Dr. Martin Luther King Jr., in "The Trumpet of Conscience" (1967), we will remember not the words of our enemies, but the silence of our friends.

Dedication

To my African brothers and sisters, both at home and in the diaspora, this guidebook is dedicated to you. It is my hope that this book becomes a valuable resource, offering you an equal opportunity to access the information pipeline that can guide you toward achieving your goals and fulfilling your purpose in life.

To my beloved son, Mr. Emeka A. Monye—a preacher in the Dominican Republic (departed on 11/04/2019)—may your soul rest in perfect peace. This book is also dedicated to you, Onyemachi T. Mokwuyem-Monye.

To my lost but found son, Messiah, never forget that you are a sojourner in this wilderness called America. Remember your roots, honor your heritage, and always pay homage to your chi.

Americaonlinevisa.com

Prologue

In this Dictionary Guide to American Visas, we present a disclaimer, and that is: The authors are neither Lawyers, Historians, nor Biblical Analysts. We are all newcomer immigrants, sharing our immigrant experiences over time within the American landscape. We are all social commentators. All information herein is based on our individual experiences and basic research. This immigration guidebook also embeds a dictionary style meanings of US visas presented in a layman's terms by alphabetical order. You will be well advised to consider this guide as both your entry to and your exit formalities from the US, but most importantly, you must consult with an attorney to help you with your specific case.

This guide must be viewed as an educational piece to introduce future immigrants to the US to our common humanity, the American way of life, and the American culture by analysing its immigration laws and policies. America is a land of laws, and the people here tend to be very obedient and respectful of their laws; and so, must you too. Yes, you can. On the other hand, however, America is a nation of extraordinary discretion and norms. This means that sometimes, the laws are thrown out of the windows, especially if the cruelty of the laws does not directly impact them- so they think! At any rate, we believe given the proper education and from a layman's point of view about American immigration laws and formalities; everyone will be a winner. After all, the American dream must still live on for those who can arrive here.

During every Presidential year in the US, it's common to hear Presidential aspirants pride themselves in demeaning immigrants. They say immigrants commit the most crimes, take over their jobs, and enjoy Americans' God-given benefits, rights, and privileges. Therefore, immigrants are not welcome. They call immigrants aliens, a derogatory term reserved for the scum of the earth. I have every reason to write this guidebook, at least if nonetheless, to keep you informed. Most Americans are immigrants, whether they know it or not. Everyone here is in pursuit of the American dream.

If you obey and follow US immigration eligibility rules and policies, you will almost certainly be a winner in your quest to secure a visa entry to the US. You are a loser if you pay people besides immigration attorneys to bring you across the border or embark upon a dangerous journey to the US by any means necessary even including attempts at extra-judicial pathways. This is not to opine that you cannot pay your passport/visa consultants and researchers like me! But please, avoid scammers! Do your due diligence research. Sometimes your failure to obtain a visa may simply be an option to try again. Re-fortify yourself regarding what is needed and required documentation, and hit the Embassy pavement again!

Background and Introduction

In studying world history from prehistoric times to the present, you would have noticed that American civilisation and its present super-power status of the world only came into being at the turn of the 20th century (popularly known as the American Century incorporating the Containment Policy, Truman Doctrine, and the Marshall Plan, etc.). Yes, not even in 1776, as one would assume, especially when the Continental Congress issued and adopted the Declaration of Independence from Great Britain, the time of the World's Superpower, but much later. In terms of superpower history, the American story is very recent.

Ancient African entities, like Sudan, Ethiopia, Egypt, Mali, and Ghana, had once occupied the superpower status long before America! People from all over Europe came to Aksum, Egypt, Alexandria, Meroe-Kush, Carthage, and Timbuktu to study and live. In those days, people didn't apply for visas, nor were they officially accorded the distinctive characteristics of being either an immigrant or a nonimmigrant. People simply wandered across the borders in search of greener pastures or in search of anyone that could speak their language and understand their customs. Nevertheless, no record nor annual reports of visa applicants existed, and notwithstanding the efforts of China's Han Dynasty and the first known census of the Babylonian empire in circa 2 CE. High-ranking officials were simply appointed goodwill ambassadors as exchange resident visitors to neighboring nations to restore or maintain comity. In today's America, you will be well served to know how, why, and what to do should you decide to apply for any of the US visas. You must know and understand your environment.

According to the US State Department's annual report of visa rejection rates of applicants from around the world, many of the visa applicants who were rejected entry into the US by the State Department lack sufficient information about visa requirements and how to obtain their visa choice. Applicants simply do not know what visa types fit their travel goals and to apply accordingly or appropriately. By 2019 figures, more than 4 million visa applicants were denied for various reasons consistently till 2022. Your lack of knowledge of the American way of life and visa procurement processes may be causing you your failure to secure any US visa of your choice. This visa guidebook is intended to help you remedy that.

There are 26 letters of the alphabet. Each of these letters is assigned a visa type, with some having several subtypes and variations; for example, the investment-based National interest waiver type, the EB-NIW visa, is an investment / employment-based visa type specifically designed to favour US government interests. It can therefore be very difficult to obtain. The EB-2 NIW visas allow the applicant to become a US permanent resident through the benefits of an EB-2 Green Card. To secure this type of visa, you must show evidence of your capacity and willingness to contribute your skills and work experience to better US society. How does that occur, you might ask? Well, the job you create or apply for must have an advanced degree in your field of study or expertise. We will discuss this later.

For a starter, most literate persons in the Anglo / American tradition know the existence of 26 letters in the English alphabet. In American visa tabulation, each letter of the alphabet is represented by a visa type. For example, A has a corresponding visa type, so is B, and so is C, D, E, F and so on till Z. To fully understand and appreciate what visa type you may need, a gentle reading of American history, especially of immigration policies from 1812 to 1986, immigrant experiences and if you care enough to explore your place in it, can be of help to you.

Nearly fifteen years ago, America had its first African descendant as President; President Barack H. Obama. It's good to know that at this point in American history, so much has been happening. Many political, social and economic changes have occurred. Today's America has an African descendant Vice President who now is vying for the Presidency, another as secretary of Defense, and yet another as Chairman, Joint Chiefs of Staff. The UN is also represented by an African American – most likely descendants of former African slaves. Nobody one hundred years ago could have foreseen these changes in the era of "Jim Crow". The reconstruction years immediately after the Civil War were no better- and, as many historians would agree, the worst period in America's Black history.

American history has been undergoing a mythological phase. In a way, at the back of your mind, you must never forget that all these changes are bound to produce backlashes from Whites. Why? Because "White grievance" is real and "White fear" is also real. White Southerners had lost the Civil War. The Civil War was fought over the slavery of African people. The issue of holding on to human bondage or vanquishing the same has persisted to this day. Whites by and large, have refused to solve these problems (Issues with White grievance) themselves; instead, they double down and pray to God for changes to be forthcoming. These fears and the human conditions they generate are always reflected in American government's policies and procedures about immigration of African peoples to the US.

If you were born or are from an African country, say, Nigeria, the American government already knows a whole lot about you, but you do not know as much about the American people, their society, and their governing structure and customs because your government does not know that much either about America. Yet do you really want to travel or immigrate to America? Well, it is conceivable to assume that the American people are ridiculously ignorant about how you go about your daily life in Africa, but this is not true as far as the American government is concerned. American government compiles data on almost every country on the face of the earth. You do not have to know what Americans are thinking in any given moment, but you should be able to know how they think, what makes them tick, unique, and in a majority of cases what governs their thought processes.

Americans are fiercely loyal people. Americans value truth and justice, although they may not always abide by it. They value the idea of fairness. More importantly, they value freedom, and in whatever form that takes. When they talk to you, they tend to believe in whatever you have to say until you can prove them wrong, and thereafter, everything else you say becomes unbelievable and irrelevant, and you cannot, therefore, be trusted. Americans do not have time for mediocrity, stupidity, and foolishness. In other words, they do not have the patience to linger long in any given topic that is irrelevant to their point of interest.

Sometimes, Americans assume, incorrectly though, that you ought to behave like them and value what they value culturally. For example, do you know that in America, when they are conversing with you in the form of an interview, they prefer to look directly into your eyes and you into theirs as they talk with you? However, as you may have noticed, in many African cultures that seemingly ignorant gesture would be considered a sign of disrespect to someone in a position of authority- yes, the authority to grant or deny you a visa.

But guess what? If the visa interview is going on and you continue to stick to your African customs of not looking back straight into- your interviewer's eyes, the Consulate official interviewer may consider you to be hiding, evading information, or outright telling lies to him or her: A reason to deny you a visa! Remember, you are guilty in the visa application process until you prove your innocence, and that burden of proof is on you if you anticipate securing a visa approval.

Do you even know how Americans live, how they think about their world, and how they survive? Simply put, you may even thinking that America is a land flowing with milk and honey. I agree, comparatively speaking. I was once in that frame of mind too! But today, I know better. For example, America's food production is enough to feed the entire world three times over and a lot more left over, yet there are food insecurities in America. Why? Well, I want you to take a moment and let that sink in. This book is about how you can apply and secure your visa approval.

Americans are simply just like us in so many ways; you and I survive rich and poor, and just like you and your family members survive daily in Africa. They, too, survive daily. You may think there are no poor people in America. You are wrong. You may think that even the poor in America are still better than the poor in Africa; again, you are wrong! I want you to read several existing treaties on self-determination, self-awareness, self-worth, self-pride, consciousness, and mind control. Then, I would hope that such exposure would help re-orient your thought processes. Nevertheless, however, you should know that most of your opinions about America are your opinions.

At any rate, I understand why you may be confusing facts about America with your opinions. There are countless valid reasons for thinking this way. Econometrics, social indicators, and statistics are often engineered and interpreted through Eurocentric frameworks—frameworks that you may have accepted unquestioningly, hook, line, and sinker. Why? Because your knowledge base has been shaped and constrained by the Western educational tradition.

There's nothing inherently wrong with this system; it's just different from what you are accustomed to. Africans, too, are inherently different in their values, perspectives, and lived experiences.

Below is a table showcasing immigration types and migrant characteristics to the U.S. from 2018 to 2022.

The table explores the variety of immigrant and nonimmigrant characteristics of those who applied and gained entry to the US, as well as those who applied but were refused entry.

No such table ever existed in the prehistoric world, notwithstanding Africa. Hint, hint…prejudicial behaviors against others existed, but there were no racism nor racist ideologies in those days even though there existed tribalism and, or differences in ethnicity! Race-baiting is a recent American phenomenon.

Table I

Immigrant and Nonimmigrant Visas Issued at Foreign Service Posts Fiscal Years 2018-2022*

*Due to the COVID-19 pandemic, posts were instructed to suspend routine visa services and provide only mission critical and emergency services in late March 2020. This had a significant impact on the provision of Immigrant and Nonimmigrant Visa-related services. Posts were only able to resume limited services on a post-by-post basis beginning in July 2020, as local conditions allowed.

	2018	2019	2020	2021	2022
Immigrant Categories					
Immediate Relatives	236,526	186,584	108,292,	170,604	212,185
Special Immigrants[1]	9,375	11,384	8,722	13,421	14,903
Vietnam Amerasian	92	96	95	63	168
Immigrants	211,641	190,938	90,435	63,858	156,800
Family Sponsored Preference	27,345	28,538	14,694	19,779	55,058
Employment-Based	0	0	0	0	0
Preference					
Armed Forces Special	48,578	44,882	18,288	17,344	54,334
Immigrants	9,028,026	8,742,068	4,013,210	2,792,083	6,815,120
Diversity Immigrants					
Total					
Nonimmigrant Categories					
Visas Issued					
(B1/B2/Border Crossing Cards)[2]	[1,032,467]	[1,106,852]	[662,536]	[512,889]	[1,244,482]
Total	9,028,026	8,742,068	4,013,210	2,792,083	6,815,120

Note: The totals on this table do not include replaced immigrant visas:

1. Special Immigrant totals include returning residents, Iraqi and Afghan translators; Iraqis and Afghans employed by or on behalf of the U.S. government, or by the International Security Assistance Force or its successor, and Iraqi and Afghan SI cases converted under Section 1244; and certain family members of U1 Nonimmigrants.
2. Combination B1/B2 visitor visa/Border Crossing Cards are issued to Mexican nationals. B1/B2/Border Crossing Card issuances are included in the "Visas Issued" line.

Organization of this Guidebook

This book is written partly as a guide and partly as a dictionary of American immigration terms and processes. It is written for those seeking to emigrate to the United States but didn't know just what to do nor know just how to go about executing their plans to obtain a visa and venture into the unknown. This book is organized into Nine sections

Section 1 explores the purpose and the definition of a US visa. An example of a visa application was presented, which was denied. And the letter of denial was attached. The approximate reasons for denial were examined and possible corrections were suggested. Section 2 focusses on finding your unique voice and knowing who you are. The assumptions here are to help you garner strength from within to guide you through the maintenance of your individual tempo in a sojourner's psychology enforced and exploited by commissioned visa issuers through the Visa interview process. You must therefore respect and appreciate your human dignity, so that others may find it difficult to violate you.

Section 2 simply wants you to know before you go! Short stories, novel accounts, immigrant experiences of America were summarized and showcased in bits and pieces from those who succeeded in the ultimate sacrifice and journey to the new world.

Section 3 is a classification of the two visa categories: Immigrant and Nonimmigrant visa types.

Section 4 also lists about 26 visa category-types in alphabetical order-A to Z. Nearly 2% of this guidebook were exhumed from the US State Department's website and or from the US Homeland Security's website. All we have done is simply get them organized and render the information readily available and understandable to the African traveler. American immigration laws, policies and procedures change yearly. You must consider this guidebook as an historical narrative, and not as a legal document. For your specific situation, please, consult an Attorney.

Section 4 focusses on Treaty Countries-these are countries with established relationships with the United States. Knowing this is important especially for immigrants from newly created African countries. Or countries that recently became independent. You must know what rules govern your immigration status, your country, and whether to apply for a diversity visa or not.

Section 5 is about Authentication certification requirements of the various document types, like birth certificate, assets, tax information, marriage, and divorce. This section is also about how to obtain your documents and which local and state governments in your country of origin are responsible for keeping each type of the required documentation.

Section 6 is on the country of Nigeria, proper. At nearly 225 million people in population, one person out of every 5 African is a Nigerian. There is a Nigerian in virtually every country of the world. Nigeria is about 3% of the world's population. This country should be a very important study in world affairs.

Section 7 is on preparing for both the US and your country's entry and exit structured interviews. These interviews are designed to generally help you to explore everything from how to make a living in the US without falling victim to the legal systems. You will learn how to avoid US law enforcement troubles, stay healthy, and stay focused with respect to your host country's laws and customs.

Section 8 Exit and Entry interviews. US immigration requirements for entry and exit formalities. Common mistakes travelers make and how to avoid them-especially with issues involving customs' declarations.

Section 9 Epilogue-went on to explore biblical references of immigration, chapters, and bible verses showcasing the bible as the ultimate immigration handbook.

Purpose of this Guidebook

Many Africans have found themselves stranded along American shores in search of obtaining an entry visa, some even wash away at high seas, dead. The purpose of this guidebook is not to make you feel bad, rather to make you feel empowered, and understand certain things you may have taken for granted but failed to examine about coming to the US. You must learn certain things about Americans if you plan to even visit here and risk it all in whatever capacity.

When you visit any American Embassy or Consulate in many African countries, you will find an unbearably long lines of individuals waiting for their visa application completion and interview. You are likely going to find both the well-prepared and the scarcely prepared visa applicants wasting both their time and the Embassy officials' time, effort and money.

Even when you are scheduled for an interview the Embassy sometimes tends to overschedule you thus creating an artificial gridlock. Some applicants even show up without an invitation. Some applicants get hoodwinked, preyed-upon by their fraudulent, money-seeking countrymen-the middlemen of visa fraudsters. You don't have to fall for this-especially if you know what you are doing. Reading this guidebook will hopefully help you as you embark upon your journey.

So, the purpose of this book is to outline a how-to-guide, a dictionary entry of some sort regarding the various visa types to help you understand who you are, what you want, and how to accomplish your goal and get what you want.

Coming to America is a noble act. Many people die along the way trying to make it. But even some immigrants that do survive the journey find themselves rotting in American prison systems because they failed to study and understand the American society before embarking on this very dangerous journey. You must know and learn to obey their laws. I shall use both historical and biblical narratives to explore and explain why your desires to travel to the US are well founded.

Your plan to travel to America is both real, moral, and justified. However, you must have adequate preparation before you go. This dictionary-style guidebook is written to help you achieve your goal.

Additionally, this book was written in honor of my late son, the Preacher, Mr. Emeka Amilio Monye. May your soul rest in peace. I miss you every day.

Yours truly,

Joseph I. Monye, Ph.D.
Basic Research Solutions, Inc.
Baltimore, Maryland, USA.
(443-750-4967) ph.
10/01/2024

SECTION ONE

What is a U.S. Visa?

Visas are foreign countries' seal or stamp of nationality on your country's issued passport or travel documents. A citizen of a foreign country who seeks to enter the United States generally must first obtain a U.S. visa, which is placed in the traveler's passport or a travel document issued by the traveler's country of citizenship.

A United State's visa approval is simply that seal or stamp of approval to come to the US. Note that this initial approval is tentative because you may be denied entry at your point or port of disembarkation. Remember that your visa was issued by the State Department abroad, usually in your home country, but it may be denied by the US Homeland Security Agency on arrival to America's shores or airport.

Does having a US visa issued by the American Consulate or Embassy in your own country of residence guarantee entry to the US? The answer is no.

Certain international travellers may be eligible to travel to the United States without a visa if they meet the requirements for visa-free travel-for example, many UK citizens travel to the US. For more information, contacting US government representatives regarding any visa questions would be wise. The Visa section in their website is all about U.S. visas for foreign citizens to travel to the United States.

(Note: U.S. citizens don't need a U.S. visa for travel, but when planning travel abroad may need a visa issued by the embassy of the country they wish to visit. In this situation, when planning to travel abroad, learn about visa requirements by country, see Country Specific Travel Information in the Passport section of any country's website.)

How Can I Use a Visa to Enter the United States?

Having a U.S. visa allows you to travel to a port of entry, airport or land border crossing and request permission to enter the United States from a Department of Homeland Security (DHS), Customs and Border Protection (CBP) inspector.

While having a visa does not guarantee entry to the United States, it does indicate a consular officer at a U.S. Embassy or Consulate abroad has determined you are eligible to seek entry for that specific purpose. DHS/CBP inspectors, guardians of the nation's borders, are responsible for the admission of travellers to the United States for a specified status and period. DHS also has responsibility for immigration matters while you are present in the United States.

What Types of Visas Are There?

There are indeed many types of US visas. However, the type of visa you must obtain is defined by U.S. immigration law and relates to the purpose of your travel. There are two main categories of U.S. visas:

In a nutshell, you have immigrant and nonimmigrant visa categories.

- Nonimmigrant visas – For travel to the United States on a temporary basis.
- Immigrant visas – For travel to live permanently in the United States.

What Does a Visa Look Like? How to read and understand a US Visa.

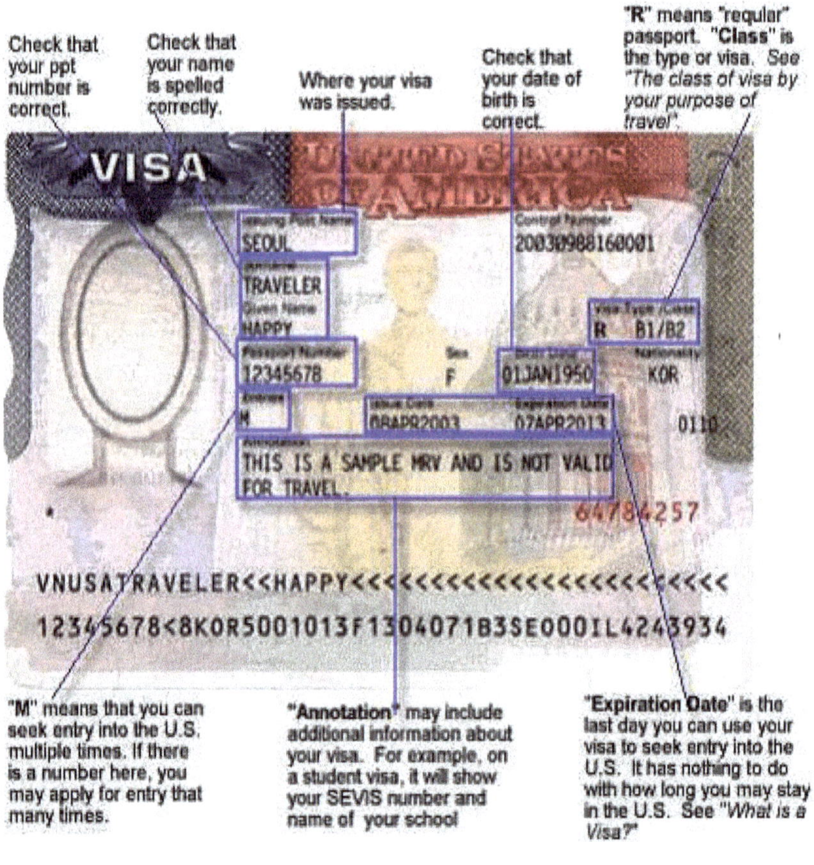

-

Most issued US visas within the past 50 years have been in the former category-for non-immigrant status. See below for an example of an online non-immigrant visa application. It is important to note that the individual applicant below was denied a visa.

We shall explore this scenario and explain why we think this visa application was denied on appearing in a face-to-face interview with the interviewer and what we think should be done as a corrective measure.

Consular Electronic Application Center - Print Application

https://ceac.state.gov/GenNIV/common/printapplication.aspx?

AA00CB3EJV

Online Non-immigrant Visa Application (DS-160)

Application - Sensitive but Unclassified (SBU)

1. Name Provided:

- **Luck, I. F.**

2. Full Name in Native Language:

- Does not apply
- **Other Names Used:** Yes

3. Other Name (1):

- **O, I. F.**
- **Telecode Name Used:** No

We do not need a printed copy of your application at any point during your interview process. Only print this application if you want a copy for your own records. If you print your application, please keep it secure.

4. Sex: Female

5. Marital Status: Married

6. Date of Birth: 02 March 1988

7. Place of Birth: Warri, Delta, Nigeria

8. Country/Region of Origin (Nationality): Nigeria

- **National Identification Number:** Does Not Apply
- **Confirmation Number:** N/A

9. U.S. Social Security Number: Does Not Apply

- **U.S. Taxpayer ID Number:** Does Not Apply

10. Home Address:

- **Street:** 4, Gold Street
- **City:** Okpe
- **State/Province:** Delta
- **Postal Zone/ZIP Code:** Does Not Apply
- **Country/Region:** Nigeria
- **Same Mailing Address?** Yes

11. Do you hold or have you held any nationality other than the one indicated above? No

12. Are you a permanent resident of a country/region other than your country of origin? No

13. Primary Phone Number: +2348157866328

- **Secondary Phone Number:** Does Not Apply
- **Work Phone Number:** Does Not Apply
- **Do you have any additional phone numbers?** No

14. Email Address: cher@gmail.com

- **Do you have any additional email addresses?** No

15. Social Media Presence:

- **Platform (1):** Facebook
    - **Social Media Identifier:** CHERISH
- **Platform (2):** Instagram
    - **Social Media Identifier:** CHERISH
- **Do you have any additional social media presence?** No

16. Passport/Travel Document Information:

- **Passport Type:** Regular Passport
- **Number:** A********12114546
- **Passport Book Number:** Does not apply
- **Country/Authority that Issued Passport:** Nigeria

- **City Where Issued:** Osogbo
- **State/Province Where Issued:** Osun
- **Issuance Date:** 06 October 2021
- **Expiration Date:** 05 October 2026
- **Have you ever lost a passport or had one stolen?** No

17. **Purpose of Trip to the U.S.:**
    - **Primary Purpose:** Temporary Business/Pleasure Visitor (B)
    - **Specify:** Business & Tourism (B1/B2)
18. **Travel Information:**
    - **Have you made specific travel plans?** Yes
    - **Date of Arrival in U.S.:** 18 October 2023
    - **Arrival City:** Jacksonville, FL
    - **Date of Departure from U.S.:** 02 November 2023
    - **Address where you will stay in the U.S.:** A-P-T Suites, Jacksonville, FL
19. **Person/Entity Paying for Your Trip:**
    - **Company/Organization:** Exxon Mobil Nigeria Unlimited
    - **Telephone Number:** +234809-000-0000
    - **Address:** Mobil House, 1 Lekki Expressway, Victoria Island, Lagos, Nigeria
20. **Are there other people traveling with you? Yes**
    - **Are you traveling as part of a group or organization?** No
    - **Name (1):** I, Luck
    - **Relationship to You:** Spouse
21. **Previous U.S. Travel History:**
    - **Have you ever been in the U.S.?** No
    - **Have you ever been issued a U.S. visa?** No
22. **U.S. Contact Information:**
    - **Contact Person Name:** Larose, Jimmy
    - **Organization Name:** National Development Institute
    - **Relationship to You:** Other
    - **Address:** P.O. BOX 1840
    - **Phone Number:** 800-200-0000

- **Email Address:** team@development.net

23. Family Information:

- **Father's Name:** Anthony O
- **Father's Date of Birth:** 30 April 1958
- **Is your father in the U.S.?** No
- **Mother's Name:** N. M. O
- **Mother's Date of Birth:** 14 April 1961
- **Is your mother in the U.S.?** No

24. Immigration History:

- **Have you ever been refused a U.S. visa or refused admission?** No
- **Do you have any immediate relatives in the U.S.?** No
- **Has anyone ever filed an immigrant petition on your behalf?** No

25. Spouse Information:

- **Full Name:** I, L.
- **Date of Birth:** 27 May 1987
- **Country of Origin:** Nigeria
- **City of Birth:** Warri, Delta
- **Current Address:** Same as Home Address
- **Primary Occupation:** Education
- **Employer/School Name:** Nursery and Primary School
- **Work Address:** P.O. Box 488, Effurun-Warri, Delta, Nigeria
- **Work Phone Number:** +23481578600000
- **Monthly Salary:** 180,000.00 Naira
- **Job Duties:** Teacher

26. Education Information:

- **Institution (1):** College of Education, Agbor, Delta State
  - **Course of Study:** Home Economics in Education
  - **Attendance Period:** September 2006 – August 2008
- **Institution (2):** University of Benin
  - **Course of Study:** B.Ed. in Home Economics
  - **Attendance Period:** September 2013 – October 2015

27. Additional Personal Information:

- **Have you attended any secondary level or higher education institutions?** Yes
- **Do you belong to a clan or tribe?** Yes
- **Clan or Tribe Name:** Igbo
- **Languages Spoken:** English, Igbo

28. Travel and Security Information:

- **Have you traveled to any other countries in the last five years?** No
- **Have you ever served in the military?** No
- **Are you or have you ever been a drug abuser or addict?** No
- **Have you ever violated any law related to controlled substances?** No
- **Have you ever been involved in money laundering?** No
- **Have you belonged to or worked for any professional, social, or charitable organizations?** Yes
    - **Name of Organization:** SWBN - Society for the Welfare of the Blind
- **Do you have any specialized skills or training (firearms, explosives, nuclear, etc.)?** No
- **Have you ever been involved with a paramilitary unit, vigilante group, rebel group, or insurgent organization?** No

Security and Background Information

Security and Background Information

29. Do you have a communicable disease of public health significance?

(Communicable diseases of public significance include chancroid, gonorrhea, granuloma inguinale, infectious leprosy, lymphogranuloma venereum, infectious stage syphilis, active tuberculosis, and other diseases as determined by the Department of Health and Human Services.)

- **No**

30. Are you a member or representative of a terrorist organization?

- **No**

31. Do you have a mental or physical disorder that poses or is likely to pose a threat to the safety or welfare of yourself or others?

- **No**

32. Have you ever ordered, incited, committed, assisted, or otherwise participated in genocide?

- **No**

33. Have you ever committed, ordered, incited, assisted, or otherwise participated in torture?

- **No**

34. Have you ever been arrested or convicted for any offense or crime, even though subject to a pardon, amnesty, or other similar action?

- **No**

35. Have you ever engaged in the recruitment or use of child soldiers?

- **No**

36. Are you coming to the United States to engage in prostitution or unlawful commercialized vice, or have you engaged in prostitution or procuring prostitutes within the past 10 years?

- **No**

37. Have you ever committed or conspired to commit a human trafficking offense in the United States or outside the United States?

- **No**

38. Have you ever committed or conspired to commit a human trafficking offense in the United States or outside the United States, and have you, within the last five years, knowingly benefited from the trafficking activities?

- **No**

39. Do you seek to engage in espionage, sabotage, export control violations, or any other illegal activity while in the United States?

- **No**

39. Do you seek to engage in terrorist activities while in the United States, or have you ever engaged in terrorist activities?

- **No**

40. Have you ever or do you intend to provide financial assistance or other support to terrorists or terrorist organizations?

- **No**

41. Have you ever provided financial assistance or other support to terrorists or terrorist organizations in the last five years?

- **No**

42. Have you committed, ordered, incited, assisted, or otherwise participated in extrajudicial

killings, political killings, or other acts of violence?

- **No**

43. Have you, while serving as a government official, been responsible for or directly carried out, at any time, particularly severe violations of religious freedom?

- **No**

Your Personal Copy -- Do Not Bring to the Interview

Consular Electronic Application Center - Print Application

https://ceac.state.gov/GenNIV/common/printapplication.aspx?p1qhi

44. Have you ever been directly involved in the coercive transplantation of human organs or bodily tissue?

- **No**

45. Have you ever been removed or deported from any country?

- **No**

46. Have you voted in the United States in violation of any law or regulation?

- **No**

47. Have you ever renounced United States citizenship for the purpose of avoiding taxation?

- **No**

48. Current Location:

- **Lagos, Nigeria**

49. Did anyone assist you in filling out this application?

- **No**

50. Have you ever been directly involved in the establishment or enforcement of the population controls forcing a woman to undergo an abortion against her free choice or a man or a woman to undergo sterilization against his or her free will?

- **No**

51. Have you ever applied for a United States immigration benefit by fraud, willful misrepresentation, or other unlawful means?

- **No**

52. Have you ever withheld custody of a U.S. citizen child outside the United States from a person granted legal custody by a U.S. court?

- **No**

53. Location where you will be submitting your application:

- **N/A**

54. Preparer of Application:

- **N/A**

55. You electronically signed your application on:

- **21-Jul-2023 03:26:10 (GMT-05:00)**

56. You were required to electronically sign your application yourself, unless otherwise exempt by regulation, even if the application was prepared by someone other than yourself. Your electronic signature certifies that you have read and understood the questions in this application and that your answers are true and correct to the best of your knowledge and belief.

57. The submission of an application containing any false or misleading statements may result in the permanent refusal of a visa or the denial of entry into the United States. All declarations made in this application are unsworn declarations made under penalty of perjury. (28 U.S.C. 1746).

An Analysis of some of the reasons you may be denied visa.

You attend the interview as requested but without adequate preparation and rehearsal of all prior statements made, all documents submitted and without a visa mock interview/examination. Above all, without a look into your finances and social economic standing.

In 2022, nearly 38 million people in the United States lived below the poverty line. That's about 12 % of the population, according to the US Census Bureau, even though the official poverty line was set at an income of $27,750.

So, you would ask, what does minimum poverty line really mean for those living through it? It's about more than just tight budgets and tough choices. Household poverty shapes individual opportunities, health, education, and even how people and families see themselves.

In terms of successfully applying for and obtaining your US visas, here are some of the issues you must consider and some of the issues you should know about poverty. These insights will help you understand the challenges poor people face and why solving the problems of visa denials may seem, at first, intractable. Here are some characteristics of poverty in the US as a benchmark for assessing your situation and why you may be denied visa so you do not become a public charge: (a)

Poor education-you or your family member (b) Poor health (c) Less access to good nutrition and general wellbeing (d) Deprivation in general and lacking in social and economic standing (e) Lacking access to safety and healthcare (f) Income of below the Federal poverty supplemental guideline- say, $30, 000.00 per annum. (g) Low levels of educational or skills attainment. In a nutshell, your interview process must include a modicum of all documentaries showing positive evidence of the above.

During the interview session, if you failed to produce documentary evidence of all statements of fact required in your application, you may likely not be approved. In the end, your visa application may be denied.

See the attached form letter below. I have approximated some reasons for why the visa was denied. Visa denial may have been based on simply by reading and analyzing the statements made during the application process. In the above application (DS 160), see number(s)

#25 Purpose of Trip to the U.S. (1) The applicant indicated> Temp. Business.; yet show no proof or documentation to demonstrate intent. Note that, further in the application form, the applicant was asked, for example, do you have a social media presence?

Instead, the applicant Specified, Business & Tourism within a (Temporary Visitor) (B1/B2) categories. But, yet, failed to answer the question about media presence in thorough manner.

Nevertheless, applicant indirectly volunteered "Instagram" on question # 14

Have you made specific travel plans? Applicant indicated -YES but failed to produce a travel itinerary or return flight tickets as proof.

25. Date of Arrival in U.S.: 18 October 2023 Arrival City: Jacksonville, Florida

26. Date of Departure from U.S.: 02 November 2023: Again, applicant has misrepresented facts in the two statements above. For example, if your date of arrival to Jacksonville, US, will be on October 2023, your planned date of departure from the US cannot be in November of 2023, if you do not have documented proof of your business intent and activities in Jacksonville, Florida.

27. Address where you will stay in the U.S.: A-P-T suites, Jacksonville, Florida. No documented proof was provided

Person/Entity Paying for Your Trip: Company/Organization

28. Company/Organization Paying for the Trip: Exxon Mobil (Nigeria) Unlimited-No documented proof was presented to Embassy officials.

29. Telephone Number: 234809-000-0000

On the travel information byline, applicant was prompted to provide a list of purposeful intent for travel to the US and (a return to your home country after business) by showing possible payment receipts and housing accommodation arrangements, in which applicant demurred.

In # 51, Applicant fails to demonstrate an ability to satisfy the "Public Charge" element of the (Immigration and Naturalization Service). The INS consideration of applicant's monthly salary in local currency (if employed) in Nigeria's 180,000.00 Naira is not enough.

The List of Purposes of Trip to the U.S. You are to provide a complete itinerary for your travel to the U.S. including flight itineraries, tickets, and or traveler's checks.

63, When prompted for tribal affiliation, applicant indicated Igbo language instead of Ika, or belonging to the Agbor ethnic group. Remember in pre-organized information dossiers of almost all the countries on earth, America may have already classified members of the Agbor people as Ika, not Igbo. Thus, the consular officer interviewing you might think that you were not being forthcoming with the truth regarding your identity-hence, another good reason to deny you visa.

Again, it appears applicant show no proof from sponsoring organizations-Exxon Mobil, nor from the Society for the welfare of the blind in Nigeria as indicated on the application, that the above organizations will be financially responsible for applicant's business trip.

Because the applicant fails to demonstrate intent with relevant documentation, the applicant had to be denied a visa.

See Consulate Letter of denial below:

CONSULATE GENERAL OF THE
UNITED STATES OF AMERICA
LAGOS, NIGERIA

Dear Applicant:

This is to inform you that you have been found ineligible for a nonimmigrant visa under Section 214(b) of the U.S. Immigration and Nationality Act. A denial under Section 214(b) means that you were not able to demonstrate that your intended activities in the United States would be consistent with the classification of the nonimmigrant visa for which you applied.

While nonimmigrant visa classifications each have their own unique requirements, one requirement shared by many of the nonimmigrant visa categories is for the applicant to demonstrate that he/she has a residence in a foreign country which he/she has no intention of abandoning. Applicants usually meet this requirement by demonstrating that they have strong ties overseas that indicate that they will return to a foreign country after a temporary visit to the United States. Such ties include professional, work, school, family, or social links to a foreign country. You have not demonstrated that you have the ties that will compel you to return to your home country after your travel to the United States.

Today's decision cannot be appealed. However, you may reapply at any time. If you decide to reapply, you must submit a new application form and photo, pay the visa application fee again, and make a new appointment to be interviewed by a consular officer. If you choose to reapply, you should be prepared to provide information that was not presented in your original application, or to demonstrate that your circumstances have changed since that application.

Sincerely,
Consular Officer
Nonimmigrant Visa Unit

If you would like to report harassment, bribery, fraud or malfeasant behavior to the U.S. Consulate General Lagos, please scan this QR code and complete the form. All submitted information will be kept anonymous.

You certify that you understand you are required to submit your visa to the United States Immigration Officer at the port where you apply to enter the United States. Possession of the visa does not entitle you to enter the United States if, upon arrival, you are found inadmissible under U.S. immigration laws.

You also certify that you understand any willfully false or misleading statement, or willful concealment of a material fact made in your application, may subject you to permanent exclusion from the United States. If admitted, it may result in criminal prosecution and/or deportation.

The information provided in your application, along with any accompanying documents, may be accessible to other government agencies with lawful authority, including for law enforcement and immigration purposes.

If fingerprints are collected during your application process, they may be compared against the FBI's Next Generation Identification (NGI) fingerprint system or its successor systems, including civil, criminal, and latent fingerprint repositories.

The photograph submitted with your application may be used for employment verification or other lawful purposes in the United States.

Onlinevisa.com lists 3 types of visas by method of application which are: **(a) Online visas (b) Embassy/consular visas and (c) Visas issued on arrival.**

Before you plan to apply for a US visa, you must be certain of the following characteristics about yourself:

1. Know who you are.
2. Know what you want and prepare for your specific goal.
3. Know how to achieve your specific goal. This is where you seek help if you do not know your specific goal. Although throughout this process, you may not need a lawyer, but an Attorney might come in handy at your zone of proximal development to help you crystalize your goal in legal jargons.

Of the three issues listed above, the most difficult part is really knowing who you are! Many of us don't know exactly who we are until very late in life. As a matter of fact, some of us will never know who we really are and die with such ignorance of life and of living. Once you can figure out who you really are and can forge and draft a goal so specific and achievable that is equally realistic and timely, the rest is history. This book guide will guide you and hopefully enable you to uncover that history; the how to

Applying for a US Visa step-by-step process chart

The first step in applying for a U.S. Visa is (a) decide whether you plan to stay, live, and work on a permanent basis. If so, then, go for immigrant visa types-listed below.

The second step in applying for a U.S. Visa is (b) decide whether you plan to stay temporary, including business, pleasure, vacationing, or visiting on a temporary basis. If so, then, go for nonimmigrant visa types-listed below. Whether immigrant or Nonimmigrant visa-types, you must complete your application online or in person, where permitted. Remember that, as far as the interviewer is concerned, your completed application covers more than enough of what they need to know about you to make a binding decision on whether to approve your application or decline your application. Thus, it is possible for a consular interviewer to deny your application in just 10 minutes after calling you to the glass window.

This visa denial can perplex you, but this scenario is very common.

It can take approximately 90 minutes to complete the entire application process.

After you submit your application and before an interview is scheduled, you would have had ample time to begin gathering your documents. However, I suggest that you gather some of your documents before filing your application. In this way, you will be well prepared on the interview day. Also, I would encourage you to pay for and attend a mock interview with an experienced service provider. Such mock interviews can greatly enhance your chances of success.

» **Write down the Application ID** displayed on the top right-hand corner of the page. If you close your browser window, you need your ID to access your application again.

» **Save your application frequently.** The system will time out after 20 minutes of inactivity, and you will lose all unsaved information.

» Read more about U.S. visas at travel.state.gov.

» Visit the website of the U.S. Embassy or Consulate in your country of origin. Learn, learn, and learn more.

FINDING YOUR VOICE AND KNOWING WHO YOU ARE

This visa guide is written for a general-purpose audience, but specifically for those of African descent, whose lifeworlds sometimes collide with the Western world's ideological framework. In the West, there is often a pretense that immigration into their so-called lands is a recent phenomenon. However, immigration is as old as humanity itself.

In the Americas—particularly North America—recent descendants of earlier immigrants to the New World, who displaced Native American Indians and dismantled their economies to seize their wealth, now claim ownership of America. Americans, it seems, have little shame. Not long ago, President Trump promised his people, "Let's build that wall... and Mexico will pay for it." The crowd responded with fervent approval. Of course, Mexico never paid for such a wall, designed to prevent Mexican and other immigrants from entering the United States.

What audacity, to suggest that Americans are so short-sighted as to forget their own immigrant origins. They seem to overlook the rich history of migration across Europe, Africa, Asia, and Latin America—including the journeys of their own forefathers from Asiatic regions. Even Christopher Columbus, seeking greener pastures in the New World, was himself an immigrant!

While Protestant Europeans were welcomed to emigrate to the New World in large numbers, Irish Catholics, Muslims, Latin Americans, and other so-called "undesirables" were systematically barred from entering the United States. American history is riddled with racism and anti-immigrant sentiment, especially during presidential election years. These attitudes are well-documented and deeply ingrained.

Africans, however, occupy a uniquely precarious position. They are perceived as "up from slavery," colonized, and in need of Christianization and "civilizing." This is the lens through which the American government—and by extension, its people—view Africans. They dismissively categorize Africans as belonging to the "Third World" while arrogantly claiming the title of the "First World" for themselves. Isn't that remarkable? Americans are indeed bold and aggressive in their assertions.

For Africans, immigrating to the New World has always been fraught with challenges—a constant push and pull. Africans are deeply religious people, much like their brothers and sisters in the diaspora, including Black Americans. While American Whites are also religious, their devotion often seems directed toward their "new god," money, with an almost neurotic emphasis on the economy.

Africans understand that seeking a better life through migration is not a crime. Yet, at every turn, they face ridicule from the American government, which simultaneously blames African nations for their challenges while exploiting their manpower and resources. Some even view Africans as heathens, unworthy of the good things in life.

This guidebook is designed to help Africans navigate this landscape. It aims to equip you with the psychological tools of a sojourner, encouraging you to set aside the prejudices of others and focus on planning your journey wisely.

If you want to understand how successive American governments have historically viewed Africa and its people, look beyond President Trump. Consider the early 20th century, during the presidency of Woodrow Wilson, the 28th President of the United States, or study America's antebellum years.

During his first year in office, Wilson openly promoted racial segregation and even justified it. Africans were dehumanized and treated as less than human. They were also portrayed as a people without religion—false narratives that the American public accepted without question.

For many Africans, the distinction between atheism and agnosticism as understood in the West is irrelevant. An atheist denies the existence of God, while an agnostic claims it's impossible to know whether God exists. However, Africans—whether adherents of traditional religions, Islam, or Christianity—often turn to their native religious practices, such as Animism, in times of need. It is not uncommon for someone to embody both agnostic and atheist beliefs simultaneously.

Let us now turn to biblical narratives of immigration in antiquity.

Below is an excerpt adapted from The Ultimate Immigration Handbook, written and presented by Rev. Joan M. Maruskin, National Administrator of the Church World Service Religious Services Program. (As of this publication, written permission for reproduction is pending, though use by individuals and congregational groups has been approved. See the Epilogue, Section 8 of this guidebook for more details.)

According to Maruskin, the Bible begins with the migration of God's Spirit and ends with John in exile on the Isle of Patmos. Between these events, the uprooted people of God seek safety, sanctuary, and refuge, while the living God provides instructions for welcoming the stranger.

As a deeply religious people, Americans must reconnect with these biblical principles and work toward a more inclusive and humane approach to immigration. By embracing the scriptural ethos of welcoming the stranger, they can inspire positive action among all nationalities.

SECTION TWO

Know Before You Go

Immigrants' Experience of America

Immigrant Experience and US immigration policies have been thoroughly researched, compiled and sponsored by Americaonlinevisa.com, Research Point, Inc, Flatiron Books and Book Riots. The theme: immigrants' experience of America is appropriate to this endeavor, **know before you go!**

On arrival to the US nearly 50 years ago, I had the opportunity to have read many books and articles on immigration topics about American immigration policies and immigrants' lives. These books were mostly written by immigrants to the US and their experiences since arrival. The reading exercises and cultural immersion were very helpful to me. The books helped form my earlier opinions of America. So, below, I have listed some more recent books to help you understand the America of your heart's desire. The proposition I am making here is that you, the sojourner, must know who you are, what you want, and how to achieve your goals. You must know these and be grounded in all the issues before you go.

Research Point authors compiled and drafted this book as a guide to help you explore who you are, what you want, and how to accomplish your goals and objectives. This book is written from the perspective of an immigrant who has a little understanding of American immigration policies, culture, politics, society, thought processes, and ideology. The information contained herein is correct and current at the point of writing for the printing press. For a more sophisticated examination of your individual situation, please, be advised to see an American immigration lawyer. This guide is not intended to supplant your need for an attorney. The authors of this guide are not Attorneys. For an understanding of your personal situation, please consult with a lawyer.

Fifteen-year-old Ana Cancion never dreamed of moving to America. But when Juan Ruiz proposes and promises to take her to New York City, she has to say yes. It does not matter that he is twice her age, that there is no love between them. Their marriage is an opportunity for her entire close-knit family to eventually immigrate from the Dominican Republic. So, in 1965, Ana leaves behind everything she knows and becomes Ana Ruiz. In bright, musical prose, Angie Cruz's Dominican is a portrait of the immigrant experience and the timeless coming of age story of a young woman finding her voice.

The story of the stranger in search of shelter, safety, and community is one of the oldest in history and one that is constantly evolving. Here are some incredible books about immigration and immigrants: heart-wrenching tales of families divided, stories of leaving everything behind in hopes of something better, accounts of dreams deferred until the next generation, reflections on identities rooted in two distinctly different cultures, and the universal search for a new self in the unknown-the American unknown.

EXIT WEST: A NOVEL BY MOHSIN HAMID

Exit West is a lyrical, heart-breaking, deeply moving reflection on migration, love, and xenophobia. Nadia and Saeed are two vastly different people thrown together in a perilous time. They must navigate, leaving a war-torn country and tending to their fledgling love affairs as they migrate country after country in search of the elusive new and better life. This book will leave you both wrecked and full to the brim, but you must attempt to find your space within it.

THE GOOD IMMIGRANT: 26 WRITERS REFLECT ON AMERICA EDITED BY NIKESH SHUKLA AND CHIMENE SULEYMAN

The Good Immigrant is so urgently necessary right now; it is a head-on account of modern immigration in America. Twenty-six authors (including Chigozie Obioma, Alexander Chee, Fatimah Asghar, and others) share their stories of immigration in the United States. The authors of The Good Immigrant give a voice to the varied and complicated realities facing so many across the country. In Home Fire by Kamila Shamsie is the story of Isma, a young British Pakistani woman who has served as the matriarch of her family since her mother's death. Isma was offered an opportunity to leave England for the U.S., but even as she escapes, she and her siblings must contend with their father's troubled past as well as the ramifications of a new man in their collective lives. A brilliantly written and unexpected book.

Sometimes poetry can convey depth and rawness of emotion in ways that prose simply cannot. Such is the case with Javier Zamora's Unaccompanied, which is his reflection on his own immigration story of crossing the border alone to meet his parents in the U.S. at the age of nine. Zamora's work is stunning, and this book is must-read.

Abdi Nor Iftin's Call Me American-a memoire, shows some reporting on a radicalized Somalia in the mid-2000s which gained him international notoriety, but also forced him to flee his homeland and leave his family behind. After a childhood spent idolizing American culture, Iftin faced the adult reality of trying to gain access to the country as an asylum seeker. His memoir explores his own experience of the Somali Civil War and his incredible journey to establishing a new and different life in America.

I stumbled upon this beautiful book while at an ethnic bookstore in South Baltimore, MD and I am so glad I did. Things Are Good Now by Djamila Ibrahim, follows migrant women in cities across the world as they sort out their new lives in foreign lands. The book explores the profound sacrifices they must make to achieve those lives and what remains when they do. A fantastic read!

In a novel by Dina Nayeri, she poses the question, what if, in the 20 years since you migrated from your home in Iran, you only got to see your father four times? How would your lives be different? Would that time apart transform you both? How would the years alter how you view home and heritage? *Refuge* explores these questions through the story of one Iranian woman who immigrated to the United States as a child. Is this the America of your dreams?

Viet Thanh Nguyen is one of the most compelling contemporary writers addressing the themes of migration and the dual cultural identity it creates. *The Refugees* is a collection of stories that spans two decades and toggles between Vietnam and America. If you love this book, try *Displaced: Refugee Writers on Refugee Lives,* a collection of essays written by seventeen refugee writers and edited by Viet Thanh Nguyen.

Cartoonist and writer Thi Bui starts her illustrated memoire; *The Best We Could Do* at the beginning: the birth of her son. What follows is a reflection on her own childhood as the daughter of Vietnamese immigrants, held up in the light of new parenthood. She recounts the many sacrifices (large and small) her parents made for the benefit of her and her siblings and contemplates what love and family really mean. Front Desk in Kelly Yang's immigrant narrative mimics a familiar story in an immigrant's experiences of culture shock. Mia Tang is a young girl who manages the front desk at her home, Calivista Motel, where her parents also clean the rooms and hide undocumented immigrants. She also wants to be a writer, even though her mother has doubts about English not being her first language. This lovely middle-grade book follows Mia as she wrestles with the issues surrounding her family's immigration status and as she discovers how to accomplish her own dreams.

In the first of two companion books by Alexandra Diaz, Jaime, a young Guatemalan boy, must leave the dangerous circumstances in his home country behind and start the treacherous journey down *The Only Road* to the United States. Jaime's story echoes the violent realities facing hundreds of thousands of immigrants across the globe every day, but life in America is especially wonderous. *Other Words for Home* by Jasmine Warga explores the lived experiences of Jude. This middle grade schoolbook focused on Jude, a young girl who immigrates with her mother from Syria to America. Jude navigates the strange newness of a new school, learning a new culture, and establishing a home and identity for herself in Cincinnati, Ohio.

But, in *The Day you Begin* by Jacqueline Woodson as illustrated by Rafael Lopez, the literary mood was on a different perspective although not exclusively about immigrants, in *The Day You Begin* reminds children of all backgrounds to love themselves, even when they think they are the exception amongst their peers. *The Day You Begin* encourages children to embrace the ways in which they are distinct and unique, no matter how they look, how they talk, or where they are from. Not only is this book told with rich, stunning illustrations, but it is also available in Spanish and English- for the bilingual enthusiasts!

René Laínez's touching picture book *From North to South* focuses on one Mexican American family whose matriarch was deported. The story pivots around the insecurity and strain that deportations place on families, especially children, and does so with aplomb. The book was written in Spanish and English and can help begin a dialogue with children facing the uncertainty of parental deportations.

In *A Different Pond* by Bao Phi as illustrated by Thi Bui, in which the story is being told from the perspective of a young Vietnamese immigrant son is quite an emotionally moving narrative. The father and son ventured out one day on a fishing trip, where the father tells the story of another pond all the way back in Vietnam. At one point, the young boy reflects, "A kid at my school said my dad's English sounds like a thick, dirty river. But to me his English sounds like a gentle rain." *A Different Pond* engages beautifully with the themes so many children of immigrants must wrestle with, specifically loving the differences embodied in their parents and their heritage.

In a book, Two White Rabbits by Jairo Buitrago as illustrated by Rafael Yockteng with translation by Elisa Amado, they use beautiful, subtle drawings to tell the story of a father and a daughter migrating from Central America to the United States. While there may be triggers for children who have had similar migration stories, it is critical reading for non-immigrant children and adults while we seek to empathize with our fellow human beings facing grave danger as they seek out a better life in America.

What other books about immigration have you read that captured your heart or pushed your imagination and thinking processes? Please, share your favorites with me by communicating via email! JMONYE04@GMAIL.COM

Fifteen-year-old Ana Cancion never dreamed of moving to America. But when Juan Ruiz proposes and promises to take her to New York City, she has to say yes. It does not matter that he is twice her age, that there is no love between them. Their marriage is an opportunity for her entire close-knit family to eventually immigrate from the Dominican. So, in 1965, Ana leaves behind everything she knows and becomes Ana Ruiz. In bright, musical prose, Angie Cruz's *Dominican* is a portrait of the immigrant experience and the timeless coming-of-age story of a young woman finding her voice.

The story of the stranger in search of shelter, safety, and community is one of the oldest known stories in antiquity and so shall it be in history and one that is constantly evolving.

SECTION THREE

CLASSIFICATION: IMMIGRANT AND NON-IMMIGRANT VISA TYPES

A Dictionary of US Visa Categories

The purpose of your intended travel and other facts will determine what type of visa is required under U.S. immigration laws. As a visa applicant, you will need to establish that you meet all requirements to receive the category of visa for which you are applying. Specifically, make sure that you satisfy the "Public Charge" provisions of their laws.

When you apply at a U.S embassy or consulate, a consular officer will determine based on the prevailing laws, whether you are eligible to receive a visa, and if so, which visa category is appropriate. Below, are two of the most frequently used visa categories: Immigrant visas and Nonimmigrant visas. We will start with the latter.

Nonimmigrant Visa Categories

The chart below contains many different purposes of temporary travel and the related nonimmigrant visa categories available in this guidebook. Select a visa category below to learn more and talk with your lawyer or service provider to help you evaluate your situation.

Purpose of Travel	Visa Category	Required: Before applying for visa*
Athlete, amateur or professional (competing for prize money only)	B-1	(NA)
Au pair (exchange visitor)	J	SEVIS
Australian professional specialty	E-3	DOL
Border Crossing Card: Mexico	BCC	(NA)
Business visitor	B-1	(NA)

CNMI-only transitional	CW-1	(USCIS)
Worker Crewmember	D	(NA)
Diplomat or foreign government official	A	(NA)
Domestic employee or nanny - must be accompanying a foreign national employer	B-1	(NA)
Employee of a designated international organization or NATO	G1-G5, NATO	(NA)
Exchange visitor	J	SEVIS
Foreign military personnel stationed in the United States	A-2, NATO1-6	(NA)
Foreign national with extraordinary ability in Sciences, Arts, Education, Business or Athletics	O	USCIS
Free Trade Agreement (FTA) Professional: Chile, Singapore	H-1B1 - Chile H-1B1 - Singapore	DOL
International cultural exchange visitor	Q	USCIS
Intra-company transferee	L	USCIS
Medical treatment, visitor for	B-2	(NA)
Media, journalist	I	(NA)
NAFTA professional worker: Mexico, Canada	TN/TD	(NA)
Performing athlete, artist, entertainer	P	USCIS
Physician	H-1B	SEVIS
Professor, scholar, teacher (exchange visitor)	J	SEVIS
Religious worker	J	USCIS
Specialty occupations in fields requiring highly specialized knowledge	R	DOL then USCIS
Student: academic, vocational	H-1B	SEVIS

Temporary agricultural worker	F, M	DOL then USCIS
Temporary worker performing other services or labor of a temporary or seasonal nature.	H-2A	DOL then USCIS
Tourism, vacation, pleasure visitor	H-2B	(NA)
Training in a program not primarily for employment	B-2	USCIS
Treaty trader/treaty investor	H-3	(NA)
Transiting the United States	E	(NA)
Victim of Criminal Activity	C	USCIS
Victim of Human Trafficking	U	USCIS
Nonimmigrant (V) Visa for Spouse and Children of a Lawful Permanent Resident (LPR)	T	(NA)
Renewals in the U.S. - A, G, and NATO Visas	V	(NA)

***What the abbreviations above mean** - Before applying for a visa at a U.S. embassy or consulate, know your purpose of travel. Click on the reporting agency in charge on your right page margins. Read up on everything. Then click on the abbreviation or the letter / the corresponding alphabet above before following the instructions as required.

- DOL = The U.S. employer must obtain foreign labor certification from the U.S. Department of Labor, prior to filing a petition with USCIS.
- USCIS = U.S. Citizenship and Immigration Services (USCIS) approval of a petition or application (The required petition or application depends on the visa category you plan to apply for.)
- SEVIS = Program approval entered in the Student and Exchange Visitor Information System (SEVIS)
- (NA) = Not Applicable - Additional approval by another U.S. government agency is not required prior to applying for a visa
- Important Notes:
- **About this chart** – It is not a complete list of all travel purposes for the visa category. Select a visa category webpage for more information. The chart lists almost all nonimmigrant visa

categories, except for several not listed above. Refer to the Foreign Affairs Manual, 9 FAM 402.1 for all nonimmigrant visa categories.

- **Canadian NAFTA Professional workers** – A visa not required; apply to U.S. Customs and Border Protection (CBP) at border port of entry.
- **K nonimmigrant visas** – For U.S. citizen fiancé(e) and spouse for immigration related purposes. Refer to Immigrant Visa Categories.

Immigrant Visa Categories

The chart below contains different purposes for immigrating to the United States, and the related immigrant visa categories for which information is available for this guidebook. Select a visa category below to learn more:

Immediate Relative & Family Sponsored	Visa Category
Spouse of a U.S. Citizen	IR1, CR1
Spouse of a U.S. Citizen awaiting approval of an I-130 immigrant petition	K-3 *
Fiancé(e) to marry U.S. Citizen & live in U.S.	K-1 *
Intercountry Adoption of Orphan Children by U.S. Citizens	IR3, IH3, IR4, IH4
Certain Family Members of U.S. Citizens	IR2, CR2, IR5, F1, F3, F4
Certain Family Members of Lawful Permanent Residents	F2A, F2B
Employer Sponsored – Employment	
Employment-Based Immigrants, including (preference group):	
• Priority workers [First]	E1
• Professionals Holding Advanced Degrees and Persons of Exceptional Ability [Second]	E2
• Professionals and Other Workers [Third]	E3, EW3
• Employment Creation/Investors [Fifth]	C5, T5, R5, I5
• Certain Special Immigrants: [Fourth]	S (many**)

Religious Workers	SD, SR
Iraqi and Afghan Translators/Interpreters	SI
Iraqis Who Worked for/on Behalf of the U.S. Government	SQ
Afghans Who Worked for/on Behalf of the U.S. Government	SQ
Other Immigrants	
Diversity Immigrant Visa	DV
Returning Resident	SB

Important Notes:

***K Visas** – Listed with immigrant visas because they are for immigration related purposes.

About this chart - This chart is a list of many immigrant visa categories, but not every immigrant visa category is contained herein.

**Refer to the Foreign Affairs Manual, 9 FAM 502.1 for a listing of all immigrant visa categories. Remember that you can always purchase US government documents for pennies. (http://www.gpo.gov).

Moving forward, below is an alphabetical list of US visa subcategories which will enable you to decide what visa type application materials might be your best fit.

A

An **A-Visa** is a type of **non-immigrant visa** that allows you to travel to the United States. The A-Visas are designed for certain **foreign government officials** and their **staff**. There are three subcategories of A-Visas: **A-1**, **A-2**, and **A-3**.

- **A-1 visas**: For **ambassadors**, **ministers**, **diplomats**, **consular officers**, and their **immediate family members**.
- **A-2 visas**: For other **government officials**, **employees**, their **immediate family members**, and their **technical and support staff**. This also includes **military personnel** and representatives from the **African Union** or **European Union**.
- **A-3 visas**: For **attendants**, **servants**, and **employees** of those in the US under **A-1** or **A-2 visas**.

A-Visa holders are generally exempt from **US taxes** and enjoy **diplomatic immunity**. However, they must apply for a visa before traveling to the US and may be subject to certain **restrictions** depending on their **status** and **purpose of travel** to the US.

Accompanying: A type of visa in which family members travel with the principal applicant, (in immigrant visa cases, within six months of issuance of an immigrant visa to the principal applicant).

Adjust Status: 1) to change from a nonimmigrant visa status or other status; or, 2) to adjust the status of a permanent resident (green card holder). Learn more on USCIS's website, as it is a Department of Homeland Security (DHS) process.

Administrative processing: Some visa applications require further administrative processing, which takes additional time after the visa applicant's interview by a consular officer. Applicants are advised of this requirement when they apply. To learn more, review our Administrative Processing webpage.

Admission: Entry into the United States is authorized by a Department of Homeland Security (DHS), Customs and Border Protection (CBP) officer. When you come from abroad and first arrive in the United States, the visa allows you to travel to the port-of-entry and request permission to enter the United States. Admission, or entering the United States, by non-U.S. citizens must be authorized by a CBP officer at the port-of-entry, who determines whether you can enter and how long you can stay here, on any visit. If you are allowed to enter, how long you can stay and the immigration classification you are given is shown as a recorded date or Duration of Status (D/S) on your admission stamp or paper Form I-94, Arrival/Departure Record. For more information, go to DHS, CBP. If you want to stay longer than the date authorized, you must request permission from DHS, U.S. Citizenship, and Immigration Services (USCIS).

Adopted Child: An unmarried child under age 21, who was adopted while under the age of sixteen, and who has been in legal custody and lived with the adopting parent(s) for at least two years. These rules do not apply to orphans adopted by U.S. Citizens. The adoption decree must give the child all the rights of a natural born child. For more adoption information visit DOS's adoption.state.gov.

Advance Parole: Permission to return to the United States after travel abroad. Advance parole must be granted by DHS prior to leaving the United States. The following categories of people may need advance parole: people on a K-1 visa, asylum applicants, parolees, people with Temporary Protected Status (TPS) and some people trying to adjust status, while in the United States. If these people do not apply for advance parole before they leave the United States, they may be unable to return. Go to DHS, USCIS to learn more.

Advisory Opinion: An opinion regarding a point of law from the Office of Visa Services in the Department of State, Washington, D.C. This opinion would be issued in response to an inquiry from a U.S. Embassy or Consulate regarding the interpretation of immigration law, or in response to an inquiry from an applicant or his/her legal representative regarding the legal correctness of the applicant's visa refusal.

Advisory Opinion ("J" Visa) Waiver of Foreign Residence Requirement, INA 212(e): A J-1 visa holder's DS 2019 or IAP 66 form will have a statement in the bottom left-hand corner of the form, as follows: "Bearer (is or is not) subject to Section 212(e). Two-year rule (does or does not) apply (name of country)". This is a preliminary endorsement of the Consular Officer or Immigration Officer regarding Section 212(e) of the INA.

When a J-1 visa holder (or his/her attorney) inquires whether the Foreign Residence Requirement under INA 212(e) applies to a particular J-1 visa holder, then a request for an Advisory Opinion is mailed to the Waiver Review Division at the Department of State. Learn more - See the "Eligibility and Application Procedures" and "FAQ" sections in the Waiver -Foreign Residence Requirement webpages.

Affidavit of Support: **(AOS)**: A document promising that the person who completes it will support an applicant financially in the United States. Family and certain employment immigration cases require the I-864 Affidavit of Support, which is legally binding. All other cases use the I-134 Affidavit of Support. Go to our I-864 information to learn more.

Affiliated: Associated or controlled by the same owner or authority.

Age Out: A child must be unmarried and under the age of 21, as defined in U.S. immigration law. A child beneficiary of an immigrant petition who will apply for an immigrant visa is considered to have **aged out** when the beneficiary no longer qualifies for an immigrant visa based on having reached age 21. The Child Status Protection Act (CSPA) changed the law, to allow many beneficiaries to still qualify as children for immigrant visa purposes even after reaching age 21. Learn more about National Visa Center processing for cases where child beneficiaries are close to aging out.

Agent: In immigrant visa processing, the applicant selects a person who receives all correspondence regarding the case and pays the immigrant visa application processing fee. The agent can be the applicant, the petitioner or another person selected by the applicant and listed on Form DS-261, Online Choice of Address and Agent.

Alien: A foreign national who is not a U.S. citizen.

Allotment: The allocation of an immigrant number to a consular office or to USCIS. This number may be used for visa issuance or adjustment of status as described in the Operation of the Immigrant Numerical Control System.

AOS: Affidavit of Support, Form I-864. A document promising that the person who completes it will support an applicant financially in the U.S. Family and certain employment immigration cases require the I-864 Affidavit of Support, which is legally binding. All other cases use the I-134 Affidavit of Support. Go to our I-864 information to learn more.

Applicant (Visa): A foreign citizen who is applying for a nonimmigrant or immigrant U.S. visa. The visa applicant may also be referred to as a beneficiary for petition-based visas.

Application Filing: The date which the Visa Office of the Department of State uses to determine when to send the Instruction Package to an immigrant visa applicant. The Instruction Package tells the applicant what documents need to be prepared for the immigrant visa application.

Appointment Package: The letter and documents that tell an applicant of the date of the immigrant visa interview. It includes forms that the applicant must complete before the interview and instructions for how to get everything ready for the interview.

Approval Notice: Notice of Action, Form I-797, issued by DHS, USCIS that says that USCIS has approved a petition, or request for extension of stay or change of status.

Asylee: A person who cannot return to his home country because of a well-founded fear of persecution. An application for asylum is made in the United States to DHS. Go to the USCIS website to learn more. See Follow-to-Join Refugees & Asylees for information for the spouse or unmarried minor children abroad following to join a refugee or asylee in the United States.

Arrival/Departure Card: Also known as Form I-94, Arrival-Departure Record. Effective May 25, 2013, a new electronic I-94 process was fully implemented at air and seaports-of-

entry. Under the new process, a CBP official at the port-of-entry provides each admitted nonimmigrant traveler (all non-U.S. citizens) with an admission stamp on their passport. CBP will no longer issue a paper form I-94, with some exceptions. Learn more on the CBP website. On the admission stamp or paper Form I-94, the CBP official records either a date or "D/S" (duration of status).

If your admission stamp or paper Form I-94 contains a specific date, then that is the date by which you must leave the United States. If you were issued a paper Form I-94, it is important to keep this card safe because it shows the length of time you are permitted and authorized by DHS to stay in the United States. It is best kept stapled with your passport, kept in a safe place. The visitors return the I-94 card when they leave the country.

Attorney of Record: An attorney or representative appointed by the petitioner, applicant, or beneficiary to receive correspondence and documentation relating to the visa petition or application. An attorney of record may be appointed by the petitioner, applicant or beneficiary by submitting to the National Visa Center or the U.S. Embassy or Consulate processing the visa application: Form G-28, Notice of Entry of Appearance as Attorney or Representative; a printed letterhead stationery showing membership in the legal profession (member of a U.S. State or District of Columbia bar association practicing in the United States) and stating that such an attorney has been retained or employed to represent the applicant; or a letter from the applicant that identifies the attorney or representative with whom the applicant established such relationship. If, as an applicant for US Visa, you have an Attorney, make sure that you verify that your lawyer is legitimate and qualified to represent you. It's your duty to trust but verify.

Searchable Keywords:

A Visa (Officials in Foreign Governments). A-3 Visa (Diplomats and Foreign Government Officials): Legal Rights and Protections Pamphlet (Wilberforce Act). AABB Testing (DNA Relationship Testing). Adjustment of Status to Permanent Resident. Administrative Processing. Admission to the United States: CBP Website. Adopting a Child. Advance Parole. Advanced Passenger Information System (APIS). Advisory Opinion for J-1

Waiver of Two-Year Foreign Residence Requirement. Affidavit of Support. Afghan and Iraqi Translators/Interpreters, Special Immigrant Visas. Afghan and Iraqi Translators/Interpreters, Special Immigrant Visas: FAQs for Applicants Living Overseas. Alien Classes Ineligible to Receive Visas. American Institute in Taiwan (AIT) Website. Americans Traveling Abroad. Arrival/Departure Record (I-94). Asylees, Follow-to-Join. Asylum: USCIS Website. Athletes, Artists, Entertainers (P Visa for Temporary Workers). Au Pairs (J-1 Exchange Visitor): ECA Website. Australian in Specialty Occupation (E-3 Visa): U.S. Embassy Canberra Website. Automatic Revalidation (Limited Re-entry with Valid Form I-94 & Expired Visa). Automatic Revalidation: CBP Website. Avian Flu.

B

The **US B-Visa** is a type of **non-immigrant visa** that allows foreign nationals to travel to the United States temporarily for **business** or **tourism** purposes. There are two subtypes of B-Visas: **B-1** and **B-2**.

- **B-1 Visa**: For **business visitors** who want to participate in activities such as **consulting**, **negotiating**, **attending conferences**, or **training**.
- **B-2 Visa**: For **tourists** who want to visit the US for **pleasure**, **medical treatment**, or **family meeting/reunion**.

Application Process

To apply for a B-Visa, you need to meet certain requirements, such as:

- Having a **valid passport**
- A **specific purpose of travel**
- **Sufficient funds** to cover your expenses

You also need to fill out an **online application form** and schedule an **interview** at a US embassy or consulate. You can find more information about the B-Visa on the official website of the **US Department of State**.

Visa Duration

The duration of a B-Visa depends on two factors:

- **Validity Period**: How long the visa may be used to enter the US, ranging from **1 month to 10 years**, depending on the **reciprocity agreement** between the US and the applicant's country.
- **Period of Stay**: How long the visa holder may remain in the US after each entry, usually up to **6 months**, with the possibility of **extensions** in some cases. The exact duration is determined by the **immigration officer** at the port of entry.

You can check the validity period on your **visa sticker** or on the official website of the **US Department of State**. The period of stay is stamped in your **passport** or on the **I-94 Arrival/Departure Record**.

Multiple Entries

The B-Visa is a **multiple-entry visa**, meaning you can enter the US more than once. There is no set limit to the number of times you can visit in a year, but each entry is subject to the **discretion of US immigration officers**. The visa is intended for **temporary, occasional visits** for business, tourism, or medical treatment — not for long-term living.

Can I Study in the US with a B-Visa?

No, you cannot study in the US with a B-Visa. The B-Visa is only for **temporary visits**. If you want to study in the US, you must apply for a **student visa (F or M)** and enroll in an **SEVP-approved school**.

A student visa (F or M) allows you to pursue a full course of study at a US academic or vocational institution. You need to meet certain requirements, such as having a valid passport, a specific purpose of travel, and sufficient funds to cover your expenses. You also need to fill out an online application form and schedule an interview at a US embassy or consulate.

A B-visa only allows you to enroll in a short recreational course of study, which is not for credit toward a degree or academic certificate. For example, you can take a cooking class or a yoga workshop as part of your tourist visit. However, you cannot enroll in a degree program, a language course, or a professional training course with a B-visa.

If you enroll in a full course of study while in a B-1, B-2 or B-1/B-2 visa status, you will be considered out of status and ineligible to extend your B status or change to F-1 or M-1 status in the future or as time and circumstances may warrant.

Searchable Keywords:

B Visa (Nonimmigrant Visitor Visa). B Visa (Nonimmigrant Visitor Visa): Refusal Rates by Nationality. B-1 Nonimmigrant Visitor Visa for domestic employees: Legal Rights and Protections Pamphlet (Wilberforce Act). Bermuda, Citizens of: Visa Requirements for Travel to United States. Border Crossing Card (BCC). Bureau of Educational and Cultural Affairs: ECA Website.

Beneficiary: An applicant for a visa as named in a petition filed with DHS, USCIS.

Biometrics: Biologically unique information used to identify individuals. This information can be used to verify identity or check against other entries in the database. The best known biometric is the fingerprint, but others include facial recognition and iris scans. Go to US Department of States' biometrics page to learn more

C

A **US C-Visa** is a type of **non-immigrant visa** for persons traveling in **immediate and continuous transit** through the United States en route to another country, with few exceptions. This means you have a **layover in the US** as part of your itinerary to your final destination, but you do not have any other privileges in the US.

There are three subtypes of C-Visas:

- **C-1 Visa**: For **general transit travelers** who need to pass through the US to reach another country.
- **C-2 Visa**: For transit travelers going **to or from the United Nations Headquarters District** in New York.
- **C-3 Visa**: For transit travelers who are **foreign government officials** or their **immediate family members**.

Application Process

To apply for a C-Visa, you must meet certain requirements, such as:

- Having a **valid passport**
- A **confirmed onward ticket**
- A **visa for your destination country** if required

You also need to fill out an **online application form** and schedule an **interview** at a US embassy or consulate.

More information about the C-Visa can be found on the official website of the **US Department of State** or on the **visa help website**.

Can I Leave the Airport During My Layover with a C-Visa?

It depends on the type of C-Visa you have and the duration of your layover. Generally, C-Visa holders are allowed to **leave the airport** during their layover, but they must **return to the airport** before their onward flight or ship departs.

However, there are some exceptions and restrictions for certain C-visa subtypes:

- C-2 visa holders are only allowed to be in the vicinity of the United Nations Headquarters District in New York City. They cannot leave the area for any reason, except to depart the US.
- C-3 visa holders are subject to the same rules as A-visa holders, which means they may

need to obtain permission from the US Department of State or the foreign mission they are representing before leaving the airport.

Additionally, C-visa holders must comply with the following requirements when leaving the airport during their layover.

They must have a valid passport, a confirmed onward ticket, and a visa for their final destination if required.

- They must not engage in any activities that are not related to their transit purpose, such as tourism, business, or study.
- They must not exceed the period of stay granted by the US immigration officer at the port of entry, which is usually up to 29 days.

How long can I stay in the airport with a C-visa?

The maximum period of stay in the airport with a C-visa is 29 days or the proposed flight or ship departure, whichever is earlier. However, this may vary depending on the discretion of the US immigration officer at the port of entry. You should check your passport stamp or your I-94 Arrival/Departure Record to confirm the exact duration of your authorized stay.

Searchable Keywords:

Canadian Citizens: Visa Requirements for Travel to United States. Camp Counselor (J-1 Exchange Visitor Visa): ECA Website. Census Bureau. Center for Disease Control and Prevention (CDC). Change of Exchange Visitor Program Category: ECA Website. Change of Status in the United States: USCIS Website. Child Status Protection Act (CSPA). Chile FTA Professional Worker (H1B1 Visa): U.S. Embassy Santiago Website. Classifications: Immigrants - Types of Immigrant Visas. Classifications: Nonimmigrants - Types of Nonimmigrant Visas. CNMI-Only Investor (E-2 CNMI Visa): USCIS Website. CNMI-Only Transitional Worker (CW-1 Visa): USCIS Website. Code of Federal Regulations (CFR). Commonwealth of the Northern Mariana Islands (CNMI) Federalization of Immigration Law: USCIS Website. Complaints About Treatment at a Port-of-Entry to the United States. Congressional Testimony. Contact a U.S. Embassy or Consulate. Contact the Visa Office, Customer Service Statement.

Cancelled Without Prejudice: A stamp a U.S. Embassy or Consulate puts on a visa when there is a mistake in the visa, or the visa is a duplicate visa (two of the same kind). It does not affect the validity of other visas in the passport. It does not mean that the passport holder will not get another visa.

Case Number: The National Visa Center (NVC) gives each immigrant petition a case number. This number has three letters followed by ten digits (numbers). The three letters are an abbreviation for the overseas embassy or consulate that will process the immigrant visa case (for example, GUZ for Guangzhou, CDJ for Ciudad Juarez).

The digits tell us exactly when NVC created the case. For example, a case with the number MNL2001747003 would be a case assigned to the U.S. Embassy in Manila. 2001 is the year in which NVC received the case from USCIS (formerly INS). The petition was received at the NVC on September 1st, which is the 247th day of the year, so 747 represents the ordinal date (247) plus 500. The 003 shows that it was the third case created for Manila on that day. This case number is not the same as the USCIS receipt number, which is written on the Notice of Action, Form I-797.

Certificate of Citizenship: A document issued by DHS as proof that the person is a U.S. citizen by birth (when born abroad) or derivation (not from naturalization). The Child Citizenship Act of 2001 gives U.S. citizenship automatically to certain foreign-born children of U.S. citizens. These children can apply for certificates of citizenship.

Certificate of Naturalization: A document issued by DHS as proof that the person has become a U.S. citizen (naturalized) after immigration to the United States.

Certified Copy: A certified copy can be any of the following:

- A photocopy of the original that has an original stamp, seal, or other endorsement from the issuing authority.
- An official transcript of the original that has an original stamp, seal, or other endorsement from the issuing authority.
- An official duplicate or replacement copy of the original that either has an original stamp, seal, or other endorsement from the issuing authority or that is printed on official stationery.

Change Status: Changing from one nonimmigrant visa status to another nonimmigrant visa status while a person is in the United States is permitted for some nonimmigrant visa holders, if approved by USCIS. The visa holder may file a request with USCIS before his or her authorized stay expires, which generally is the date on the visa holder's admission stamp or paper Form I-94,

Arrival/Departure Record (except for visa holders admitted to the U.S. for duration of status, stamped D/S). See Change My Nonimmigrant Status on the USCIS website to learn more.

Charge/Chargeable: There are numerical limits on the number of immigrant visas that can be granted to aliens from any one foreign country. This limit is the same for all countries. The limit is based on place of birth, not citizenship. Where the immigrant is "charged", means that person is counted towards a given country's numerical limit. For example, an immigrant born in Ethiopia is "charged" to Ethiopia, and therefore counted towards reaching the numerical limit for that country. The person would be "charged" to Ethiopia, even if the immigrant born in Ethiopia was born of Yemeni parents and has a passport from Yemen. For more information visit USCIS's webpage on the topic.

Although immigrants are normally "charged" to their country of birth, an immigrant is sometimes able to claim another for the sake of immigration. You will do this if it helps the immigrant in reaching the "cut-off date" date faster. For example, suppose you were born in India, but your spouse was born in Sudan. The "cut-off date" for a person born in India is earlier in family fourth preference immigration category than the "cut-off date" for a person born in Sudan.

The US government can "charge" you to Sudan, rather than India, and you can use the more favorable cut-off date for Sudan. Therefore, you would be able to immigrate years earlier with a chargeability to Sudan than a chargeability to India.

Child: Unmarried child under the age of 21 years. A child may be natural born, step or adopted. If the child is a stepchild, the marriage between the parent and the U.S. citizen must have occurred when the child was under the age of 18.

If the child is adopted, he/she must have been adopted with a full and final adoption when the child was under the age of 16, and the child must have lived with and been in the legal custody of the parent for at least two years. An orphan may qualify as a child if he/she has been adopted abroad by an U.S. citizen or if the U.S. citizen parent has filed an immediate-relative (IR) visa petition for him/her to go to the United States for adoption by the U.S. citizen.

In certain visa cases a child continues to be classified as a child after he/she becomes 21 if the petition was filed for him/her when he/she was still under 21 years of age. For example, an IR-2 child of an U.S. citizen remains a child after the age of 21 if a petition was filed for him/her on or after August 6, 2002, when he/she was still under 21 years old. The child must meet other requirements of a child as listed above.

Child Status Protection Act (CSPA):

Child Status Protection Act (CSPA): The Child Status Protection Act (CSPA) is a U.S. federal law. CSPA allows some people to apply for an immigrant visa as a child even after they turn 21 years old. (In U.S. immigration law, to be considered a child, you must be under 21 years of age and unmarried.) The law allows an applicant to lower their age by subtracting the time their petition was being reviewed at U.S. Citizenship and Immigration Services (USCIS) from their age on the day a visa became available. If the applicant's age *after* this calculation is less than 21 years, he or she can continue to apply as a "child" in their original visa category. To take advantage of CSPA protections you must have pursued your immigrant visa within a year of a visa becoming available. This is commonly called the "seek to acquire" rule.

Code of Federal Regulations: The Code of Federal Regulations contains useful information on the laws regulating U.S. visa policy.

Cohabit: To live together without a legal marriage ceremony.

Common-law marriage: An agreement between a man and woman to enter marriage without a civil or religious ceremony. It may not be recognized as a marriage for immigration purposes.

Conditional Residence (CR) Visa: If you have been married for less than two years when your husband or wife (spouse) gets lawful permanent resident status (gets a green card), then your spouse gets residence on a conditional basis.

After two years, you and your spouse must apply together to DHS to remove the condition to the residence. Learn how to apply for a CR visa on our Immigrant Visa for a Spouse webpage.

The investor visa (EB5 or T5/C5) is also a conditional residence visa. After two years, it requires an application procedure to remove the condition on permanent residence.

Current/non-current: There are numerical limits on the number of immigrant visas granted to aliens from any foreign country. The limit is based on place of birth, not citizenship.

Because of the numerical limits, there is a waiting time before the immigrant visa can be granted. The terms current/non-current refer to the priority date of a petition in family or employment preference-based immigrant visa cases in relation to the immigrant cut-off date. If your priority date is before the cut-off date, according to the monthly Visa Bulletin, your case is current.

This means your immigrant visa case can now be processed. However, if your priority date is later/comes after the cut-off date, you will need to wait longer, until your priority date is reached (becomes current). To find out whether a preference case is current, see the Visa

Bulletin or call them in Washington, DC @ (202) 485-7699.

Immediate relative immigrant visa cases do not have country numerical limits, but waiting times are longer because of the country limits. The terms priority date, cut-off date and current/non-current do not apply for immediate relative cases.

D

A US D-visa type is a non-immigrant visa for crewmembers who work on board commercial sea vessels or international airlines in the United States.

This visa allows crewmembers to enter the US to provide services required for the normal operation of their vessel or aircraft. They must intend to depart the US on the same vessel or any other vessel within 29 days.

If they travel to the US to join their vessel or aircraft, they also need a transit (C-1) visa or a combination C-1/D visa.

To apply for a D-visa, they need to have a valid passport, a confirmed onward ticket, and fill out an online application form. They also need to schedule an interview at a US embassy or consulate.

You can find more information about the D-visa on the official website of the US Department of State or on the Travel website. How long does it take to get a D-Visa?

The processing time for a D-visa may vary depending on the location and workload of the US embassy or consulate where you apply. According to the official website of the US Department of State, the estimated wait time to receive a nonimmigrant visa interview appointment is based on staff availability and can change from week to week.

However, some websites provide more specific information about the processing time for a D-visa based on the country of application. For example, according to the Embassy of Serbia website, the processing time for employment Visa D usually takes up to 15 days. In some cases, this may take longer, but not more than 30 days.

You can check the estimated wait time for a nonimmigrant visa interview appointment at a US embassy or consulate by selecting your country's location. You can also check the processing times for other types of visas too. Can I work with a D-visa?

No, you cannot work with a D-visa in the United States. A D-visa is only for crewmembers who work on board commercial sea vessels or international airlines that operate in the United

States. You cannot work for any other employer or engage in any other form of activities that are not related to your crewmember status or duties.

If you want to work in the United States, you need to apply for a different type of visa that provides employment authorization, such as an H-1B, L-1, or O-1 visa-types. You also need a U.S. employer who is willing to sponsor you and file a petition on your behalf.

The official website of the U.S. Citizenship and Immigration Services provides more information about working in the United States and the different types of work visas.

How long can I stay in the US with a D-Visa?

The maximum period of stay in the US with a D-Visa is 29 days or the proposed flight or ship departure, whichever is earlier. However, this may vary depending on the discretion of the US immigration officer at the port of entry. You should check your passport stamp or your I-94 Arrival/Departure Record to confirm the exact duration of your authorized stay.

Searchable Keywords:

Denials, Visas. Denials, Visas: Ineligibilities for a Visa. Department of Health & Human Services. Department of Justice. Department of Labor. DHS Trip: For Complaints About Treatment at Port-of-Entry to the United States. Diplomats and Foreign Government Officials. Diplomats and Government Officials, Employee of (A-3 Visa): Legal Rights and Protections Pamphlet (Wilberforce Act). VisitTheUSA.com: U.S. Travel and Tourism Website. Diversity Lottery: USCIS Website. Diversity Visa Program (DV). DNA Relationship Testing Procedures. Dual Citizenship. Duration of Stay.

Denomination/Sect: A religious group or community.

Department of Homeland Security (DHS): DHS is comprised of three main organizations responsible for immigration policies, procedures, implementation, and enforcement of U.S. laws, and more. These DHS organizations include United States Citizenship and Immigration Services (USCIS), Customs and Border Protection (CBP) and Immigration and Customs Enforcement (ICE).

Together, the above US government agencies provide the basic governmental framework for regulating the flow of visitors, workers, and immigrants to the United States.

USCIS is responsible for the approval of all immigrant and nonimmigrant petitions, the authorization of permission to work in the United States, the issuance of extensions of stay, change or adjustment of an applicant's status while the applicant is in the United States, and more.

CBP is responsible for admission of all travelers seeking entry into the United States, and determining the length of authorized stay, if the traveler is admitted. Once in the United States, the traveler falls under the jurisdiction of DHS.

Visit the DHS website for more information.

Department of Labor (DOL): A cabinet level unit/ministry of the U.S. government responsible for labor issues. It has the responsibility for deciding whether certain foreign workers can work in the U.S. Hiring foreign workers for employment in the United States normally requires approval from several government agencies. First, employers must seek labor certification through the DOL. Once the application is certified (approved), the employer must petition USCIS for approval of the petition before applying for a visa.

Derivative Status is getting a status (visa) through another applicant, as provided under immigration law for certain visa categories. For example, the spouse and children of an exchange visitor (J visa holder) would be granted derivative status as J-2 visa holders. Derivative status is only possible if the principal applicant is issued a visa.

Diversity Visa Program: The Department of State has an annual lottery for immigration to the United States. Up to 55,000 immigrants can enter the United States each year from countries with low rates of immigration to the United States. See our information on the Diversity Visa Program.

Documentarily Qualified: The applicant has submitted all documents specified by the consular officer or the National Visa Center (NVC) as sufficient to meet the formal visa application requirements, and necessary processing procedures of the consular office or NVC have been completed.

DOL: U.S. Department of Labor. A cabinet level unit/ministry of the U.S. government that has responsibility for labor issues. It has the responsibility for deciding whether certain foreign workers can work in the United States. Hiring foreign workers for employment in the United States normally requires approval from several government agencies. First, employers must seek labor certification through the DOL. Once the application is certified (approved), the employer must petition USCIS for approval of the petition before applying for a visa.

Domicile: Place where a person has his or her principal residence. The person must intend to keep that residence for the foreseeable future. The sponsor of an immigrant must have domicile in the United States before the visa can be issued. This generally means that the sponsor must be living in the United States. In certain circumstances, however, one can be considered to have a domicile while living temporarily living overseas.

Duration of Status: In certain visa categories, such as diplomats, students and exchange visitors, the alien may be admitted into the United States for as long as the person is still doing the activity for which the visa was issued rather than being admitted until a specific departure date. This is called admission for "duration of status". For students, the time during which a student is in a full course of

study plus any authorized practical training, and following that, the authorized time to depart the country is the duration of status.
The length of time depends upon the course of study. For an undergraduate degree this is commonly four years (eight semesters). Normally the immigration officer gives a student permission to stay in the United States for "duration of status". Duration of Status (or D/S) is recorded on the traveler's admission stamp or paper Form I-94, Arrival/Departure Record. See Arrival/Departure Record above. For more information visit the USCIS website.
DV: See Diversity Visa.

E

A **US E-Visa** is a **non-immigrant visa** for certain foreign nationals engaged in **trade, investment, or specialty occupations** in the United States. There are three subtypes of E-Visas:

- **E-1 Visa**: For **treaty traders** who conduct substantial trade in **goods, services, or technology** between the US and their country of nationality.
- **E-2 Visa**: For **treaty investors** who direct the operations of an enterprise in which they have invested, or are actively investing, a **substantial amount of money** in the US.
- **E-3 Visa**: For **Australian specialty occupation workers** who perform services in a specialty occupation that requires a **bachelor's degree or higher** in the US.

E-3 Visa Special Conditions

The **E-3 visa** classification applies only to **Australian nationals**, their **spouses**, and their **children under the age of 21**. However, their spouses or children **do not need to be Australian citizens**. E-3 principal applicants must be going to the US mainly to work in a specialty area such as:

- Medicine
- Law
- Education
- Biotechnology
- Healthcare

Applicants must have a **bachelor's degree** or its equivalent to apply.

Application Process

To apply for an E-Visa, you need:

- A **valid passport**
- Fill out an **online application form**
- Schedule an **interview** at a US embassy or consulate

You must also provide **evidence of your eligibility**, such as proof of your trade, investment, or employment, as described above.

How long does it take to get an E-visa?

The processing time for an E-visa may vary depending on the location and workload of the US embassy or consulate where you apply. According to the official website of the US Department of State, the estimated wait time to receive a nonimmigrant visa interview appointment is based on staff availability and can change from week to week.

However, some websites provide more specific information about the processing time for an E-visa based on the country of application. Again, according to the Embassy of Serbia's website, the processing time for employment Visa D usually takes up to 15 days. This may take longer, but not more than 30 days in some cases

You can check the estimated wait time for a nonimmigrant visa interview appointment at a US embassy or consulate by selecting your location in your home country.

How much does it cost to get an E-Visa?

The cost of obtaining an E-Visa varies based on the visa subtype and the applicant's country of origin. According to the official website of the U.S. Department of State, the fee for treaty trader, treaty investor, and specialty occupation applicants (nonimmigrant E category) increased from $205 to $315 as of June 17, 2023.

Additionally, some countries may impose supplementary charges or have varying fee structures for E-Visas. For instance, the cost of an E-Visa for Vietnam ranges from $47 to $180 per person, depending on the selected processing time.

You can check the fee for your specific E-Visa subtype and country of application on the official website of the US Department of State here or on the website of the US embassy or consulate where you apply. You can also search for other websites that provide information about E-Visa fees for different countries.

To be clear, the E-1 nonimmigrant classification allows a national of a treaty country (a country with which the United States maintains a treaty of commerce and navigation, or which the United States maintains a qualifying international agreement, or which has been deemed a qualifying country by legislation) to be admitted to the United States solely to engage in international trade on his or her own behalf.

Certain employees of such a person or of a qualifying organization may also be eligible for this classification. (For dependent family members, see “Family of E-1 Treaty Traders and Employees” below.)

See the excerpts below from the “U.S. Department of State's Treaty Countries for a current list of countries with which the United States maintains a treaty of commerce and navigation”. Retrieved on September 10, 2022.

“Who May File for Change of Status to E-1 Classification

If the treaty trader is currently in the United States in a lawful nonimmigrant status, they may file Form I-129 to request a change of status to E-1 classification. If the desired employee is currently in the United States in a lawful nonimmigrant status, the qualifying employer may file Form I-129 on the employee's behalf.

How to Obtain E-1 Classification if Outside the United States

A request for E-1 classification may not be made on Form I-129 if you are physically outside the United States. Interested parties should refer to the U.S. Department of State website for further information about applying for an E-1 nonimmigrant visa abroad. Upon issuance of a visa, the person may seek admission at a United States port of entry as an E-1 nonimmigrant.

General Qualifications of a Treaty Trader

To qualify for E-1 classification, the treaty trader must:

- Be a national of a country with which the United States maintains a treaty of commerce and navigation or with which the United States maintains a qualifying international agreement, or which has been deemed a qualifying country by legislation.
- Carry on substantial trade; and
- Carry on principal trade between the United States and the treaty country which qualified the treaty trader for E-1 classification.

Trade is the existing international exchange of items of trade for consideration between the United States and the treaty country. Items of trade include but are not limited to:

- Goods
- Services
- International banking
- Insurance
- Transportation
- Tourism
- Technology and its transfer
- Some news-gathering activities.

See 8 CFR 214.2(e)(9) for additional examples and discussion.

Substantial trade generally refers to an amount of trade sufficient to ensure a **continuous flow of international trade items** between the United States and the treaty country. The continuous flow involves **numerous transactions over time**, without a specific minimum requirement for the

monetary value or **volume** of each transaction.

While the **monetary value** of transactions is an important factor, **greater weight** is given to **more numerous exchanges of greater value**. For smaller businesses, the income derived from numerous transactions that **support the treaty trader and their family** is considered favorable.

Refer to **8 CFR 214.2(e)(10)** for further details.

Principal Trade Requirement

Principal trade between the United States and the treaty country exists when **over 50% of the volume of international trade** of the treaty trader is between the United States and the treaty trader's country of nationality.

See **8 CFR 214.2(e)(11)** for more information.

General Qualifications of the Employee of a Treaty Trader

To qualify for **E-1 classification**, the employee of a treaty trader must:

- Be the **same nationality** as the principal noncitizen employer (who must have the nationality of the treaty country)
- Meet the definition of **"employee"** under relevant law
- Engage in **executive or supervisory duties** or, if employed in a lesser capacity, possess **special qualifications** essential to the efficient operation of the treaty enterprise

If the principal noncitizen employer is not an individual, the enterprise or organization must be at least **50% owned by persons in the United States** who have the nationality of the treaty country.

These owners must either:

- Maintain **nonimmigrant treaty trader status** or
- If not in the United States, be **classifiable as nonimmigrant treaty traders** if they seek admission to the country

See **8 CFR 214.2(e)(3)(ii)** for more information.

Executive or Supervisory Duties

Duties of an **executive or supervisory character** involve providing the employee with **ultimate control and responsibility** over the treaty enterprise's overall operation or a **major component** of it.

For a full definition, refer to **8 CFR 214.2(e)(17)**.

Special Qualifications

Special qualifications are skills or aptitudes that make the employee's services **essential** to the treaty enterprise. Factors that may meet this requirement include:

- Proven **expertise** in the employee's area of operations
- Whether others **possess the same skills**
- The **salary** the qualifications can command
- Whether the skills are **readily available** in the United States

Knowledge of a **foreign language** or **culture** alone does not meet this requirement. Additionally, a skill that is essential at one time may become **commonplace** later, making it no longer qualify.

Refer to **8 CFR 214.2(e)(18)** for more information.

Period of Stay

Qualified treaty traders and employees will be allowed a maximum initial stay of two years. Requests for extension of stay in, or changes of status to, E-1 classification may be granted in increments of up to two years each. There is no limit to the number of extensions an E-1 nonimmigrant may be granted. All E-1 nonimmigrants, however, must maintain an intention to depart the United States when their status expires or is terminated.

An E-1 nonimmigrant who travels abroad may generally be granted, if determined admissible by a U.S. Customs and Border Patrol Officer, an automatic two-year period of readmission when returning to the United States.

Terms and Conditions of E-1 Status

A **treaty trader** or **employee** may only work in the activity for which they were approved at the time the classification was granted. However, an **E-1 employee** may also work for the treaty organization's **parent company** or one of its **subsidiaries**, provided that:

- The **relationship between the organizations** is established
- The subsidiary employment requires **executive, supervisory, or essential skills**
- The **terms and conditions of employment** have not otherwise changed

Refer to **8 CFR 214.2(e)(8)(ii)** for further details.

Substantive Changes in Employment

USCIS must approve any **substantive change** in the terms or conditions of E-1 status. A **substantive change** is a fundamental alteration in the employer's basic characteristics that would affect the noncitizen's eligibility for E classification. Examples of substantive changes include:

- A **merger**
- An **acquisition**

- The **sale of the division** where the noncitizen is employed
- Any other event that affects the treaty trader or employee's previously approved relationship with the treaty enterprise

Filing a New Application

If there has been a substantive change, the treaty trader or enterprise must notify USCIS by filing a new **Form I-129** (Petition for a Nonimmigrant Worker) with the applicable fee. The petition may simultaneously request an **extension of stay** for the treaty trader or affected employee.

The petition must include evidence to show that the treaty trader or affected employee continues to qualify for E-1 classification. An employer who no longer employs an E-1 nonimmigrant is urged to inform USCIS of this upon termination of the E-1 nonimmigrant's employment.

A treaty trader is not required to file a new Form I-129 to notify USCIS about non-substantive changes. A treaty trader or E-1 employee enterprise may seek advice from USCIS, however, to determine whether a change is considered substantive. To request advice, the treaty trader or enterprise must file Form I-129 with a fee and a complete description of the change.

See 8 CFR 214.2(e)(8) for more information on terms and conditions of E-1 treaty trader status.

A strike or other labor dispute involving a work stoppage at the intended place of employment may affect a Canadian or Mexican treaty trader or employee's ability to obtain E-1 status. See 8 CFR 214.2(e)(22) for details.

Family of E-1 Treaty Traders and Employees

Treaty traders and employees may be accompanied or followed by spouses and unmarried children who are under 21 years of age. Their nationalities need not be the same as the treaty trader or employee. Spouses and children may seek E-1 nonimmigrant classification as dependents and, if approved, generally will be granted the same period of stay as the employee.

If the family members are already in the United States and seeking changes of status to or extensions of stay in an E-1 dependent classification, they may apply by filing a single Form I-539, Application to Change/Extend Nonimmigrant Status, with fee.

Spouses of E-1 workers in valid E-1 or E-1S status are considered employment authorized incident to status, except for spouses of employees of the Taipei Economic and Cultural Representative Office (TECRO) and Taipei Economic and Cultural Offices (TECO), who continue to be required to apply for employment authorization per 8 CFR 274a.12(c)(2).

Department of Homeland Security (DHS)-issued evidence of such employment authorization, particularly that may be presented to employers for completion of Form I-9, Employment Eligibility Verification, including:

1. **An unexpired Form I-94 with a notation reflecting E-1S nonimmigrant status.** As of Jan. 30, 2022, USCIS and CBP began issuing Form I-94 with a new admission code for certain spouses of E-1 workers: **E-1S**. An unexpired Form I-94 reflecting this new code is acceptable as evidence of employment authorization under **List C** of Form I-9.
2. **An unexpired Form I-94 with a notation reflecting E-1 nonimmigrant status, together with a notice from USCIS regarding the new admission code.**
   USCIS will send E spouses with a Form I-94 issued by USCIS before Jan. 30, 2022, that was notated with **E-1 nonimmigrant status** and who are employment authorized incident to status, a notice regarding the new admission code that, together with an unexpired Form I-94 reflecting **E-1 nonimmigrant status**, serves as evidence of employment authorization for such spouses under **List C** of Form I-9.
3. **An unexpired Employment Authorization Document (EAD).**
   E spouses who are employment authorized incident to status are not required to request employment authorization by filing **Form I-765, Application for Employment Authorization**, but may still file Form I-765, with fee, to obtain an **Employment Authorization Document (Form I-766 EAD)**. Form I-766 EAD can be presented to employers as evidence of both **identity and employment authorization** acceptable under **List A** of Form I-9.
4. **An expired EAD with additional documentation to show the EAD is automatically extended (as discussed below).**
   Certain E spouses qualify for the **automatic extension** of their existing Form I-766 EADs if they meet the following conditions:
   - They timely filed a renewal **Form I-765, Application for Employment Authorization**, based on the same E nonimmigrant status; and
   - They have an unexpired Form I-94 showing their status as an **E-1 or E-1S nonimmigrant**.

Normally, DHS regulations provide for an **automatic extension period of up to 180 days** from the expiration date stated in the EAD. However, DHS has published a temporary final rule increasing the automatic extension period.

Temporary Extension Period

Effective **May 4, 2022**, DHS is temporarily increasing the automatic extension period and providing **up to 360 days** of additional automatic extension time, for a total of **up to 540 days**, to eligible renewal applicants.

The automatic EAD extension will therefore continue until whichever comes first:

- The end date on the dependent spouse's **Form I-94** showing valid **L-2 or L-2S nonimmigrant status**, as applicable.
- The date USCIS approves or denies their application to renew the previous EAD; or
- **540 days** from the "Card Expires" date on the front of the previous EAD.

Additional information on the temporary increase of the automatic extension period is available on the **Automatic Employment Authorization Document (EAD) Extension page**.

Evidence of Automatic EAD Extension

Eligible E spouses may present the following evidence of the automatic EAD extension to employers for Form I-9 purposes:

- Form I-94 indicating the unexpired **E-1 or E-1S nonimmigrant status**.
- **Form I-797C** for a timely-filed EAD renewal application (**Form I-765**) stating "Class requested" as **"(a)(17)"**.
- The expired EAD issued under the same category, **Category A17**.

Travel Abroad and Readmission

As discussed above, the **E-1 treaty trader or employee** may travel abroad and will generally be granted an automatic **two-year period of admission** when returning to the United States. Unless the family members are accompanying the E-1 treaty trader or employee at the time the latter seeks admission to the United States, or the family members separately travel abroad and return to the United States within the new readmission period, the new readmission period will not apply to the family members.

To remain lawfully in the United States, family members must carefully note the **period of stay** they have been granted in **E status** and apply for an **extension of stay** before their own validity expires.

Excerpts from "U.S. Department of State's Treaty Countries for a current list of countries with which the United States maintains a treaty of commerce and navigation". Retrieved on September 10, 2022.

Searchable Keywords

E-1/E-2 Visa (Treaty Traders and Treaty Investors). E-3 Visa (Australian in Specialty Occupation): U.S. Embassy Canberra Website. E-Verify: USCIS Website.

Emergency Travel: USCIS Website. Employment Authorization / Employment Authorization Document (EAD) Visit USCIS Website. Employment, Labor Certification: DOL Website. Employment-BasedEmployment Based Visas, Nonimmigrant. Employment (H-1B, H1B1, H-2A, H-2B Visas): Legal Rights and Protections Pamphlet (Wilberforce Act). Employment: Iraqi or Afghan translators/interpreters. Employment: Iraqis -Worked for/on behalf of the US Government. Enhanced Border Security and Visa Entry Reform Act. Entertainers P Visa for Temporary Workers. ESTA (Electronic System for Travel Authorization) for VWP Travelers: CBP Website. ESTA (Electronic System for Travel Authorization) for VWP Travelers.

Exchange Visitor (J-1 Visa) Skills List - 2009. Exchange Visitor (J-1 Visa) Two-Year Home-Country Physical Presence (Foreign Residence) Requirement. Exchange Visitor (J-1 Visa): Legal Rights and Protections Pamphlet (Wilberforce Act). Exchange Visitor (J-1 Visa) Program: Private Sector Programs. Exchange Visitors and Students, Arrival Procedures: CBP Website. Exchange Visitors (J-1 Visa). Expired Visa: Limited Re-entry. my stay in the United States. How do I do it? Extending Stay in the United States and Program Extension, Exchange Visitors (J-1 Visas): ECA Website. Extension of Stay vs. Visa Expiration Date. Extraordinary Ability (O Visa for Temporary Workers).

Educational and Cultural Affairs: The Bureau of Educational and Cultural Affairs (ECA) of the U.S. Department of State fosters mutual understanding between the people of the United States and the people of other countries to promote friendly, sympathetic, and peaceful relations. ECA administers a variety of exchange programs for non-U.S. secondary, undergraduate, graduate students, and professionals, along with other duties. Visit the ECA website.

ESTA: Electronic System for Travel Authorization (ESTA) is an automated system that determines the eligibility of visitors (nationals from 38 participating countries) to travel to the United States without a visa under the Visa Waiver Program (VWP). A valid ESTA approval is required for all VWP travel to the United States. ESTA applications may be submitted at any time prior to travel, though it is recommended travelers apply when they begin preparing travel plans.

To learn whether you may be able to travel on the VWP, and therefore whether you need an ESTA authorization, see our Visa Waiver Program webpage. For more information about ESTA and/or to apply, see the DHS, Custom and Border Protection's ESTA website.

Exchange Visitor: A foreign citizen coming to the United States to participate in a particular program in education, training, research, or other authorized exchange visitor program. See the Educational and Cultural Affairs website and our Exchange Visitor webpage for more information.

Exchange Visitor Skills List: The Exchange Visitor Skills List (J visas) is a list of fields of specialized knowledge and skills that are deemed necessary for the development of an exchange visitor's home country. When you agree to participate in an Exchange Visitor Program, if your skill is on your country's Skills List you are subject to the two-year foreign residence (home-country physical presence) requirement, which requires you to return to your home country for two years at the end of your exchange visitor program, under U.S. law. Review the Exchange Visitor webpage to learn more.

Extension of Stay: Extending the length of time a visa holder is authorized to stay in the United States, when approved by USCIS. The visa holder may file a request with USCIS before his or her authorized stay expires, which generally is the admitted-until date on the traveler's admission stamp or paper Form I-94, Arrival/Departure Record (except for visa holders admitted to the U.S. for duration of status, stamped D/S). See Extend Your Stay on the USCIS website to learn more.

F

A **US F-visa type** is a **non-immigrant visa** for students who want to pursue **academic** or **vocational studies** in the United States. There are two subtypes of F-visas: **F-1** and **F-2**.

- **F-1 visas** are for full-time students who enroll in an accredited **college**, **university**, **seminary**, **conservatory**, **academic high school**, **elementary school**, or **language training program**. They must maintain a **full course of study** and be **proficient in English**. They may also work **on or off campus** under certain conditions and restrictions.
- **F-2 visas** are for **dependents** of F-1 visa holders, such as **spouses** and **unmarried children under the age of 21**. They may accompany or join the F-1 visa holder in the US, but they **cannot work** or **study full-time**.

F-Visa Application Process

To apply for an F-visa, you must:

- Possess a **valid passport**.
- Obtain a **Certificate of Eligibility for Nonimmigrant Student Status (Form I-20)** from your school.
- Complete the **online application form (DS-160)**.
- Schedule an **interview** at a U.S. embassy or consulate.
- Pay the **necessary fees**.

For further details about the F-visa, visit the official website of the U.S. Department of State or the USCIS website.

The processing time for an F-visa may vary depending on the location and workload of the US embassy or consulate where you apply. According to the official website of the US Department of State, the estimated wait time to receive a nonimmigrant visa interview appointment is based on the availability of staff and can change from week to week.

However, some websites provide more specific information about the processing time for an F-visa based on the country of application.

You can check the estimated wait time for a nonimmigrant visa interview appointment at a US embassy or consulate by selecting your location on their designated webpage. You can also check the processing times for other types of visas.

Can I work in the US with an F-visa? It depends on the type of F-visa you have and the conditions of your employment. Generally, F-1 visa holders can work on campus for up to 20 hours per week during the academic year and 40 hours per week during the breaks. They can also work off-campus after completing one academic year, but only with authorization from their school and the USCIS.

The F-visa holders can choose from three types of off-campus employment: (1) Curricular Practical Training (CPT), (2) Optional Practical Training (OPT), or (3) STEM OPT Extension.

F-2 visa holders, who are dependents of F-1 visa holders, are not allowed to work in the US at all. They can only accompany or join the F-1 visa holder in the US, but they cannot study or work full-time.

If you want to work in the US with an F-visa, you need to follow the rules and regulations of your visa category and your employer. You also need to maintain your student status and report any changes to your school and the USCIS.

Searchable Keywords

F Visa (Academic Students). Family Based Immigrants. Fees, Visa Services. Fees and Forms: USCIS Website. Fiancé(e) or Spouse of an American Citizen (K Visa).

Fingerprints: USCIS Website. Flight Training (J-1 Visa): ECA Website. Follow-to-Join Refugees & Asylees. Food, Prohibitions about bringing food into the United States: CBP Website. Foreign Affairs Manual (FAM). Foreign Media, Press and Radio Visas (I Visa). Foreign Residency Requirement (J-1 Visa). Foreign Worker Labor Certification: DOL Website. Forms, Immigration: USCIS Website. Forms, I-94 Arrival/Departure Record: CBP Website. Forms, Visa Application. Fraud, Reporting. FTA, Chile Professional Worker (H1B1 Visa). FTA, Singapore Professional Worker (H1B1 Visa).

Family First Preference: A category of family immigration (F1) for unmarried sons and daughters of U.S. citizens, and their children. Visit our Family Based Immigration webpage for more info.

Family Second Preference: A category of family immigration (F2) for spouses, children and unmarried sons and daughters of lawful permanent residents. Visit our Family Based Immigration webpage for more info.

Family Third Preference: A category of family immigration (F3) for married sons and daughters of U.S. citizens and their spouses and children. Before 1992 this was known as fourth preference (P-4). Visit our Family Based Immigration webpage for more info.

Family Fourth Preference: A category of family immigration (F4) for brothers and sisters of U.S. citizens and their spouses and children. The American citizen must be 21 years of age or older before he/she can file the petition. Before 1992, this was known as the fifth preference (P-5). Visit the State Department's Family Based Immigration webpage for more info.

Federal Poverty Guidelines: See Poverty Guidelines. The Department of Health and Human Services publishes a list every year giving the lowest income acceptable for a family of a particular size so that the family does not live in poverty. Consular officers use these figures in immigrant visa cases to determine whether a sponsor's income is sufficient to support a new immigrant, in accordance with U.S. immigration laws. Visit USCIS's Poverty Guidelines webpage for more information.

Fiancé(e): A person who plans or is contracted to marry another person. The foreign fiancé(e) of a U.S. citizen may enter the United States on a K-1 visa to marry the U.S. citizen. Visit our Fiancé(e) webpage to learn more.

Final Action Dates: The date that determines whether a preferred immigrant visa applicant can be scheduled for an immigrant visa interview in any given month. When "C" (meaning Current) is listed instead of a specific date, that means all priority dates are eligible for processing.

The final action date is the priority date of the first applicant who could not be scheduled for a visa interview for a given month. Applicants with a priority date earlier than the final action date can be scheduled. However, if your priority date is on or later than the final action date, you will need to wait until your priority date is reached (becomes current). To find out whether a preference case can be scheduled, see the Visa Bulletin.

First Preference: A category of family immigration (F1) for unmarried sons and daughters of U.S. citizens and their children. Visit our Family Based Immigration webpage for more info.

Fiscal Year: The budget year for the U.S. government. It begins on October 1 and ends on September 30 of the following year.

Following to Join: A type of derivative visa status when the family member gets a visa after the principal applicant.

Foreign Affairs Manual (9 FAM): 9 FAM Chapter 400 relates to nonimmigrant visas. 9 FAM Chapter 500 covers immigrant visas. 9 FAM Chapter 300 relates to visa ineligibility and waivers. Go to our site to review the FAM relating to visas.

Fourth Preference: A category of family immigration (F4) for brothers and sisters of U.S. citizens and their spouses and children. The U.S. citizen must be 21 years of age or older before he/she can file a petition under this category. Before 1992, this was known as fifth preference (P-5). Visit the Family Based Immigration webpage for more info.

Full and Final Adoption: A legal adoption in which the child receives all the rights of a natural born, legitimate child. For more adoptions information visit our Adoptions website.

G

A US G-visa type is a category of official visas issued to diplomats, government officials, and international organization employees who are visiting the United States temporarily for a governmental purpose. G visas may also be issued to immediate family members of the principal visa holder.

There are five visas in the G visa category: G-1, G-2, G-3, G-4, and G-5. Each visa has different eligibility criteria and requirements depending on the status and purpose of the visitor. For more information, you can visit the official website of the U.S. Department of State.

What is the difference between G-1 and G-2 visas?

The key distinction between a G-1 and a G-2 visa lies in their purposes:

- A **G-1 visa** is issued to permanent mission members of a recognized government assigned to a designated international organization in the United States.
- A **G-2 visa** is granted to representatives of a recognized government traveling temporarily to the U.S. to participate in meetings of a designated international organization.

Both visas fall under the broader **G visa category**, which is designed for diplomats, government officials, and employees of international organizations visiting the U.S. temporarily for governmental purposes. For more details, refer to the University of Texas at San Antonio's guide on Visas for Employees of International Organizations and NATO.

Duration of Stay with a G Visa

The length of your stay in the U.S. with a G visa depends on the visa type and the purpose of your visit. General guidelines include:

- **G-1, G-2, G-3, and G-4 visas**: You can remain in the U.S. as long as the Secretary of State recognizes you as a member of the diplomatic category. There is no need to apply for an extension of stay.
- **G-5 visas**: You may stay for up to three years and can apply for an extension if you continue to meet the eligibility criteria.
- **Expired G visas**: If your visa expires, you have 30 days to leave the country. Staying beyond this period would result in illegal status.

For more specific information, you should contact the US embassy or consulate where you applied for your visa or visit the official website of the US Department of State.

See the following sources on Visas for Employees of International Organizations and NATO -Travel : Diplomatic G Visas G1, G2, G3, G4 | Tucker, Nong & Associates : How Long Will Your U.S. Visa Allow You to Stay? | Nolo : Visas for Employees of International Organizations and NATO – Travel.

Can I travel outside of the US with a G-visa?

In other words, if I have a G-visa, am I allowed to travel outside of the US?

The answer to your question may depend on the type of **G visa** you have, the **purpose and duration of your travel**, and the **country you are visiting**. According to the web search results, here are some general guidelines:

- **G-1, G-2, G-3, or G-4 visa:** You may travel outside of the US for **official** or **personal reasons** if you maintain your status and have a **valid visa** to reenter the US. You may also be eligible for **visa-free travel** to certain countries under the **Visa Waiver Program** or other **bilateral agreements**.
- **G-5 visa:** You may travel outside of the US for **personal reasons**, but you must have a **valid visa** to reenter the US. You may also need a **visa to enter the country** you are visiting, depending on their visa requirements.
- If you plan to travel outside of the US for **more than one year**, you may need to apply for a **new visa** at a US embassy or consulate abroad, regardless of your visa type. You may also need to obtain a **re-entry permit** from the US Citizenship and Immigration Services (**USCIS**) before you leave the US.

For more specific information, you should contact the **US embassy or consulate** where you applied for your visa or visit the **official website** of the US Department of State. You may also consult the **World Bank Group** if you are an employee of an international organization.

G-Visa Processing Time

How long does it take to get a G-visa?

The processing time for a G-visa may vary depending on the type of G-visa, the location where you apply, and the workload of the US embassy or consulate. According to the web search results, here are some general guidelines:

- The **estimated wait time** to receive a nonimmigrant visa interview appointment at a US embassy or consulate is based on the availability of slots and can change from week to week. You can check the current wait time for your location using this tool.
- After the interview, your visa application may be subject to further **administrative**

processing (221(g)), which can take additional time. This is issued when the consular officer needs more information or documents to plan and settle on a decision in your case. The processing time for **221(g)** varies from case to case and can range from **a few days to several months**. You can track the status of your case online using the **reference ID** provided by the visa consulate.

- If your visa is approved, you will receive your **passport with the visa stamp** within a few days. The exact delivery time depends on the **courier service** you choose.

Searchable Keywords

G Visa (International Organizations & NATO). G-5 Visa (Employees of an International Organization): Legal Rights and Protections Pamphlet (Wilberforce Act). Genetic Testing, DNA Relationship Testing Procedures. Glossary of Visa Terms. Government Officials, Foreign. Green Card (LPR): USCIS Website. **Green card**: Permanent Resident Card, Form I-551 (formerly called Alien Registration Card, also known as *green card),* is a wallet-sized card showing that the person is a lawful permanent resident (immigrant) in the United States. For more information visit the USCIS website.

H

A **US H-visa type** is a category of **nonimmigrant visas** issued to **temporary workers** who are coming to the United States to perform a **specific job** or **service**. There are several types of H visas, each with different **eligibility criteria** and **requirements**.

Some of the most common H visas are:

- **H-1B:** For **specialty occupations** in fields requiring **highly specialized knowledge**, such as science, engineering, medicine, law, etc.
- **H-1B1:** For professionals from **Chile and Singapore** who are engaged in a **specialty occupation**.
- **H-2A:** For **temporary agricultural workers** who are needed to perform **seasonal or temporary labor** or services.
- **H-2B:** For **temporary non-agricultural workers** who are needed to perform **seasonal or temporary labor** or services.
- **H-3:** For **trainees** who are coming to the United States to receive training in any field of endeavor, except **graduate medical education or training**.

To apply for an H visa, you must have:

- A **valid job offer** from a US employer who is willing to **sponsor** you.
- The employer must file a **petition** on your behalf with the US Citizenship and Immigration Services (**USCIS**).
- You must also meet the **specific qualifications** for the visa type you are seeking.

For more information, you can visit the official website of the US Department of State or the official website of the USCIS. You can explore the following websites and sources further: Visas for Temporary Workers - Travel : H-1B Specialty Occupations, DOD Cooperative Research and Development Project Workers, and Fashion Models. USCIS : H-1B1 Chile/Singapore Free Trade Agreement. USCIS : H-2A Temporary Agricultural Workers | USCIS : H-2B Temporary Non-Agricultural Workers. USCIS: H-3 Nonimmigrant Trainee or Special Education Exchange Visitor. USCIS: Working in the United States. USCIS.

Can my family come with me on an H-visa? Yes, your family members can come with you on an H-visa if they qualify as dependents. According to the question answering results, dependents are defined as spouses, children under 21 years of age, and parents of the H-1B visa holder.

Your dependents will need to apply for an H-4 visa, which allows them to live, study, and travel in the US, but not work, unless you have an approved Form I-140.

The H-4 visa is valid for the same period as your H-1B visa, and you will need to provide proof of your relationship, financial support, and medical examination records.

How long can I and my family stay in the US with an H-visa? The duration of your stay in the US with an H-visa depends on the type of H-visa you have and the purpose of your visit. Below are some general guidelines:

- **H-1B Visa:** You can stay in the US for up to **six years**. The initial petition is valid for **three years** but can be extended for another **three years**.
- **H-2A or H-2B Visa:** You can stay in the US for the period authorized on your **Form I-94**, which is usually the same as the period of your approved petition. The maximum period of stay is **three years**.
- **H-3 Visa:** You can stay in the US for the period authorized on your **Form I-94**, which is usually the same as the period of your approved petition. The maximum period of stay is **two years**.

Your **family members** who accompany you on an **H-4 visa** can stay in the US for the **same period** as you, as long as they maintain their status.

Traveling Outside of the US with an H-Visa

Yes, you can travel outside of the US with an **H-visa** if you have valid documentation and meet certain conditions. Here are important points to know before traveling:

- You will need a **valid passport**, a **valid H-visa stamp**, and a **valid I-94 form** to reenter the US.
- You may also need a **visitor's visa** to enter the country you are visiting, depending on their visa requirements.
- If you are traveling to **Canada or Mexico** for less than **30 days**, you may be able to reenter the US with an **expired visa stamp** under the **Automatic Visa Revalidation** procedure.
- If you plan to travel outside the US for more than **one year**, you may need to apply for a **new visa stamp** at a US embassy or consulate abroad and obtain a **re-entry permit** from the USCIS before you leave.
- If you need to obtain a **new visa stamp** while abroad, the process can take **six weeks or more** due to **security clearances**.

- Your **family members** on **H-4 visas** can travel with you, but they must also have **valid documentation** and meet the same conditions.

For more specific and detailed information, it's always best to contact the U.S. embassy or consulate where you applied for your visa. Alternatively, you can visit the official website of the U.S. Department of State for accurate and up-to-date guidance.

Sources:

- Visas for Temporary Workers – Travel
- How to Travel Internationally on an H-1B Visa | Visa2us
- Travel Outside the U.S.: H-1B Visas: Scholars: Office of International Services: Indiana University
- Travel Visa Pro
- Can I Travel While My H-1B Application Is Pending at USCIS? – Nolo
- H-3 Nonimmigrant Trainee or Special Education Exchange Visitor | USCIS
- Working in the United States | USCIS
- H4 Visa – All You Need To Know (January 2024 Update) – India USA Travel (Retrieved January 5, 2024)

Notes: First, if you were to ask, can an H-visa type holder apply for a Green Card? The answer would be yes, you can. An H-visa is a type of nonimmigrant visa that allows you to work temporarily in the United States. However, it also has a dual intent, which means that you can apply for a permanent residence (Green Card) while you are on an H-visa.

There are different steps and requirements to apply for a Green Card with an H-visa, depending on the type of H-visa you have and the category of Green Card you are seeking. Generally, you will need to have a U.S. employer who is willing to sponsor you and file a petition on your behalf. You will also need to meet the eligibility criteria for the specific Green Card category you are applying under.

Some of the common **Green Card** categories for **H-visa holders** are:

- **EB-1:** For priority workers with **extraordinary ability**, **outstanding professors or researchers**, or **multinational executives or managers**.
- **EB-2:** For professionals holding **advanced degrees** or persons of **exceptional ability**.
- **EB-3:** For **skilled workers**, **professionals**, or **other workers**.

The processing time for a Green Card with an H-visa may vary depending on the type of H-visa, the category of Green Card, the availability of visas, and the workload of the U.S. immigration agencies.

It can take from several months to several years.

For more information, you can visit the official website of the U.S. Department of State or the U.S. Citizenship and Immigration Services.

Searchable Keywords

H Visa for Temporary Workers. H-1B, H1B1, H-2A, and H-2B Visas: Legal Rights and Protections Pamphlet (Wilberforce Act). HIV, Removal from List of Communicable Diseases of Public Health Significance (HIV Final Rule). Holiday (B-2 Visitor Visa). Homeland Security, Department of (DHS). Humanitarian Parole: USCIS Website.

Homeless: Persons from countries that do not have a U.S. Embassy or Consulate where they can apply for immigrant visas are "homeless". For example, the U.S. government does not have an embassy in Iran. Residents of Iran are "homeless" for visa purposes.

Household Income: The income used to determine whether a sponsor meets the minimum income requirements under Section 213A of the Immigration and Nationality Act (INA) for some immigrant visa cases.

Household Member: A "household member" is an individual who is promising to make his or her income and/or assets available to the sponsor (signer of Form I-864) to help support the sponsored immigrant(s). Household members must complete Form I-864A, Contract Between Sponsor and Household Member.

A **household member** can be one of the following individuals:

- A **relative** who has the same **principal residence** as the sponsor and is related to the sponsor as a **spouse**, **adult child** (must be at least **18 years of age**), **parent**, or **sibling**.
- A **relative** or **other person** whom the sponsor has **lawfully claimed as a dependent** on the sponsor's most recent **Federal income tax return**, even if that person does **not live at the same residence** as the sponsor.
- The **principal applicant**, under either of the following circumstances:
    - If the principal applicant has the same **principal residence** as the sponsor and the intending immigrant can establish that his or her **income will continue from the same source**, even after acquiring **permanent residence**.
    - If the principal applicant is the sponsor's **spouse** and can show that his or her **income will continue from the same source** after acquiring **permanent residence**.

I

A U.S. I-visa type: An I-visa is a type of nonimmigrant visa for representatives of the foreign media, including members of the press, radio, film, and print industries, who are traveling temporarily to the United States to work in their profession.

To qualify for an I-visa, you must be engaged in informational or educational media activities that are essential to the foreign media function. You must also have a home office in a foreign country and seek to enter the United States solely for your work as a foreign media representative.

An I-visa is usually valid for the duration of your media project or assignment, up to a maximum of one year. You may apply for extensions of stay if necessary. You may also bring your spouse and unmarried children under 21 years of age with you on an I-visa, but they are not allowed to work in the United States.

For additional information, visit the official website of the U.S. Department of State. To explore specific topics, consider searching for the following resources:

- Visas for Temporary Workers – Travel
- Employment-Based Immigration: First Preference (EB-1) – USCIS
- Employment-Based Immigration: Second Preference (EB-2) – USCIS
- Employment-Based Immigration: Third Preference (EB-3) – USCIS
- Visas for Members of the Foreign Media, Press, and Radio – Travel

Can an I-visa holder switch from I-visa to permanent work in the US? No, you cannot switch from an I-visa to a permanent work in the United States. An I-visa is a type of nonimmigrant visa for representatives of the foreign media, who are only allowed to work in their profession while they are in the United States temporarily.

To become a **permanent worker** in the United States, you must apply for an **employment-based immigrant visa**, which follows a different process and eligibility criteria than an **I-visa**. You will also need a **U.S. employer** who is willing to **sponsor you** and file a petition on your behalf with the **U.S. Citizenship and Immigration Services (USCIS)**.

Some of the common **employment-based immigrant visa categories** are:

- **EB-1**: For priority workers with **extraordinary ability**, **outstanding professors or researchers**, or **multinational executives or managers**.
- **EB-2**: For **professionals holding advanced degrees** or **persons of exceptional ability**.

- **EB-3**: For **skilled workers**, **professionals**, or **other workers**.

The processing time for an employment-based immigrant visa may vary depending on the category, the availability of visas, and the workload of the U.S. immigration agencies. It can take from several months to several years.

For more information, visit the official website of the U.S. Department of State or the USCIS. You can also explore the following resources:

- Visas: Working in the United States | USCIS
- Employment-Based Immigration: First Preference (EB-1) | USCIS
- Employment-Based Immigration: Second Preference (EB-2) | USCIS
- Employment-Based Immigration: Third Preference (EB-3) | USCIS

Searchable Keywords

I-Visa for Journalist, Media, Press. Immigrant Visas. Immigrant Visa Statistics. Immigration Statistics: DHS Website. Immigration and Nationality Act (INA): USCIS Website. Immigration Classifications and Visa Categories. Import and Export: U.S. Dept. of Agriculture Website. Ineligibilities for a Visa. Information for Nonimmigrants Present in the United States and Visiting Canada or Mexico. International Cultural Exchange (Q Visa for Temporary Workers). International Flights to the United States, Security Measures: TSA website. International Organizations & NATO (G Visa). International Organization (G-5 Visa): Legal Rights and Protections Pamphlet (Wilberforce Act). Intracompany Transferee (L Visa for Temporary Workers). Iraqi and Afghan Translators/Interpreters, Special Immigrant Visas: FAQs for Applicants Living Overseas. Iraqis Employed by/on Behalf of U.S. Government (Special Immigrant Visa). Iraqi "H" series Passports: A & G visas FAQ. Iraqi "M" and "N" series Passports: A & G visas FAQ. Iraqi "M" and "N" series Passports: general visa FAQ. Iraqi "S" series Passport: A & G visas FAQ. Iraqi "S" series Passport: general visa FAQ. Iraqi Refugee Processing, Fact Sheet: USCIS Website.

I-551 (Green Card): Permanent residence card or alien registration receipt card or "green card." See Lawful Permanent Resident.

Immediate Relative: Spouse, widow(er) and unmarried children under the age of 21 of a U.S. citizen. A parent is an immediate relative if the U.S. citizen is 21 years of age or older. There are no numerical limits to the immigration of immediate relatives.

Immigrant Visa: A visa for a person who plans to live indefinitely and permanently in the United

States. Visit the Immigrant Visa section of this website.

Immigration and Nationality Act (INA): U.S. immigration law. The Immigration and Nationality Act, or INA, was created in 1952, Public Law No. 82-414. The INA has been amended many times over the years but is still the basic body of immigration law. See INA for additional information.

Immigration and Naturalization Service (INS): A branch of the Department of Justice that formerly existed and had responsibility for immigration and naturalization. INS was renamed and became part of DHS on March 1, 2003. To learn more, go to the DHS website.

INA: See Immigration and Nationality Act.

Ineligible/Ineligibility: Immigration law says that certain conditions and actions prevent a person from entering the United States. These conditions and activities are called ineligibilities, and the applicant is ineligible for (cannot get) a visa. Examples are selling drugs, active tuberculosis, being a terrorist, and using fraud to get a visa. Read our information on the Classes of Aliens Ineligible to Receive Visas to learn more.

In Status: It's important to understand the concept of immigration status and the consequences of violating that status. Being aware of the requirements and possible consequences will make it more likely that you can avoid problems with maintaining your status. Every visa is issued for a particular purpose and for a specific class of visitor.

Each visa classification has a set of requirements that the visa holder must follow and maintain. Those who follow the requirements maintain their status and ensure their ability to remain in the United States. Those who do not follow the requirements violate their status and are considered "out of status".

For more information see "Out of Status" below. In Status means you are following the requirements of your visa type under immigration law. For example, you are a foreign student who entered the United States on a student visa. If you are a full-time student and pursuing your course of study, and are not engaged in unauthorized employment, you are "in status". If you work full-time in your uncle's convenience store and do not study, you are "out of status". See the DHS, USCIS website Extension of Stay and Change of Status.

IV: Immigrant Visa.

J

A **US J-visa type** is a category of **nonimmigrant visas** for foreign nationals who wish to participate in **exchange visitor programs** in the United States. These programs are designed to promote the **interchange of persons, knowledge, and skills** in the fields of **education**, **arts**, and **science**.

There are different types of **J-visas**, depending on the purpose and duration of the exchange program. Some of the common J-visas are below:

- **J-1**: For **exchange visitors** who are coming to the United States to **teach**, **study**, **research**, **train**, or **work** in various fields.
- **J-2**: For **spouses and dependents** of J-1 visa holders, who are allowed to accompany them and **apply for work authorization**.

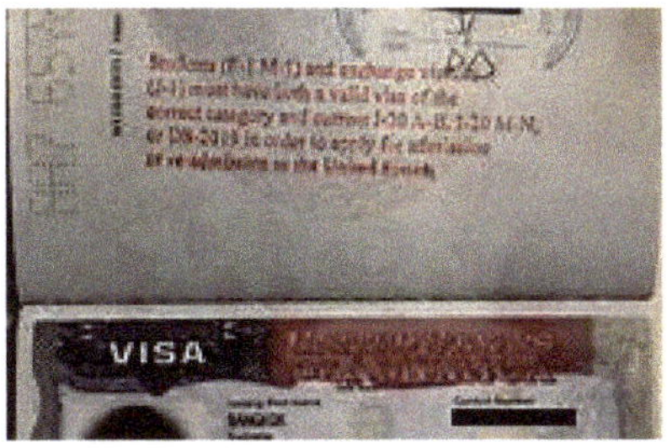

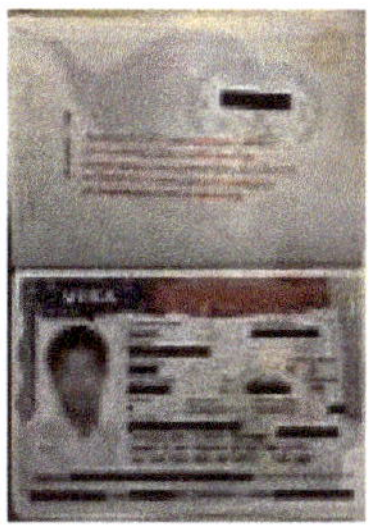

To apply for a J-visa, you must first be accepted into an approved exchange visitor program by a designated sponsor in the United States. You must also pay the SEVIS I-901 fee and schedule an interview at a U.S. embassy or consulate.

For more information, you can visit the official website of the U.S. Department of State or the U.S. Citizenship and Immigration Services.

How Long Can I Stay in the US with a J-Visa?

The duration of your stay in the US with a **J-visa** depends on the **type and category** of your exchange program. According to the web search results, here are some general guidelines:

- **J-1 Exchange Visitor**: You can stay in the US for the period **authorized on your Form DS-2019**, which is issued by your **program sponsor**. This period may vary from a **few weeks to several years**, depending on the nature and purpose of your program.
- **J-2 Dependent**: You can stay in the US for the **same period as the J-1 principal**, as long as you maintain your status.

- **Two-Year Home-Country Physical Presence Requirement**: If you are subject to this rule, you **must return to your home country for at least two years** before you can **change or adjust** your status to another visa category in the US.
- **Changing or Adjusting Status**: If you **are not subject** to the two-year requirement, you **may be eligible** to change or adjust your status to another visa category in the US, if you meet the criteria and follow the procedures.
- **J-Visa Expiration & Grace Period**: If your **J-visa expires**, you have a **30-day grace period** to **depart the US**. During this period, you **are not allowed** to **work, study, or travel** within the US.

For more specific information, you should contact your **program sponsor**, the **US embassy or consulate** where you applied for your visa, or visit the **official website of the US Department of State**. You can also explore the following resources:

- **Exchange Visitor Visa - Travel**
- **J-1 Visa - Categories**
- **J-2 Visa: Spouse or Child of J-1 Visa Holder**
- **Waiver of the Exchange Visitor Two-Year Home-Country Physical Presence Requirement - Travel**
- **J-1 Visa Grace Period - What You Need to Know - Visa Nation**

Can I Apply for a Green Card with a J-Visa?

Yes, you **can apply** for a **Green Card** with a **J-visa**, but the process **is not easy**. A **J-visa** is a **nonimmigrant visa** for **exchange visitors** who come to the US for a **temporary period**. However, some **J-visa holders may be eligible** to apply for a **Green Card**, which grants **permanent residence** in the US.

There are two main challenges that J-visa holders face when applying for a green card. The first one is the issue of immigrant intent. This means that when you applied for your J-visa, you had to show that you intended to return to your home country after your exchange program ended. To apply for a green card, you must show that your circumstances have changed and that you now want to stay in the US permanently.

The second challenge is the two-year foreign residence requirement. This applies to some J-visa holders who must return to their home country for at least two years before they can apply for a green card or another visa in the US. This requirement applies if your exchange program was funded by the

US or your home government, if your home country needs your skills or knowledge, or if you received medical training in the US

If you are subject to the two-year requirement, you can try to get a waiver from the US Department of State. There are several grounds for getting a waiver, such as having a US citizen
or permanent resident spouse or child, facing persecution in your home country, or getting a no-objection statement from your home government.

To apply for a green card with a J-visa, you will need to have a valid basis for your application, such as family sponsorship, employment sponsorship, or diversity lottery. You will also need to follow the steps and procedures for the specific green card category you are applying under.

The process of getting a green card with a J-visa can be complicated, lengthy, and costly. It can take from several months to several years, depending on your situation and the availability of visas. You may also need to hire an immigration lawyer to help you with your case.

For more information, you can visit the official website of the US Department of State or the US Citizenship and Immigration Services.

Can my family come with me on a J-visa? Yes, your family members can come with you on a J-visa if they qualify as dependents. According to the question answering results, dependents are defined as spouses and children under 21 years of age of the J-1 visa holder.

Your dependents will need to apply for a J-2 visa, which allows them to live, study, and travel in the US, but not work, unless you have an approved Form I-140

The J-2 visa is valid for the same period as your J-1 visa, and you will need to provide proof of your relationship, financial support, and medical examination records

For more information, visit the official website of the U.S. Department of State or the USCIS official website. You can also explore the following resources:

- Exchange Visitor Visa - Travel
- J-2 Visa: Spouse or Child of J-1 Visa Holder
- Dependents – J-2 Status | US Forest Service
- J-2: Family of the J-1 - Academic Personnel

How long can I stay in the US with a J-visa?

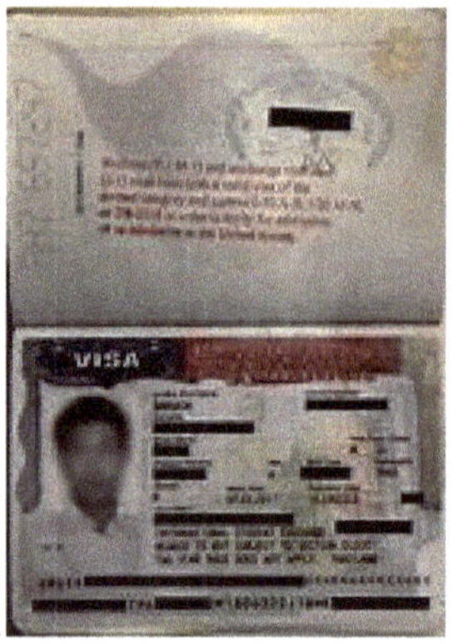

Ex. Visa notations on a passport. 1

Ex. Visa notations on a passport. 2

Exploring the **duration of your stay in the US** with a **J-visa category** will depend on the **type and structure** of your exchange program. According to the web search results, here are some general guidelines:

- **J-1 Exchange Visitor**: You can stay in the US for the period **authorized on your Form DS-2019**, which is issued by your **program sponsor**. This period may vary from **a few weeks to several years**, depending on the nature and purpose of your program.
- **J-2 Dependent**: You can stay in the US for the **same period** as the J-1 principal, as long as you maintain your status.
- **Two-Year Home-Country Physical Presence Requirement**: If you are subject to this rule, you **must return to your home country for at least two years** before you can **change or adjust** your status to another visa category in the US.
- **Change or Adjustment of Status**: If you are **not subject** to the two-year requirement, you **may be eligible** to change or adjust your status to another visa category in the US, if you meet the criteria and follow the procedures.
- **J-Visa Expiration & Grace Period**: If your **J-visa expires**, you have a **30-day grace period** to **depart the US**. You are **not allowed** to **work, study, or travel** within the US during this period.

For more specific information, you should contact your **program sponsor**, the **US embassy or consulate** where you applied for your visa, or visit the **official website of the US Department of State**.

Can I Apply to Extend My Stay in the US on a J-Visa?

Yes, you **can extend** your stay on a **J-visa**, but you will need to meet **certain conditions** and follow **specific procedures**. According to the web search results, here are some general guidelines:

- **Request Extension from Original Sponsor**: You can only request an extension from the **original sponsor** who issued your **Form DS-2019**. You **cannot change** your sponsor or program category.
- **Timing**: Initiate your request **at least 30 days before** your current DS-2019 expires. Your sponsor will need to approve your request and issue you a **new DS-2019** with the extended date.
- **Required Documents**: Provide evidence of **financial support**, **health insurance**, and **valid reasons** for extending your stay. You may also need to pay a **SEVIS fee again**, depending on your program category.
- **Maximum Period**: You **cannot extend your stay** beyond the **maximum period allowed** for your program category. For example:
    - Professors or Researchers: **Maximum period is five years**
    - Students: **Length of your academic program**

For more specific information, you should contact your **program sponsor**, the **US embassy or consulate** where you applied for your visa, or visit the **official website of the US Department of State**.

Searchable Keywords

J-1 Exchange Visitors Skill List - 2009. J-1 Exchange Visitor Visa: Legal Rights and Protections Pamphlet (Wilberforce Act). J Visa (Exchange Visitor). J-1 Visa – Two-Year Home-Country Physical Presence Requirement (212e). J-1 Visas, Advisory Opinion for Waiver of
Two-Year Home-Country Physical Presence Requirement. J-1 Waiver of Two-Year Home-Country Physical Presence Requirement. J-1 Waiver of Two-Year Home-Country Physical Presence Requirement: Application Process. Journalists, Foreign Media (I Visa).

Joint Sponsor: A person who accepts legal responsibility for supporting an immigrant with an I-864 Affidavit of Support along with the sponsor. The joint sponsor must be at least 18 years of age, a U.S. citizen or lawful permanent resident and have a domicile in the United States. The joint sponsor and his/her household must meet the 125 percent income requirement for the immigrant that he/she sponsors.

Jurisdiction: Authority to apply the law in each territory or region. For example, the DHS USCIS district office in the area where a person lives has jurisdiction or authority to decide on a fiancé(e) petition.

K

Can a K-Visa Holder Work in the U.S.?

Yes, K-visa holders can work in the U.S., but they must first apply for a work permit from U.S. Citizenship and Immigration Services (USCIS). Below are general guidelines based on the type of K-visa:

- **K-1 Visa (Fiancé(e) of a U.S. Citizen):** You may apply for a work permit (Form I-765) immediately upon entering the U.S. However, this work permit is only valid for **90 days**. Alternatively, after marrying your U.S. citizen fiancé(e), you can apply for a green card and subsequently a work permit based on your pending green card application.
- **K-3 Visa (Spouse of a U.S. Citizen):** You can apply for a work permit (Form I-765) at any time after entering the U.S. Additionally, if you have a pending green card application, you may apply for a work permit based on that.
- **K-2 and K-4 Visas (Children of K-1 and K-3 Visa Holders):** You may apply for a work permit (Form I-765) at any time after entry. However, the permit is valid only until your **21st birthday**. If you have a pending green card application, you may also apply for a work permit based on that.

For more details, visit the USCIS website. Additional resources include:

- **Directory of Visa Categories – U.S. Department of State**
- **Visas for Fiancé(e)s of U.S. Citizens – USCIS**
- **K-3/K-4 Nonimmigrant Visas – USCIS**
- **K-1 Visa Timeline, Fees, and Requirements – Boundless**
- **Fiancé(e) Visa Timeline – Visa Nation**
- **USCIS Processing for Form I-129F – Nolo**

How to Differentiate Between K-1 and CR-1 Visa Types

The primary difference between a K-1 and CR-1 visa lies in their purpose and application process:

- **K-1 Visa:** Designed for fiancé(e)s of U.S. citizens planning to marry within 90 days of arriving in the U.S.
- **CR-1 Visa:** Issued to spouses of U.S. citizens who are already married and wish to immigrate to the U.S.

Key Differences:

1. **Visa Type:**

    - K-1 is a **nonimmigrant visa** requiring adjustment of status for permanent residency after marriage.
    - CR-1 is an **immigrant visa** granting permanent residency upon arrival.
2. **Marriage Requirements:**
    - K-1 requires marriage within **90 days** of entry into the U.S.
    - CR-1 requires applicants to be already **married** before filing.
3. **Application Process:**
    - K-1 involves filing **Form I-129F** (Petition for Alien Fiancé(e)) with USCIS, followed by visa application at a U.S. consulate.
    - CR-1 requires filing **Form I-130** (Petition for Alien Relative) with USCIS and waiting for approval before applying for a visa.
4. **Processing Time:**
    - K-1 generally has a **shorter processing time**, but the adjustment of status post-marriage can take several months or years.
    - CR-1 has a **longer processing time**, but permanent residency is granted immediately upon arrival.
5. **Cost:**
    - K-1 is **more expensive** due to fees for the petition, visa, adjustment of status, and green card application.
    - CR-1 is **less costly** as it involves fewer steps and associated fees.

For additional information, consult the following resources:

- U.S. Department of State – Directory of Visa Categories
- **Fiancé(e) Visa (K-1) vs. Marriage Visa (CR-1) – HLG**
- **Fiancé Visa (K-1) vs. Marriage-Based Green Card – USCIS**

Searchable Keywords

K Visa, Fiancé(e)/Spouse (Married Abroad). Kentucky Consular Center (KCC). Kentucky Consular Center (KCC): A U.S. Department of State facility located in Williamsburg, Kentucky. It gives domestic (U.S.) support to the worldwide operations of the Bureau of Consular Affairs Visa Office. It manages the Diversity Visa (DV) Program.

L

What is a US L-Visa?

An **L-visa** is an immigration document used to enter the United States for the purposes of **work in L-1 status**. It is a **non-immigrant visa** and is valid for a relatively **short amount of time** by design—mostly for **intra-company transferees**.

Processing Time for an L-Visa Application

The processing time for an L-visa application depends on several factors, such as:

- The **type of L-visa**
- The **location of the US embassy or consulate**
- Whether the applicant chooses **premium processing** for expedited delivery or not

Here are some general estimates based on the web search results:

- **Standard Processing**: Usually takes between **2 to 4 months**. This includes processing of the **I-129 petition**, which can take up to **six months**, and **consulate processing**, which can take up to six months or longer.
- **Premium Processing**: An optional service that costs an additional **$2,500** and guarantees a decision on the case within **15 business days**. This only applies to the **I-129 petition** and does not affect the **consulate processing time**.
- **Blanket L Processing**: A special option for **large multinational companies** with a pre-approved L-1 visa program. This can reduce the processing time to **1-3 weeks**, as the applicant does not need to file a separate **I-129 petition**.

Please note that these are approximate timelines and may vary depending on the specific circumstances of each case. You can:

- Check the **current wait time** for a nonimmigrant visa interview appointment at a US embassy or consulate using the **online tool**.
- Check the **status of your case online**.
- Contact the **USCIS** or the **embassy or consulate** where you applied for more information.

L-Visa Application Fees

The cost of applying for an L-visa depends on:

- The **type of L-visa**
- The **location of the US embassy or consulate**

- Whether you choose **premium processing**

Here are some of the fees you may have to pay:

- **Base Petition Fee**: Fee for filing **Form I-129, Petition for a Nonimmigrant Worker** with the USCIS – **$460**
- **Fraud Prevention and Detection Fee**: For certain L-visa applicants to prevent and detect fraud – **$500** (only paid once under a blanket L petition)
- **Nonimmigrant Visa Fee**: For applying at a US embassy or consulate
  - **$265** for **L-1 visas**
  - **$190** for **L-2 visas**
- **Premium Processing Fee**: Optional fee for expedited processing within **15 business days** – **$2,500**
- **Additional Fee for Certain Employers**: Applies to employers with **50 or more employees in the US** and **more than 50% of them are in H-1B or L-1 status** – **$4,500**
- **Immigration Attorney Fee**: Varies depending on the **lawyer** and the **complexity** of your case

Important Notes

- These fees are **subject to change** and may not include all costs associated with your application.
- Always check the **official websites** of the **USCIS** and the **Department of State** for the most updated information.
- Consult an **immigration attorney** for specific advice on your situation.

For more information, visit:

- **USCIS**: H and L Filing Fees for Form I-129
- **Visa Nation**: L-1 Visa Application | Process, Checklist, and Fees
- **Travel.State.Gov**
- **Visa-Pro**: Blanket L Petition Approval Process

Searchable Keywords

L Visa (Intracompany Transferee). Labor Certification, Foreign Workers: DOL Website. Laser Visa - See Border Crossing Card. Lawful Permanent Resident (LPR), Green Card: CBP Website. Lawful Permanent Resident (LPR), Green Card: USCIS Website. Legal Rights and Protections: Employment and Education Based Nonimmigrants. Locate an Embassy Website: Locate American Institute in Taiwan (AIT) Website: Lost and Stolen Documents. Lottery, Diversity: Immigrant Visa Program.

Labor Certification: The initial stage of the process by which certain foreign workers get permission to work in the United States. The employer is responsible for getting the labor certification from the Department of Labor. In general, the process works to make sure that the work of foreign workers in the United States will not adversely affect job opportunities, wages and working conditions of U.S. workers.

Labor Condition Application (LCA): A request to the Department of Labor for a foreign worker to work in the United States.

Lawful Permanent Resident (LPR): A person who has immigrated legally, admitted to the United States by DHS as a permanent resident of the United States, and has a Permanent Resident Card, Form I-551 (formerly called Alien Registration Card, also known as *green card).* Form I-551 is a wallet-sized card showing that the person is a lawful permanent resident (immigrant) in the United States.

Permanent resident status is not the same as being a U.S. citizen. However, you have authority to live and work in the United States permanently, as well as other rights and responsibilities. Learn more about Lawful Permanent Residents, including how to replace or renew a Permanent Resident Card, on the USCIS Website. Learn about the requirements for entry into the United States on the CBP website.

This person may also be called a legal permanent resident, a green card holder, a permanent resident alien, a legal permanent resident alien (LPRA) and resident alien permit holder.

Lawful Permanent Resident Alien (LPRA): Lawful permanent resident.

Laws (immigration and visa-related laws): The Code of Federal Regulations contains useful information on the laws regulating U.S. visa policy.

Lay Worker: A person who works in a religious organization but is not a member of the formal clergy.

LEA: See Local Educational Agency.

Legitimation: The legal process that a natural father can use to acknowledge legally his children who were born out of wedlock (outside of marriage). A **legitimated child** can be considered a **"child"** under immigration law under these conditions:

- The **legitimation** took place according to the **law of the child's residence** or the **father's**

residence.

- The **father proved (established)** that he is the child's **natural father**.
- The child was **under the age of 18**.
- The child was in the **legal custody** of the father, who legitimated the child when the legal process of **legitimation** took place.

LIFE Act: Legal Immigration Family Equity (LIFE) Act and amendments. This act of Congress allows foreign spouses of U.S. citizens, the children of those foreign spouses, and spouses and children of certain lawful permanent residents (LPR) to come to the United States to complete the processing for their permanent residence. This Act became effective on December 21, 2000.

Local Educational Agency: School or school district. Also called LEA. This term is used for deciding tuition charges for secondary school students with F-1 visa status.

Lose Status: To stay in the United States longer than the period which DHS gave to a person when they entered the United States, or to fail to meet the requirements or violate the terms of the visa classification. The person becomes "out of status". For example, you entered the United States on a student visa to study at a university. You work at your uncle's convenience store without authorization and do not study. You have lost status. You are out of status.

Lottery: See the diversity visa program.

LPR or LPRA: See lawful permanent resident (LPR).

Special Constable TransfereeAttestation | Author unknown: Retrieved on September 10, 2024

M

US M-visa type-visa: A US M-visa type is a nonimmigrant visa for students who wish to enroll in a vocational or non-academic program in the US, such as cooking, design, or programming. Unlike the F-visa, which is for academic students, the M-visa does not allow students to take language courses or change their field of study. The M-visa is valid for the duration of the program, plus 30 days, and cannot exceed one year. M-visa holders are not eligible for practical training or employment except for certain limited circumstances. They can bring their spouses and children under 21 years old as dependents under the M-2 visa category, but they cannot work or study in the US.

To apply for an M-visa, you will need to obtain a Form I-20 from the vocational school you plan to attend, pay the SEVIS fee and the visa application fee, and schedule an interview at a US embassy or consulate. You will also need to provide proof of your financial ability, English proficiency, and ties to your home country

You may explore the following websites for detailed information:

- Directory of Visa Categories – Travel
- Students and Employment | USCIS
- Differences Between F, M, and J Visas | File Right
- M-1 Visa Information
- U.S. Study and Exchange Visas: F-1, M-1, J-1, and Q-1 Visas – US Visa-Help

How long does it take to process an M-visa application?

The processing time for an M-visa application varies depending on several factors, such as the type of M-visa, the location of the US embassy or consulate, and whether you choose premium processing or not. Here are some general estimates based on the web search results:

- **Standard Processing:** This typically takes between **2 to 4 months**. The processing of the **I-20 form** can take up to **six months**, and consulate processing may also require **six months or more**. Applicants should plan accordingly, as delays can occur.
- **Premium Processing:** This optional service costs an additional **$2,500** and ensures a decision on the case within **15 business days**. However, it applies only to the **I-20 form** and does not expedite the consulate processing time.
- **China Processing:** For applicants applying for an M-visa in China, the standard processing time is usually **4 business days**. For those needing faster service, **express and rush options** are available, which can significantly reduce the processing time.

Service is also available if you want to pick up your M-visa earlier. An additional **USD 30** should be paid for the **same-day collection** and **third-day collection**.

- **Japan Processing:** If you are applying for an M-visa in Japan, the time required from visa application to visa issuance is **5 working days** from the day following the date of receipt of the application if there is no problem with the content of the application.

Please note that these are just approximate timelines and may vary depending on the specific circumstances of each case. You can check the current wait time for a nonimmigrant visa interview appointment at a US embassy or consulate using the tool below. You can also check the status of your case online or contact the **USCIS** or the embassy or consulate where you applied for more information.

Processing Times – USCIS

China Business

The M-1 Student Visa, Explained – Boundless

Visa Processing Time | Ministry of Foreign Affairs of Japan

How much does it cost to apply for an M-visa?

The cost of applying for an M-visa consists of several fees, such as:

- **SEVIS I-901 fee:** This is a fee for the **Student and Exchange Visitor Information System**. The current amount is **$330**.
- **Application fee:** This is a fee for processing your visa application. The current amount is **$185**.
- **Issuance fee:** This is a fee for issuing your visa, also known as a **reciprocity fee**. The amount varies depending on your country of citizenship. You can check the reciprocity fee for your country using the tool below.

Please note that these fees are subject to change and may not include all the costs associated with your application. You should check the official websites of the **USCIS** and the **Department of State** for the most updated information. You should also consult an immigration attorney for specific advice on your situation.

Sources:

- Students
- M1 Visa for Vocational Students - Requirements and How to Apply
- Visa Fees | Official U.S. Department of State Visa Appointment Service

- Nonimmigrant Visa Fee Increases to Take Effect June 17, 2023 – Travel

Can I Expedite My Consulate Processing?

You may be eligible to expedite your consulate processing in cases of urgent or exceptional circumstances, such as:

- A medical emergency
- A family crisis
- An imminent school deadline

However, expedited processing is not guaranteed. Approval depends on the consulate's availability and discretion.

To request expedited processing, send an email to **NVCExpedite@state.gov** with the following details:

- Your full name and contact information
- Your case number or relevant reference details
- A clear explanation of the emergency or exceptional circumstance
- Supporting documentation to substantiate your request

Keep in mind that each request is reviewed on a case-by-case basis, and you should submit your request as early as possible to allow time for processing.

- Your **NVC case number** and **invoice number** are in the subject line and the body of the email.
- Your **full name** and **date of birth** as the **beneficiary (applicant)** in the body of the email.
- The **full name** and **date of birth** of the **petitioner (sponsor)** in the body of the email.
- The **reason for the expedited request** and any supporting evidence, such as a **doctor's letter**, a **psychological evaluation**, or a **school letter** in the body of the email and as attachments.
- At least **two phone numbers** where you can be contacted.

You should also pay the **NVC fees**, complete the **DS-260 form**, and submit the **required documents** online as soon as possible, as these are necessary for your visa interview.

You will receive a response from NVC within a few weeks, either approving or denying your expedite request. If your request is approved, your case will be forwarded to the Consulate, and you will be notified of your interview date. If your request is denied, your case will continue to process normally.

Please note that the processing times and fees for visa applications can vary depending on your visa type, country of citizenship, and the Consulate's location. For the most up-to-date information, consult the official websites of the USCIS and the Department of State.

Additionally, you can explore the following resources for guidance:

- Immigrant Visas Processing – General FAQs – Travel
- National Visa Center (NVC) Expedite Requests for Consular Process Cases
- How to Make an NVC Expedite Request for Hardship: Step by Step – Visa-Nation
- Guide to Expedited Case Processing at the National Visa Center
- Fees for Visa Services – Travel

Searchable Keywords

M-Visa (Nonacademic Student). Media, Journalists (I Visa). Medical Exam/Panel Physician Information.

Machine-Readable Passport (MRP): A passport that has biographic information entered on the data page according to international specifications. A machine-readable passport is required to travel without a visa on the Visa Waiver Program (VWP). See the VWP that to learn more about the requirements.

Machine Readable Visa (MRV): A visa that contains biometric information about the passport holder. A visa that immigration officers read with special machines when the applicants enter the United States. It gives biographic information about the passport holder and tells the DHS information about the type of visa. It is also called MRV.

Maintain Status: To follow the requirements of the visa status and comply with any limitations on duration of stay.

Missionary Work: Work performed for a religious organization to spread the faith (religion) and advance the principles and doctrines of the religion. Such work may include religious instruction, help for the elderly and needy and proselytizing.

MRV: See Machine Readable Visa.

N

US N-visa type: A US N-visa is a special immigrant visa for certain children of parents who have been granted special immigrant status under the Hague Convention on Protection of Children and Co-operation in Respect of Intercountry Adoption. The N-visa allows these children to enter the US as lawful permanent residents and join their adoptive parents.

The N-Visa: Categories and Application Process

The N-visa is a specialized visa category with two subcategories:

1. **N-8 Visa**: For children who have been adopted or will be adopted by a U.S. citizen outside the United States.
2. **N-9 Visa**: For biological siblings of an N-8 child who will also be adopted by the same U.S. citizen.

Eligibility Requirements

To qualify for an N-visa, the child must meet the following conditions:

- Be under 16 years old.
- Be unmarried.
- Be eligible for adoption under the Hague Convention.

Application Process

1. **Filing the Petition**:
   - The adoptive parent must file **Form I-800, Petition to Classify Convention Adoptee as an Immediate Relative**, with the U.S. Citizenship and Immigration Services (USCIS).
   - A provisional or final approval must be obtained before proceeding.
2. **Hague Adoption Certificate or Declaration**:
   - The child must have a **Hague Adoption Certificate** or a **Hague Custody Declaration** issued by the Central Authority of their country of origin, ensuring compliance with Hague Convention standards.
3. **Visa Application and Processing**:
   - The child must apply for an immigrant visa through the Hague Convention process at

a U.S. embassy or consulate.

- This includes:
  - Undergoing a medical examination.
  - Attending an interview.

4. **Travel to the United States**:
   - Once approved, the child will receive an N-visa and a travel document to enter the United States as a lawful permanent resident.

Additional Information

For further details, refer to **USCIS: N-8 and N-9 Visa – Hague Process** and the **U.S. Department of State's Hague Adoption Process** resources.

What is the Hague Convention processes on Protection of Children and Co-operation in Respect of Intercountry Adoption?

The Hague Convention on Protection of Children and Co-operation in Respect of Intercountry Adoption has virtually every country on earth as a signatory to its mission statement.

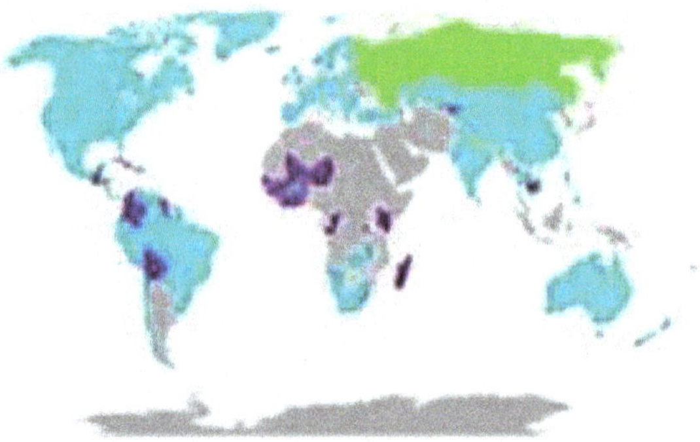

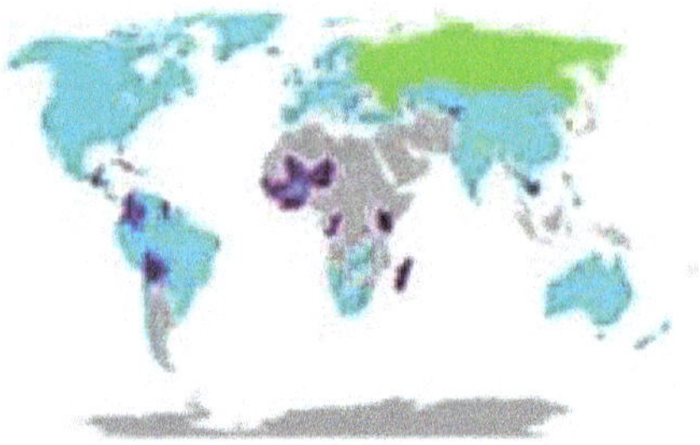

The Hague Convention on Protection of Children and Co-operation in Respect of Intercountry Adoption, or the **Hague Adoption Convention**, is an international treaty that aims to protect the rights and interests of children, birth parents, and adoptive parents involved in intercountry adoptions.

The Convention establishes common standards and procedures for intercountry adoptions, such as:

- Ensuring that **intercountry adoptions** are made in the **best interests of the child** and with respect for their **fundamental rights**.
- Preventing the **abduction**, **sale**, or **trafficking of children** for adoption purposes.
- Creating a system of **cooperation and communication** among the countries that are parties to the Convention.
- Securing the **recognition of intercountry adoptions** in the countries that are parties to the Convention.

The Convention was drafted by the **Hague Conference on Private International Law** and was concluded on **May 29, 1993**. It entered into force on **May 1, 1995**, and as of **March 2019**, it has been ratified by **99 countries**.

If you are interested in learning more about the Hague Adoption Convention, you can visit the following websites:

- **Hague Conference on Private International Law**: This is the official website of the organization that drafted and administers the Convention. It provides the full text and outline of the Convention, as well as information on its implementation and operation.
- **U.S. Department of State**: This is the website of the U.S. Central Authority for the Convention. It provides information on the U.S. adoption process, the countries that are parties to the Convention, and the resources and services available for adoptive families and children.
- **USCIS**: This is the website of the U.S. Citizenship and Immigration Services, which is responsible for adjudicating immigration petitions for children adopted through the Convention. It provides information on the eligibility requirements, the application forms, and the fees for the Hague Process.

Searchable Keywords

National Visa Center (NVC). NATO Visa. NATO-7 Visa: Legal Rights and Protections Pamphlet (Wilberforce Act). News, Visa. Nonimmigrant Classifications and Types of Nonimmigrant Visas. Nonimmigrants: Legal Rights and Protections for Certain Education or Employment Based Nonimmigrant Visas. Nonimmigrant Visas. Nonimmigrant Visa Statistics. Nonimmigrant Visitor (B) Visa Refusal Rates by Nationality.

NAFTA: North American Free-Trade Agreement.

National Interest Waiver: This is for physicians and doctors who work in an area without adequate health care workers or who work in Veterans Affairs facilities. These physicians and doctors can file immigrant visa petitions for themselves without first applying for a labor certification.

National Visa Center (NVC): A Department of State facility located in Portsmouth, New Hampshire. It supports the worldwide immigrant visa operations of the Bureau of Consular Affairs Visa Office. The NVC processes immigrant visa petitions from DHS for people who will apply for their immigrant visas at U.S. Embassies and Consulates abroad. It also collects fees associated with immigrant visa processing. Go to the NVC webpage for more information.

Native: A person born in a particular country is a native of that country.

Naturalization: A citizen who acquires nationality of a country after birth. That is, the person did not become a citizen by birth but by a legal procedure. See the USCIS website for more information.

Nonimmigrant Visa (NIV): A U.S. visa allows the bearer, a foreign citizen, to apply to enter the United States temporarily for a specific purpose. Nonimmigrant visas are primarily classified according to the principal purpose of travel. With few exceptions, while in the United States, nonimmigrants are restricted to the activity or reason for which their visa was issued. Examples of persons who may receive nonimmigrant visas are tourists, students, diplomats, and temporary workers. For more information, see Temporary Visitors to the U.S.

Notice of Action (Form I-797): A DHS, USCIS immigration form that says that USCIS has received a petition you submitted, acted, approved a petition, or denied a petition.

NSEERS: Effective April 28, 2011, the Department of Homeland Security (DHS) no longer requires registration of foreign citizens entering and exiting the United States under the National Security Entry-Exit Registration System (NSEERS), also known as Special Registration. More information is available in the Federal Register notice from DHS dated April 28, 2011.

NVC: See National Visa Center.

O

The following paragraph is excerpted from the Department of Homeland Security website:

The **US O-Visa** is a **non-immigrant temporary worker visa** granted by the United States to individuals who possess **extraordinary ability** in various fields. Here are the key points about O-Visas:

1. **O-1A Visa**: This category is for individuals with **extraordinary ability in the sciences, education, business, or athletics** (excluding arts, motion pictures, or television industry).
2. **O-1B Visa**: Reserved for individuals with **extraordinary ability in the arts** or **extraordinary achievement in the motion picture or television industry**.
3. **O-2 Visa**: Accompanies an **O-1 artist or athlete** to assist in a specific event or performance.
4. **O-3 Visa**: For **spouses or children** of O-1 and O-2 visa holders.

O-Visa and Green Card

- The **Green Card** is a **permanent resident card** that allows you to live and work in the U.S. permanently.
- You can apply for a Green Card while on an O-Visa, but you must meet certain eligibility criteria and go through a **complex application process**. You must also maintain your O-Visa status until your Green Card is approved.
- The difference between the **O-1A** and the **O-1B** visas is that the O-1A is for individuals with extraordinary ability in the **sciences, education, business, or athletics**, while the O-1B is for individuals with extraordinary ability in the **arts or extraordinary achievement in the motion picture or television industry**. The **criteria and evidence** required for each category are different.

O-Visa Processing Times

The processing time for an O-Visa petition can vary depending on:

- The **service center**
- The **type of petition**
- Whether you request **premium processing**

The average processing time ranges from **2 weeks to 4 months**. The processing time for a Green Card application can also vary depending on:

- The **category**

- The **country of origin**
- The **availability of visa numbers**

The average processing time ranges from **6 months to 2 years**.

Overstay of Visas: Visa Overstays in the US by Some African Countries

According to the **DHS report for FY 2019**, Nigeria had the highest number of visa overstays in the US, with **29,723**, followed by **South Africa** with **10,616** and **Ghana** with **9,474**.

The African country with the highest **overstay rate** (the percentage of expected departures that did not occur) was **Djibouti**, with **44.67%**, followed by **Chad**, with **30.14%**, and **Liberia**, with **28.21%**.

You can explore the data on **visa overstays by country**.

According to the **Department of Homeland Security (DHS)**, about **650,000 to 850,000 nonimmigrant admissions** result in an **overstay** each year for the fiscal years between **2016 and 2020**. This represents about **1-2% of all nonimmigrant admissions**.

The majority of overstays come from countries such as:

- **Venezuela**
- **Mexico**
- **India**
- **China**
- **Brazil**

Overstaying a visa can have **serious consequences**, such as being barred from **re-entry** or **applying for a Green Card**.

Consequences of Overstaying a Visa in the U.S.

Overstaying a visa in the U.S. can result in:

- Being barred from returning to the U.S. for **three or ten years**, depending on the duration of the overstay
- Being restricted from applying for an **extension of stay** or a **change of status**
- Having your existing visa **voided** and being unable to obtain a new visa except in your **country of origin**
- Being unable to **adjust your status** to a permanent resident or a citizen, even if you are otherwise eligible

Searchable Keywords

What is the US, O-visa type? Google Top Top Media Results. See examples below. Working in the United States Temporary Workers O-1 Visa: Individuals with Extraordinary Ability or Achievement O-1 Visa: Individuals with Extraordinary Ability or Achievement.

Opt-out: A U.S. federal law called the Child Status Protection Act (CSPA) provides a type of relief referred to as the "opt-out." This is very limited in scope and applies only to immigrant visa applicants in the family second preference (F2B) category for unmarried adult children (age 21 or older) of a Lawful Permanent Resident (LPR). If the LPR petitioner naturalizes before his/her adult child receives an immigrant visa, the applicant's visa category automatically converts to the family first preference (F1) visa category.

Under "opt-out," the visa applicant can choose to remain an F2B visa applicant. This may be beneficial because sometimes the waiting time for an F2B visa is shorter than the waiting time for an F1 visa. Please always ask questions and read the instructions for applying for opt-out approval.

Original Document: An original document is the actual document that was issued when an authority recorded an event (e.g., birth, marriage, divorce, adoption, etc.).

Orphan: A child who has no parents because of death, disappearance, desertion, or abandonment of the parents. A child may also be considered an orphan if the child has an unwed mother or a single living parent who cannot care for the child and has released him/her them irrevocably (permanently) for adoption and emigration. Adoptive parents must make sure that a child meets the legal definition of an "orphan" before adopting a child from another country. For more information, visit our Adoptions website.

Orphan Petition: Form I-600.

Out of Status: A U.S. visa allows the bearer to apply for entry to the United States in a certain classification for a specific purpose, such as student (F), visitor (B), or temporary worker (H). Every visa is issued for a particular purpose and a specific class of visitor. Each visa classification has a set of requirements that the visa holder must follow and maintain.

Arrival and Admission Process in the United States

Upon arriving in the United States, a Department of Homeland Security (DHS) Customs and Border Protection (CBP) inspector will determine:

- Whether you are eligible for admission.
- The length of your authorized stay.
- Any conditions attached to your stay.

If admitted, you will receive an **admission stamp** in your passport or a paper **Form I-94 (Arrival/Departure Record)**. This document specifies the date by which you must depart the United States.

It's important to note that the date on the admission stamp or Form I-94 governs your authorized length of stay, regardless of the validity of your visa. Always ensure you leave the U.S. by the date indicated to remain in compliance with immigration laws.

the the length of your stay and the conditions of your stay. When admitted,

You are considered out of status if you remain in the United States without authorization after the expiration date on your admission stamp or paper Form I-94. It is important to understand the concept of immigration status and the consequences of violating that status.

Failure to maintain status can result in arrest, and violators may be required to leave the United States. Violation of status also can affect the prospect of readmission to the United States for a period, by making you ineligible for a visa. Most people who violate the terms of their status are barred from lawfully returning to the United States for years. See our Visa Expiration Date page for more information.

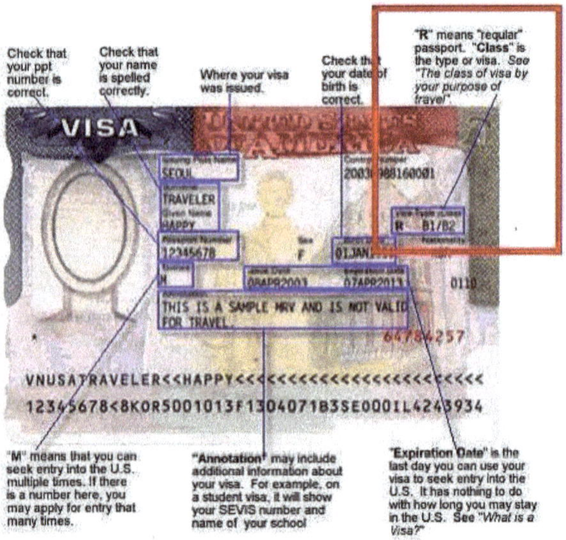

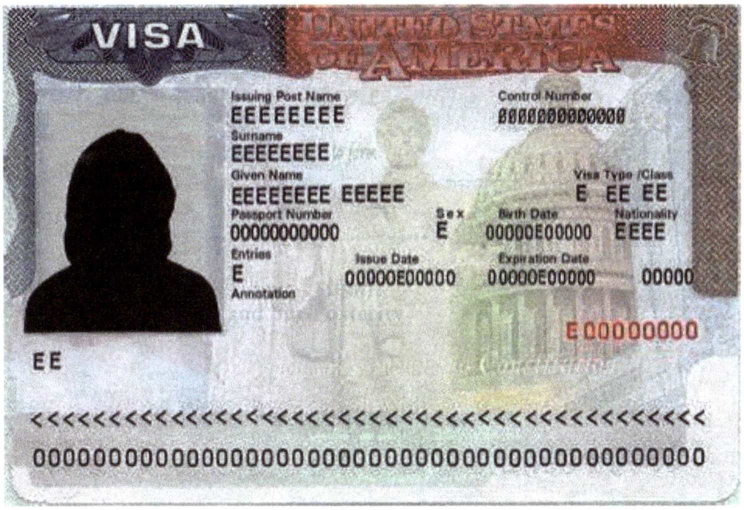

Overstay: An "overstay" occurs when a visitor stays longer than permitted, as shown on their electric admission stamp or paper Form I-94 Arrival/Departure Record. A violation of the CBP-defined length of admission may make you ineligible for a visa in the future.

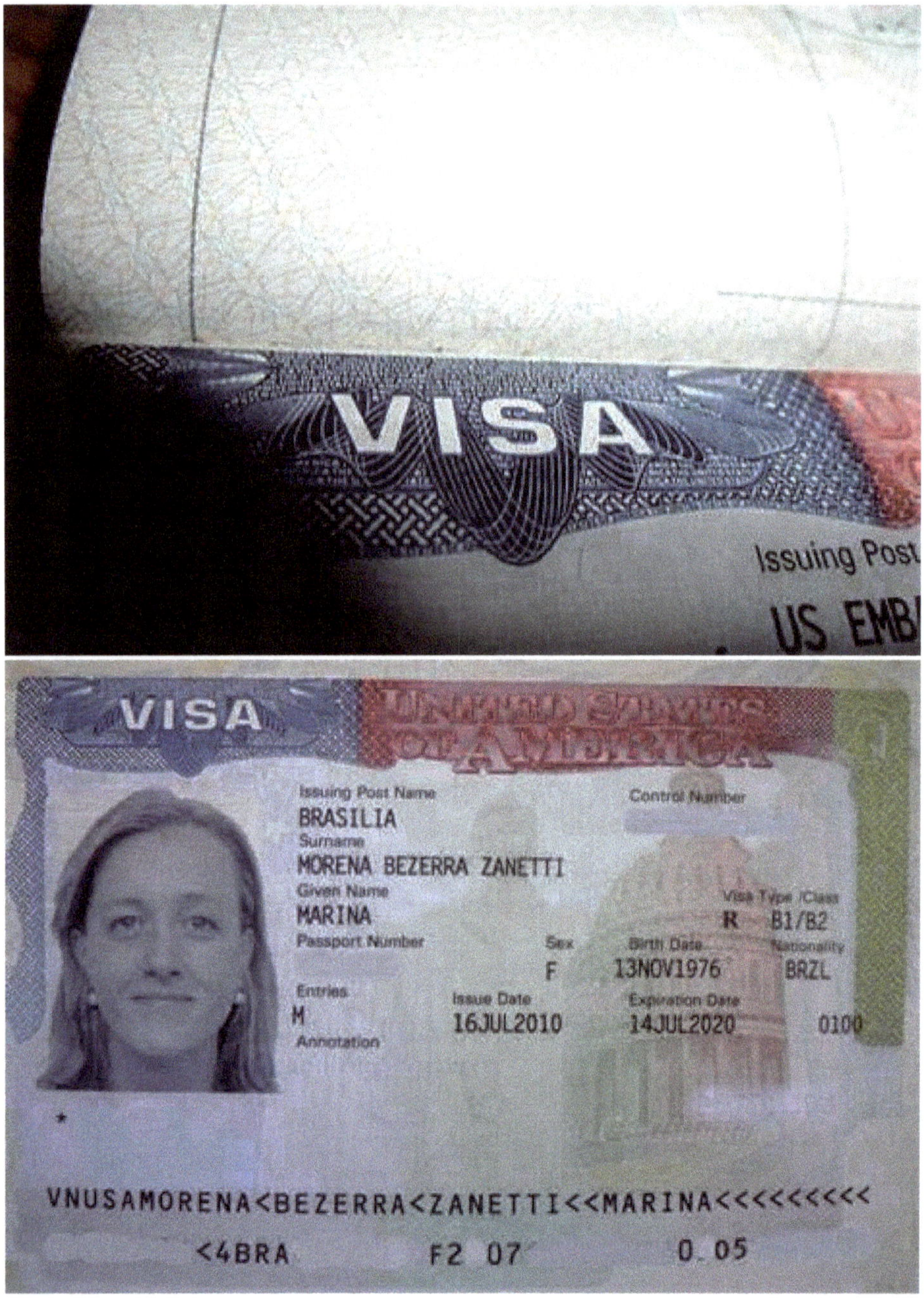

Ex. Visa notations on a passport, what they mean and how to interpret them.

Ex. Visa notations on a passport. 3.

Retrieved on October 19, 2024.

Internet source. Unknown Author: Retrieved February 13, 2024.

Internet source. Unknown Author: Retrieved February 13, 2024.

According to a dictionary definition, the ability is simply the possession of a particular skill-set skill set, talent, or proficiency in an area of human endeavor.

P

Searching for a US P-visa type: A US P-visa is a type of temporary employment visa for athletes, artists, and entertainers who have a job offer from a U.S. employer and are internationally recognized or culturally unique. There are different subcategories of P-visas depending on the specific occupation and purpose of the visit.

For example, P-1A is for individual or team athletes, P-2 is for artists or entertainers in a reciprocal exchange program, and P-3 is for artists or entertainers in a culturally unique program. P-visas also allow the principal applicant's spouse and children to accompany them to the U.S. as P-4 visa holders. Visit the USCIS or the U.S. Department of State websites to learn more about the eligibility criteria, application process, and period of stay for each P-visa type

(P-3 Artist or Entertainer Coming to Be Part of a Culturally Unique Program | USCIS: Directory of Visa Categories - Travel : P visa - Wikipedia: What is a Type P Visa | Herman Legal Group).

Can I apply for a green card with a P-visa? The answer to your question depends on your specific situation and goals. A P-visa is a nonimmigrant visa that does not directly lead to a green card or permanent residency in the U.S.

However, there may be some scenarios where you can change your status to another visa category that allows you to apply for a green card, such as an H-1B visa for skilled workers. Alternatively, you may be eligible for a green card through family-based immigration, such as marrying a U.S. citizen or being sponsored by a close relative who is a U.S. citizen or permanent resident.

If you are interested in pursuing a green card with a P-visa, you should consult with an immigration attorney who can advise you on the best course of action for your case. You

should also be aware of the requirements and procedures for applying for a green card, such as filing the appropriate forms, paying the fees, submitting the evidence, and attending the interviews. The process can be complex and lengthy, so you should be prepared and informed before you start.

P-1A Athlete | USCIS: Complete Guide to the P1 Visa in the U.S. [2024] - Stilt: Can I Apply for a Green Card if I am in the U.S. on a P-1 Athletic Visa ...: Green Card Processes and Procedures | USCIS webpages.

How long can I stay in the US with a P-visa? What is the difference between a P-1 and an O-1 visa type?

Searching for: P-visa period of stay.

Searching for: P-1 vs O-1 visa.

The length of stay for a P-visa holder depends on the type of P-visa and the specific event or activity for which they were admitted. According to the USCIS website, an individual P-1 athlete can stay for up to five years with extensions not to exceed a total of 10 years. Other P-1, P-2, and P-3 visa holders, including their support personnel, can stay for the time needed to complete the event or activity, not to exceed one year. They can also request extensions in increments of one year.

The main difference between a P-1 and an O-1 visa is the level of achievement or recognition required for each category. A P-1 visa is for athletes, artists, and entertainers who are internationally recognized or culturally unique. An O-1 visa is for individuals who

have extraordinary ability or extraordinary achievement in the fields of art, science, education, business, or athletics, as demonstrated by sustained national or international acclaim. The O-1 visa also has some advantages over the P-1 visa, such as not requiring a residence abroad, allowing solo performances, and having no limit on the period of stay.

If you need more information, you can visit the U.S. Department of State website or consult with an immigration attorney.

P-1A Athlete | USCIS : Directory of Visa Categories - Travel : O-1 and P-1 Visas (Artists/ Entertainers) | Greenwood Hanlon Kendrick

Can I bring my family with me on a P-1 visa? Yes, you can bring your family with you on a P-1 visa. Your spouse and unmarried children under the age of 21 may obtain P-4 status, which allows them to accompany you to the U.S. for the duration of your stay. However, P-4 visa holders are not authorized to work in the U.S., but they may attend school or college.

See the following web pages: P-1A Athlete | USCIS: What is a You may contact law firms, Searching for The P-visa application process: How do I apply for a P-visa type?

To apply for a **P-Visa Type**, you need to follow these steps:

1. **Petition Filing**
   - You need to have a **U.S. employer or sponsor** who will file a petition on your behalf with the **USCIS**.
   - The employer or sponsor must submit **Form I-129**, *Petition for Nonimmigrant Worker*, along with the **required documents and fees**.
   - The petition must be filed no more than **six months** before the scheduled event or performance.

2. **Advisory Opinion**
    - Obtain an **advisory opinion** from a **labor organization** that represents your field of work.
    - If no such organization exists, submit evidence proving this.
    - The advisory opinion should state:
        - Whether you meet the criteria for the P-Visa type
        - Whether your participation will affect the working conditions of U.S. workers
3. **Visa Application**
    - Apply for a **P-Visa** at a **U.S. embassy or consulate** in your home country.
    - Complete **Form DS-160**, *Online Nonimmigrant Visa Application.*
    - Schedule an **interview** with a consular officer.
    - Bring the following documents to the interview:
        - **Passport**
        - **Photo**
        - Copy of the **approved petition**
        - Any other **supporting documents**

By following these steps, you can ensure a smoother P-Visa application process.

The P-visa application process can vary depending on your specific situation and the type of P-visa you are applying for. Therefore, it is advisable to consult with an immigration attorney who can guide you through the process and help you avoid any potential pitfalls.

P-1A Athlete | USCIS : P Visa Guide: Everything You Need to Know | Ashoori Law : P Visa Application - P1, P2, P3 Visa Application Process: P-1 Visa for Internationally – Recognized Athletes and Artists: P1 Visa - US Athlete Visa Application and Requirements – Visa-Guide. World / US-Visa

Can I apply for multiple P-visas at once? According to the P Visa Guide, there is no limit on how many P visas can be granted per year. However, you cannot have two valid visas of the same type at the same time. Therefore, you can apply for multiple P visas at once if they are different subcategories, such as P-1A, P-2, or P-3.

For example, you could apply for a P-1A visa as an individual athlete and a P-3 visa as a member of a culturally unique entertainment group. However, you could not apply for two P-1A visas for different athletic events or teams.

To apply for multiple P visas, you need to follow the same steps as applying for a single P visa, but you need to submit separate petitions and applications for each visa category. You also need to pay the fees and attend the interviews for each visa category. You can find more information about the P visa application process in my previous response or on the U.S. Department of State website.

How long does it take to process a P-visa application? The processing time . This service center handles the petition, and whether you request premium processing or not depends on the type of P-visa. This service center handles the petition and whether you request premium processing. According to the USCIS website, the current processing times for P-visas range from 2.5 weeks to 4.5 months. However, these times may change due to various factors, such as workload, demand, and emergencies. You can check the latest processing times for your specific case on the USCIS website by selecting your form, form category, and the office that is processing your case.

If you want to expedite your P-visa application, you can request premium processing for an additional fee of US $1,440. Premium processing guarantees that the USCIS will adjudicate your petition within 15 calendar days. However, premium processing does not guarantee that your petition will be approved, nor does it affect the processing time of your visa application at the U.S. embassy or consulate.

Searchable Keywords

Pamphlet, Rights, Protections, and Resources (for Certain Employment and Education Based Nonimmigrants). Panel Physician/Medical Exam Information. Parole,

Humanitarian: USCIS Website. Permanent Immigrants to the United States. Permanent Resident, Advance Parole, Re-entry Permit: CBP Website. Permanent Resident, Processes and Procedures: USCIS Website. Photograph Requirements. Physician (Exchange Visitor). ECA Website. Poverty Guidelines. Premium Processing Service for Temporary Workers: USCIS Website. Professor (J-1 Exchange Visitor): ECA Website.

Panel Physician: U.S. Embassies and Consulates which issue immigrant visas have selected certain doctors to do the medical examinations for immigrant visa applicants. Please visit our Medical Examination webpage to find your local Panel Physician.

Permanent Resident (correctly called Lawful Permanent Resident (LPR)): See Lawful Permanent Resident (LPR).

Petitioner: A U.S. citizen or lawful permanent resident family member or employer (or the employer's agent) who files a family-based or employment-based immigrant visa petition with

USCIS.

Photocopy: A photocopy is a mechanical reproduction of the original document that does not contain an original stamp, seal, or other endorsement from the issuing authority. Note: A photocopy of a certified copy (i.e., the stamp, seal, endorsement, or security paper is not original) is considered a photocopy.

Physical Presence: The place where a person is physically located.

Polygamy: Having more than one husband or wife at the same time. Polygamy is illegal under U.S. law.

Port-of-Entry: Place (often an airport) where a person requests admission to the U.S. by the DHS, CBP officer. Learn more on the CBP website.

Post: U.S. Embassy, Consulate, or other diplomatic mission abroad. Not all U.S. Embassies, Consulates and Missions are visa-issuing posts. Visit a list of U.S. Embassies, Consulates, and Missions.

Poverty Guidelines: The Department of Health and Human Services publishes a list every year giving the lowest income acceptable for a family of a particular size so that the family does not live in poverty. Consular officers use these figures in immigrant visa cases to determine whether a sponsor's income is sufficient to support a new immigrant, in accordance with U.S. immigration laws. Go to the Federal Poverty Guidelines to learn more.

Preference Immigration: A system for determining which and when people can immigrate to the U.S. within the limits of immigration set by Congress. In family immigration, preference is based on the status of the petitioner (U.S. citizen or lawful permanent resident) and his/her relationship to the applicant. Visit the Family Based Immigration webpage for more info. In employment immigration, it is based on the qualifications of the applicant and labor needs in the U.S. Visit Employment Based Immigration webpage for more info.

Principal Applicant: The person named in the petition. For example, a U.S. citizen may file a petition for his married daughter to immigrate to the United States. His daughter will be the principal applicant, and her family members will get visas from her position. They will get derivative status. Or a company may file a petition for a worker. The worker is the principal applicant. Family members get derivative status.

Priority Date: The priority date determines a person's turn to apply for an immigrant visa. In family immigration, the priority date is the date when the petition was filed at a DHS office or submitted to a U.S. Embassy or Consulate abroad. In employment immigration, the priority date may be the date the labor certification application was received by the Department of Labor (DOL).

Public Charge: Following U.S. immigration law, an applicant is ineligible for a visa if he/she is likely at any time to become a public charge.

Q

Searching for: US Q-visa type. A US Q-visa is a type of non-immigrant visa that allows you to travel to the United States to participate in an international cultural exchange

program. The purpose of the program is to provide practical training and employment and to share the history, culture, and traditions of your home country with the United States.

To be eligible for a Q-visa, you must have a U.S. employer or sponsor who will file a petition on your behalf with the USCIS, and you must obtain an advisory opinion from a labor organization that represents your field of work. You can stay in the U.S. for the duration of your program, not to exceed 15 months, and you cannot change your status to another visa category while in the U.S.

Research the Following Webpages

- **Q Cultural Exchange**
- **USCIS: Directory of Visa Categories - Travel**
- **Q-1 Visa - Wikipedia**
- **A Q-1 Visa to the U.S.: Who Qualifies?**
- **Nolo.com**

These resources can provide answers to some relevant questions, such as:

- What is the difference between a **Q-Visa** and an **H-Visa**?
- How do I apply for a **Q-Visa**?
- Can I bring my family with me on a **Q-1 Visa**?

Searchable Keywords

- Q Visa (International Cultural Exchange Visitor)
- Questions About Visas: What Visa Type?

R

The US R-visa type: A US R-visa type is a nonimmigrant visa for religious workers who want to work temporarily in the United States. Religious workers include ministers, priests, monks, nuns, rabbis, imams, and other persons authorized by a recognized religious denomination to conduct religious worship and perform other duties usually performed by members of the clergy.

To Qualify for an R-Visa, the Applicant Must Meet the Following Requirements:

- Be a member of a **religious denomination** that has a **bona fide non-profit religious organization** in the United States for at least **two years** immediately before the filing of the petition.
- Be coming to the United States solely to work as a **minister** of that denomination or in a **religious occupation or vocation** for that organization (or its **nonprofit affiliate**).
- Have been working in one of these capacities for at least **two years**, immediately before the filing of the petition.

The R-visa is valid for an initial period of up to 30 months, and can be extended for another 30 months, for a maximum stay of 60 months. The spouse and unmarried children under 21 of and are eligible to study in the United States

The processing time for an R-visa depends on several factors, such as the type of petition, the evidence submitted, and the workload of USCIS. According to some sources, it usually takes around 6 months for USCIS to review and process the required documents.

However, this may vary depending on the case. If the religious organization has already been approved, the employer can request premium processing for an additional fee of about $1,225, which could reduce the waiting time to two weeks. You can check the current processing times on the USCIS website.People made refugees by US 'war on terror' – Middle East. by Unknown Author. Retrieved on February 23, 2023.

People made refugees by US 'war on terror' – Middle East. by Unknown Author. Retrieved on February 23, 2023.

Ethnic girl standing near refugee tents · Photo by Unknown Author. Retrieved on February 15, 2023.

Searchable Keywords

Reciprocity. Refugees: Department of State, PRM Website. Refugees, Follow-to-Join. Refugees, Iraqi Refugee Processing: USCIS Website. Refugees: U.N. High Commission on Refugees

(UNHCR) Website. Refugees: USCIS Website. Refugee Resettlement: Health and Human Services Website. Refusal Rates: Nonimmigrant B Visa Refusal Rates by Nationality. Religious Workers (Temporary). Renewing your A, G, or NATO Visas. Replacing your lost or stolen Visa. Report of the Visa Office: Visa Statistics. Returning Resident Alien. Rights and Protections: Employment and Education Based Nonimmigrant.

Rank Order Number: The number that Kentucky Consular Center gives to the entries of DV Program (lottery) as the computer selects them. The first entries are chosen to have the lowest numbers. The Visa Office of the Department of State gives winning entries a chance to apply for immigration according to their rank order number for their region. Visit our DV Program webpage for more information on the Diversity Visa Lottery Program.

Receipt Notice: A DHS, USCIS Notice of Action, Form I-797, which says that DHS has received a petition.

Re-entry Permit: A travel document that DHS issues to lawful permanent residents (LPRs) who want to stay outside of the United States for more than one year and less than two years. LPRs who cannot get a passport from their country of nationality can also apply for a re-entry permit. You can put visas for foreign countries in a re-entry permit.

Refugee: A person who has a well-founded fear of persecution if he/she should return to his/her home country. He/she applies to come to the United States in another country and enters the United States as a refugee. See the DHS, USCIS website Refugee information to learn more. See Follow-to-Join Refugees & Asylees for information for the spouse or unmarried minor children abroad following to join a refugee or asylee in the United States.

Retrogression: Sometimes, a case that is current one month will not be current the next month. This occurs when the annual numerical limit has been reached. This usually happens near the end of a fiscal year (October 1 to September 30 of the next year). When the new fiscal year begins, the Visa Office gets a new supply of visa numbers and usually brings back the cut-off dates to where they were before retrogression.

Returning Residents: Lawful permanent residents who want to return to the United States after staying abroad for more than one year or beyond the expiration of their re-entry permits. For more information, visit our Returning Resident Visas webpage.

Revalidation or Renewal of a Visa: Nonimmigrant visa applicants who currently have a visa and are seeking renewal or revalidation of their visa for future travel to the U.S. must apply abroad, generally in their country of residence. The exception is the renewal or revalidation of A, G, and NATO diplomatic and official visas (except A-3, G-5 and NATO-7), which continue to be processed in Washington and at the U.S. Mission to the United Nations in New York. See Visa Renewal to learn more.

Revocation of a Visa: Cancellation of a visa. The visa is no longer good (valid) for travel to the United States.

S

The US S-visa category: A US S-visa category is a type of visa for individuals who have assisted a law enforcement agency as a witness or informant. A law enforcement agency may apply for permanent residence (a Green Card) on behalf of a witness or informant when the individual has completed the terms and conditions of his or her S classification.

The S-Visa: Informant or "Snitch" Visa

The S-visa category is a specialized nonimmigrant visa under U.S. immigration law, often referred to as the "informant visa" or the "snitch visa." Below is an overview of its purpose, eligibility, and application process:

1. Purpose of the S-Visa

- The S-visa is designed for individuals who serve as witnesses or informants in criminal investigations or prosecutions.
- These individuals provide critical information to law enforcement agencies, aiding in solving or preventing crimes.
- It allows them to enter the United States temporarily to assist in legal proceedings.

2. Eligibility Criteria

To qualify for an S-visa, an individual must meet the following conditions:

- Be a witness or informant with information related to a specific criminal activity.
- Have provided substantial assistance to law enforcement agencies.
- Be willing to cooperate further with the investigation or prosecution.
- Demonstrate that their presence in the U.S. is necessary for the case.

3. Application Process

The application process involves these steps:

- **Law Enforcement Certification**: The law enforcement agency handling the case must certify the individual's eligibility and need for an S-visa.
- **Form I-854 Submission**: The agency submits Form I-854 (Interagency Alien Witness and Informant Record) to U.S. Citizenship and Immigration Services (USCIS).
- **Consular Processing**: If approved, the individual applies for the S-visa at a U.S. embassy or

consulate.

4. Benefits of the S-Visa

S-visa holders enjoy several benefits:

- **Entry to the U.S.**: They can legally enter the United States.
- **Work Authorization**: They are eligible for employment authorization.
- **Dependent Visas**: Immediate family members (spouse and unmarried children under 21) can accompany them as dependents.

5. Duration and Extensions

- The initial S-visa is valid for up to 3 years.
- Extensions may be granted if the individual continues to cooperate with law enforcement.

The S-visa is a vital tool for U.S. law enforcement agencies. It enables them to access key information from informants while providing temporary legal status and protections for those individuals.

Remember that the S-visa is a specialized category, and its issuance is based on specific circumstances related to criminal investigations. If you know someone who might qualify, they should consult with legal professionals or law enforcement agencies for guidance.

Searchable Keywords

Safety and Security of U.S. Borders. Scholar: ECA Website. Security Measures for International Flights to the United States: TSA website. Services, Visa Issuing Posts (U.S. Embassy/Consulate). Skills List 2009, For J-1 Exchange Visitors. Singapore FTA Professional Worker (H1B1 Visa). Social Security Administration (SSA) Website. Social Security Card, How to Apply (Non-citizens/Immigration). Social Security Card, How to Replace Your Card. Special Immigrant Visas for Iraqi and Afghan Translators/Interpreters. Special Immigrant Visas for Iraqis Employed by/on Behalf of U.S. Government. Special Immigrant Visas for Afghans Employed by/on Behalf of U.S. Government. Spouse /Fiancé(e) of a U.S. Citizen (K Visa). State Sponsors of Terrorism countries, visa applicants from: Processing procedures and FAQs. Statistics, Immigration: DHS Website. Statistics, Visa Students: Department of State, ECA Website. Students Abroad, for U.S. Citizens. Students and Exchange Visitors, Arrival Procedures: CBP Website. Student and Exchange Visitor Information System (SEVIS): ICE Website. Student Visa (F Visa). Students: USCIS Website. Study Abroad for U.S.

Students: ECA Website. Summer Work/Travel (J-1 Exchange Visitor): ECA Website.

SAW: See Special Agricultural Worker.

Schedule "A" Occupations: The Department of Labor (DOL) has given DHS authority to approve labor certifications for these occupations. These occupations are physical therapists, professional nurses and people of exceptional ability in the sciences or arts.

Second Preference: A category of family immigration (F2) for spouses, children and unmarried sons and daughters of lawful permanent residents. Visit the Family Based Immigration webpage for more info.

Section 213A: A section of the Immigration and Nationality Act (INA) establishes that sponsors have a legal duty to support immigrants they want to bring (sponsor) to the United States. They must complete Form I-864, Affidavit of Support.

Sibling: Brother or sister.

Skills List: The Exchange Visitor Skills List (J Visas) is a list of fields of specialized knowledge and skills that are deemed necessary for the development of an exchange visitor's home country. When you agree to participate in an Exchange Visitor Program, if your skill is on your country's Skills List, you are subject to the two-year foreign residence (home-country physical presence) requirement, which requires you to return to your home country for two years at the end of your exchange visitor program, under U.S. law. Review the Exchange Visitor webpage to learn more.

Son/daughter (married/unmarried): In immigration law, a child becomes a son or daughter when he/she turns 21 or marries. A son or daughter must have once met the definition of a child. Under U.S. immigration law, an unmarried "son or daughter" is a person who was once a "child" but who is now 21 years of age or older. A "married son or daughter" is a person who also satisfies the definition of child but who is also married, regardless of age.

Special Agricultural Worker: Farm workers in perishable products who worked for a specified period and were able to adjust their status to lawful permanent residents according to the Immigration Reform and Control Act of 1986.

Special Immigrant: A special category of immigrant visas (E-4) for persons who lost their citizenship by marriage; persons who lost citizenship by serving in foreign armed forces; certain foreign medical school graduates; Panama Canal immigrants; and certain others. Visit our Employment-based Visas webpage for more information.

Sponsor: A sponsor can be one of the following:

- **The petitioner** (The petitioner must submit an **I-864** or **I-864EZ**)
- **A relative** with a significant ownership interest in the petitioning entity (**I-140s only**)
- **A substitute** in the case of a deceased petitioner (This person is approved as a substitute by **USCIS only**)

A sponsor must be at least **18 years old** and domiciled in the **United States** or its **territories** or **possessions**.

Note: A sponsor must be an individual and may not be an enterprise, business, or any other type of organization

Sponsored Immigrant: An immigrant who has had an Affidavit of Support filed for her.

Spouse: Legally married husband or wife. A cohabiting partner does not qualify as a spouse for immigration purposes. A common-law husband or wife may or may not qualify as a spouse for immigration purposes, depending on the laws of the country where the relationship occurs.

State Workforce Agency: The agency or bureau in each State that deals with employment and labor issues. For the address of workforce agency in each State go to the U.S. Department of Labor, Foreign Labor Certification site.

Stepchild: A spouse's child from a previous marriage or other relationship. In order for a stepchild to be able to immigrate as a "child," the marriage creating the stepchild/stepparent relationship must have happened before the stepchild was 18 years of age.

Substitute Sponsor: A substitute sponsor is a sponsor who is completing a Form I-864 on behalf of an intending immigrant whose original I-130 petitioner is deceased after USCIS approved the Form I-130. The substitute sponsor can only be approved by USCIS.

Successor Mission: The International Security Assistance Force (ISAF) mission in Afghanistan ended on December 31, 2014, and the NATO-led Resolute Support Mission (RSM) began on January 1, 2015. Section 1227 of the National Defense Authorization Act (NDAA) for FY 2015 expanded the Afghan SIV program, authorized under section 602(b) of the Afghan Allies Protection Act of 2009, as amended, to certain Afghans who had been employed by ISAF, but did not provide for SIVs for Afghans employed by successor missions. Section 1216 of the NDAA for FY 2016 expands qualification to now include Afghans employed by ISAF successor missions.

Certain Afghans employed by RSM, as well as any future successor missions to ISAF, may now qualify for the Afghan SIV program. Applicants who were employed by ISAF, RSM, a successor mission, or a combination of these entities must meet all of the SIV program requirements explained in Step 1 on the Afghan SIV Program webpage.

Surviving Parent: A child's living parent when the child's other parent is dead, and the living parent has not remarried.

SWA: See State Workforce Agency.

T

In the US, T nonimmigrant status, commonly referred to as a T visa, is a temporary immigration benefit that allows certain victims of severe human trafficking to remain in the United States. Here are the key points about T's nonimmigrant status.

1. **Eligibility:**
    - Victims of a severe form of trafficking in persons may qualify.
    - This includes both sex trafficking (where force, fraud, or coercion is used for commercial sex acts) and labor trafficking (where individuals are forced into labor or services through coercion).
    - T nonimmigrant status is also available to certain qualifying family members of trafficking victims.
2. **Benefits:**
    - T nonimmigrants are eligible for employment authorization and certain federal and state benefits and services.
    - They may also be able to adjust their status and become lawful permanent residents (obtain a Green Card).
3. **Application Process:**
    - Victims must submit Form I-914, Application for T Nonimmigrant Status.
    - To be eligible, they must have complied with any reasonable request for assistance from law enforcement in the detection, investigation, or prosecution of human trafficking.
4. **Family Members:**
    - Eligible family members include:
        - Spouse
        - Unmarried children under 21 years old
        - Parents
        - Unmarried siblings under 18 years old
5. **Purpose:**
    - T visas offer protection to victims and strengthen law enforcement agencies' ability to detect, investigate, and prosecute human trafficking.

Green Card Application Process for T Visa Holders:

1. **Determine Eligibility:**
    - First, ensure that you meet the eligibility criteria for a Green Card.
    - Victims of severe human trafficking who hold T visas are eligible to apply.
2. **File an Immigrant Petition:**
    - You or someone else (such as a family member or employer) must file an immigrant petition on your behalf. This step is necessary if applicable.
3. **Check Visa Availability:**
    - If applicable, check whether there is a visa number available for your category. Some categories have numerical limits.
4. **File Form I-485:**
    - Submit Form I-485, Application to Register Permanent Residence or Adjust Status.
    - This form allows you to apply for a Green Card while you are present in the United States.
5. **Application Support Center Appointment:**
    - Attend your Application Support Center appointment for biometrics (fingerprinting and photograph).
6. **Interview (if applicable):**
    - You may be required to attend an interview with a USCIS officer.
7. **Respond to Requests for Evidence (if applicable):**
    - If USCIS requests additional evidence, promptly provide the requested documents.
8. **Check Your Case Status:**
    - Keep track of your case status through USCIS updates.
9. **Receive a Decision:**
    - USCIS will review your application and decide on your Green Card application.

US T-Visa Type:

A US T-visa type is a nonimmigrant visa for victims of human trafficking who are willing to assist law enforcement in the investigation or prosecution of the traffickers. Human trafficking is a form of modern slavery that involves the use of force, fraud, or coercion to exploit someone for labor or commercial sex. To qualify for a T-visa, the applicant must meet the following requirements:

- Be or have been a victim of a severe form of trafficking in persons, as defined by U.S. law.
- Be physically present in the United States, American Samoa, the Commonwealth of the Northern Mariana Islands, or at a port of entry due to trafficking.

- Comply with any reasonable request from a law enforcement agency for assistance in the investigation or prosecution of human trafficking (or be under 18 years of age or unable to cooperate due to physical or psychological trauma).
- Demonstrate that they would suffer extreme hardship involving unusual and severe harm if they were removed from the United States.
- Be admissible to the United States (or apply for a waiver of inadmissibility).

The T-visa is valid for up to four years and can be extended if the victim's presence is needed to investigate or prosecute the traffickers or if the victim has a pending application for adjustment of status. The T-visa holder may also apply for permanent residence (a green card) after three years of continuous presence in the United States or upon completion of the investigation or prosecution, whichever occurs earlier. The spouse, children, parents, and unmarried siblings under 18 of the T-visa holders may also accompany or follow to join the principal applicant and are eligible to work and apply for permanent residence in the United States.

Efforts to End Human Trafficking in Kumasi (Ghana) Author, unknown. Retrieved on April 14, 2024.

Organ Trafficking – The Cause and Consequences of Human Trafficking... by Unknown Author. Retrieved on March 18, 2021

Searchable Keyword

For detailed instructions and forms, visit the USCIS Victims of Human Trafficking: T Nonimmigrant Status page. If you're ready to apply, you can find the application form (Form I-914) on the USCIS website.

Again, if you have a T nonimmigrant status (T visa), you may be eligible to apply for a Green Card (lawful permanent resident status) without having to go through a more complex route. Remember that seeking legal advice from an immigration attorney is recommended during this process. For detailed instructions and forms, visit the USCIS Victims of Human Trafficking: T Nonimmigrant Status page. You may consult the websites below:

uscis.gov visaandgreencard.com committocitizenship.org immigrationhelp.org

Learn how you might return to your home country for visa processing as you follow the steps to adjust your status from a T visa to a Green Card. Taiwan, American Institute in Taiwan (AIT) Website. Temporary Religious Workers. Temporary Protected Status for Haitian Nationals, Press Release: DHS Website. Temporary Protected Status: USCIS Website. Temporary Worker (H-1B, H1B1, H-2A, H-2B Visas): Legal Rights and Protections Pamphlet (Wilberforce Act). Temporary Workers, Overview. Tourism (B-2 Visitor Visa).

Tourism: VisitTheUSA.com. Trainees (H-3 Visa for Temporary Workers). Transit Visas. Translators/Interpreters, Iraqi and Afghan: Special Immigrant Visas. Transportation Security Administration (TSA) Website. Travel Documents. Traveler Complaints About Treatment at Port-of-Entry to the United States. Traveler Redress for Complaints About Treatment at Port-of-Entry to the United States. Treaty Traders & Treaty Investors (E Visa).

Tax-exempt: A condition of the law in which an organization or people in some kinds of work do not have to pay taxes which regular citizens or businesses must pay. Religious organizations are often tax-exempt.

Temporary Worker: A foreign worker who will work in the United States for a limited period. Some visas classes for temporary workers are H, L, O, P, Q and R. If you are seeking to come to the United States for employment as a temporary worker in the United States (H, L, O, P, and Q visas), your prospective employer must file a petition with DHS, USCIS.

This petition must be approved by USCIS before you can apply for a visa.

Select temporary workers to visit the USCIS website and learn more. Select temporary worker visas to go to the Department of State website to learn more, and review information about NAFTA workers (TN visa) and treaty traders/investors (E visas).

Termination of a Case: If the applicant fails to reply to the inquiry correspondence sent by the U.S. Embassy or Consulate, or the National Visa Center (NVC), termination of their visa application will begin.

The U.S. Embassy or Consulate, or NVC, will first send a Follow-up Letter and Instruction Package to the applicant. If the applicant does not answer within one year, a termination letter is sent.

At this point the applicant has one more year to activate the immigrant visa case. If there is no answer in one year, the case is terminated. You can stop termination of a case by notifying the U.S. Embassy or Consulate, or NVC, before the prescribed time has lapsed, that the applicant does not want the case to be closed (terminated).

Third Country National: Someone who is not a U.S. citizen and not a citizen of the country in which he or she is applying for a visa. Suppose you are a Kenyan visiting Mexico. If you apply for a visa to visit the United States while you are in Mexico, we will consider you a third country national.

Third Preference: A category of family immigration (F3) for married sons and daughters of U.S. citizens and their spouses and children. Before 1992 this was known as fourth preference (P-4). Visit

Family Based Immigration webpage for more info.

Two-Year Home-Country Physical Presence Requirement: This refers to (J) exchange visitors who are required to return to their home country for two years at the end of their exchange visitor program, under U.S. immigration law. To learn more review the Exchange Visitor webpage

U

The US U-visa category. A US U-visa category is a type of nonimmigrant visa for victims of certain crimes who have suffered mental or physical abuse and are helpful to law enforcement or government officials in the investigation or prosecution of criminal activity.

This visa category is also known as the victim of criminal activity visa or the humanitarian visa. Some of the benefits of the U visa are that it allows the applicant to stay in the U.S. for up to four years, work legally, apply for certain family members, and eventually seek permanent residence.

However, the U visa also has some limitations, such as a numerical cap of 10,000 visas per fiscal year, a lengthy processing time, and a high evidentiary standard[2].

To qualify for a U visa, the applicant must meet the following criteria:

- The applicant must have been a victim of qualifying criminal activity.
- The applicant must have suffered substantial physical or mental abuse because of having been a victim of criminal activity.
- The applicant must have information about criminal activity. If under the age of 16 or unable to provide information due to a disability, a parent, guardian, or next friend may possess the information about the crime on your behalf (If available, see glossary for definition of 'next friend' or investigate searchable keywords).
- The applicant must have been helpful, are being helpful, or are likely to be helpful to law enforcement in the investigation or prosecution of the crime. If you are under the age of 16 or unable to provide information due to a disability, a parent, guardian, or next friend may assist law enforcement on your behalf.
- The crime must have occurred in the United States or violated U.S. laws.
- The applicant must be admissible to the United States. If not admissible, the applicant may apply for a waiver on a Form I-192, *Application for Advance Permission to Enter as a Nonimmigrant.*

Searchable Keywords

U.N. High Commission on Refugees (UNHCR) Website. USA.gov. U.S. Citizens Traveling Abroad. U.S. Citizenship and Immigration Services (USCIS). U.S. Customs and Border Protection (CBP). U.S. Department of Homeland Security (DHS). U.S. Embassies and Consulates Overseas, Locate

U.S. Immigration and Customs Enforcement (ICE). USCIS.GOV. Explore the following topics / webpages: Victims of Criminal Activity: U Nonimmigrant Status USCIS : [U Visa for Victims of Crime - Immigration Law of Montana, P.C.].

Upgrade a Petition: If you naturalize (become a U.S. citizen) you may ask to change the petitions you filed for family members when you were a lawful permanent resident (LPR) from one category to another. This is called upgrading. For example, a petition for a spouse will be changed/upgraded from F2 to IR1. That is, the petition changes from a preference category with numerical limits to an immediate relative category without numerical limits.

The applicant no longer must wait for her/his priority date to be reached.

Upgrading a petition sometimes has consequences. A preference petition for a spouse permits derivative status for children. An immediate relative petition does not. You, the petitioner, would need to file separate petitions for each of your children.

V

Searching for a US V-visa type:

A US V-visa is a nonimmigrant visa for spouses and children of lawful permanent residents who are waiting for their immigrant visas to be processed. It allows them to stay in the United States with their family members and work legally.

To qualify for a V-visa, the applicant must meet certain criteria, such as having a petition filed by their spouse or parent before December 21, 2000, having a priority date that is not current, and complying with law enforcement requests if they are victims of human trafficking.

The V-visa is valid for up to four years and can be extended under certain circumstances. The V-visa holder may also apply for permanent residence after three years of continuous presence in the United States or upon completion of the investigation or prosecution of the traffickers, whichever occurs earlier.

- What is the difference between V-visa and K-visa?
- How long does it take to process an immigrant visa for a spouse or child of a US citizen?

Searchable Keywords

Generally, a citizen of a foreign country who wishes to enter the United States must first obtain a visa, either a nonimmigrant visa for a temporary stay or an immigrant visa for permanent residence. Visitor **visas** are nonimmigrant **visas** for persons who want to enter the United States temporarily for business (visa category B-1), for tourism (visa category B-2), or a combination of both purposes (B-1/B-2). Vacation (B-2) Visitor Visa. Vacation: VisitTheUSA.com

Vaccination Requirements for Immigrant Visa Applicants. Visa Bulletin. Visa Categories. Visa Denials. Visa Issuing Posts (Embassy/Consulate). Visa Policy, U.S. Visa, Reading Your Visa. Visa Reciprocity Table. Visa Refusal Rates: Nonimmigrant B Visa Refusal

Rates by Nationality. Visa Services, Who We Are. Visa Statistics. Visa Types for Permanent Immigrants. Visa Types for Temporary Visitors (Nonimmigrant). Visa Wait Times. Visa Waiver Program (VWP): TSG Website. Visa Waiver Program (VWP), ESTA (Electronic System for Travel Authorization): CBP Website. Visa Waiver Program (VWP), ESTA (Electronic System for Travel Authorization): TSG Website. Visa Waiver Program (VWP): DHS Website. Visitor (B-1) Visa for Domestic Employees: Legal Rights and Protections Pamphlet (Wilberforce Act). Visitor Visa for

Business and Pleasure (B Visa). Visitor Visa Refusal Rates by Nationality. Visitor Visas - Business and Pleasure (PDF).

Visa: A citizen of a foreign country wishing to enter the United States generally must first obtain a visa, either a nonimmigrant visa for temporary stay or an immigrant visa for permanent residence. Visa applicants will need to apply overseas, at the U.S. Embassy or Consulate, generally in their country of permanent residence.

The type of visa you must have been defined by immigration law and relates to the purpose of your travel. A visa allows a foreign citizen to travel to the U.S. port-of-entry,port of entry and request permission from the U.S. immigration inspector to enter the United States. Issuance of a visa does not guarantee entry to the United States. The CBP Officer at the port of entry determines whether you can be admitted and decides how long you can stay for any visit.

Visa Expiration Date: The visa expiration date is shown on the visa. This means the visa is valid, or can be used, from the date it is issued until the date it expires, for travel for the same purpose, when the visa is issued for multiple entries. This time, from the visa issuance date to visa expiration date, as shown on the visa, is called visa validity. If you travel frequently as a tourist, for example, with a multiple entry visa, you do not have to apply for a new visa each time you want to travel to the United States.

As an example of travel for the same purpose, if you have a visitor visa, it cannot be used to enter later to study in the United States. The visa validity is the length of time you are permitted to travel to a port-of-entry in the United States to request permission from the U.S. immigration inspector to permit you to enter the United States. The visa does not guarantee entry to the United States.

The Expiration Date for the visa should not be confused with the authorized length of your stay in the United States, given to you by the U.S. immigration inspector at port-of-entry, on the electronic I-94 admission stamp or paper Form I-94, Arrival/Departure Record. The visa expiration date has nothing to do with the authorized length of your stay in the United States for any given visit.

There are circumstances that can serve to void or cancel the period your visa is valid. If you overstay the end date of your authorized stay, as provided by the DHS's U.S. immigration officer at port of entry, or USCIS, then this action on your part generally will automatically void or cancel your visa.

However, if you have filed an application in a timely manner for extension of stay or a change of status, and that application is pending and not frivolous, and if you did not engage in unauthorized employment, then this normally does not automatically cancel your visa. If you have applied for adjustment of status to become a permanent resident alien ("green card" holder), you should contact USCIS regarding obtaining Advance Parole before leaving the United States.

Visa Numbers: Congress establishes the amount of immigration each year. Immigration for immediate relatives is unlimited; however, family and employment preference categories are limited. To distribute the visas fairly among all categories of immigration, the Visa Office in the Department of State distributes the visas by providing visa numbers according to preference and priority date. To learn more on how the numbers are created each month, review Operation of the Immigrant Numerical Control System webpage.

Visa Validity: This generally means the visa is valid or can be used from the date it is issued until the date it expires for travel for the same purpose for visas, when the visa is issued for multiple entries. The visa expiration date is shown on the visa. Depending on the alien's nationality, visas can be issued for any number of entries, from as little as one entry to as many as multiple (unlimited) entries, for the same purpose of travel.

If you travel frequently as a tourist for example, with a multiple entry visa, you do not have to apply for a new visa each time you want to travel to the United States. As an example of travel for the same purpose, if you have a visitor visa, it cannot be used to enter later to study in the United States. The visa validity is the length of time you are permitted to travel to a port-of-entry in the United States to request permission of the U.S. immigration inspector to enter the United States.

The visa does not guarantee entry to the United States. The Expiration Date for the visa should not be confused with the authorized length of your stay in the United States, given to you by the U.S. immigration inspector at port-of-entry, on the admission stamp or paper Form I-94 Arrival/Departure Record.

The visa expiration date has nothing to do with the authorized length of your stay in the United States for any given visit. There are circumstances which can serve to void or cancel the period your visa is valid. If you overstay the end date of your authorized stay, as provided by the DHS's U.S. immigration officer at port of entry, or USCIS, then this action on your part generally will automatically void or cancel your visa.

However, if you have filed an application in a timely manner for extension of stay or a change of status, and that application is pending and not frivolous, and if you did not engage in UnauthorizedUnauthorized employment, then this normally does not automatically cancel your visa.

Suppose you have applied for adjustment of status to become a permanent resident alien ("green card" holder). In that case, you should contact USCIS regarding obtaining Advance Parole before leaving the U.S. See Visa Expiration Date.

Visa Waiver Program (VWP): Citizens of participating countries meeting the Visa Waiver Program requirements may be allowed to enter the United States as visitors for pleasure or business without first getting a visa. Visitors can stay only 90 days and cannot extend their stay. Go to our information on the Visa Waiver Program to learn more, or visit the Department of Homeland Security (DHS) website.

Voluntary Service Program: An organized project that a religious or nonprofit charitable organization does to provide help to the poor or needy or to further a religious or charitable cause. Participants may be eligible for B visas.

W

Searching for: US W-visa type: A US W-visa type is a proposed nonimmigrant visa for lower-wage workers who want to work temporarily in the United States. It was part of the Border Security, Economic Opportunity, and Immigration Modernization Act of

2013 (S.744), which was passed by the Senate but not by the House of Representatives.

to enacted, the W-visa program various occupations, such as housekeepers, landscapers, retail workers, restaurant staff, and some construction workers.

To qualify for a W-visa, the applicant would have to meet certain requirements, such as having a job offer from a registered employer, passing a background check, paying a fee, and demonstrating basic English skills.

The W-visa would be valid for up to three years and could be renewed for another three years. The W-visa holder would also be able to change employers and apply for permanent residence after one year of employment. The spouse and children of the W-visa holder would also be able to accompany or follow the principal applicant and would be eligible to work and study in the United States.

- The W-visa program, if enacted, would have an annual cap of 20,000 visas in the first year, increasing to 75,000 visas in the fourth year, and then adjusting based on a formula that considers the unemployment rate, the number of job openings and the demand for workers. The program would also have a limit of 15,000 visas per year for construction workers and a limit of 33% of visas per year for workers from any single country. The program would be overseen by a new federal agency called the **Bureau of Immigration and Labor Market Research**, which would monitor the labor market and recommend changes to the program.

The W-visa program was part of the Border Security, Economic Opportunity, and Immigration Modernization Act of 2013, which passed the Senate but not the House of Representatives. The W-visa program would apply to workers in occupations such as

Housekeeping The W-visa holders would be sponsored by registered employers and would have some rights and benefits, such as portability, health care, and a path to permanent residency. However, the W-visa program has not been implemented yet and its future is uncertain.

What is the status of immigration reform in the US? Immigration reform is a complex and controversial issue in the US, and there is no clear consensus or action on how to address it. Here are some key points about the status of immigration reform in the US:

- President Biden has proposed a comprehensive immigration reform bill that would create a pathway to citizenship for millions of unauthorized immigrants, update the family-based and employment-based immigration systems, and increase the number of diversity visas. However, the bill faces strong opposition from Republicans and has not been voted on by Congress.
- The Senate is considering some immigration provisions in a spending bill, the Build Back Better Act, that the House passed in November 2021. The bill would grant protection from deportation, work permits, and driver's licenses to about 7 million unauthorized immigrants. However, the bill's fate is uncertain, as it requires the support of all 50 Democratic senators and faces legal challenges from Republican states.
- Amid a record number of migrant encounters at the U.S.-Mexico border, Biden reinstated in December 2021 a Trump-era policy that requires asylum seekers to wait in Mexico while their claims are processed. Biden had earlier ended the policy, known as the Migration Protection Protocols or "Remain in Mexico", but was forced to restart it after the Supreme Court upheld a lawsuit by Texas and Missouri that challenged the program's closure.
- The Biden administration has also announced new measures to manage regional migration, such as expanding legal pathways for protection, increasing humanitarian assistance, and enhancing cooperation with Mexico and Central American countries. The administration hopes to address the root causes of migration and reduce the pressure on the U.S. border.

As you can see, immigration reform in the US is a dynamic and evolving topic, and there is no simple or definitive answer to anybody's questions and concerns.

Why was the W-visa type not implemented yet?

The W-visa type was part of a comprehensive immigration reform bill that passed the Senate in 2013, but not the House of Representatives. The bill faced opposition from some lawmakers who argued that it would increase competition for American workers, lower wages, and create a new bureaucracy. Since then, the W-visa type has not been revived or included in any other immigration legislation. Therefore, the W-visa type remains a proposed but not implemented category of nonimmigrant visas.

What is the Wilberforce Act and how is it related to avoidance of human trafficking? The Wilberforce Act, also known as the William Wilberforce Trafficking Victims Protection.

Reauthorization Act of 2008 is a U.S. federal law that aims to combat both international and domestic trafficking in persons.

It expands the law enforcement authority and the criminal penalties for human trafficking offenses, as well as the protection and assistance for trafficking victims. It also establishes programs to prevent and deter trafficking in persons, including related assistance to foreign governments. Modern prohibitions of human trafficking in the United States have their roots in the 13th Amendment to the U.S. Constitution, which barred slavery and involuntary servitude in 1865.

The Wilberforce Act is named after William Wilberforce, a British abolitionist who led the movement to end the slave trade in the 19th century. The Wilberforce Act is one of the most significant legislation in the area of human trafficking, as it represents the U.S. government's commitment to fight this global problem and protect the human rights of the victims.

Visit the following websites: justice.gov, congress.gov, crsreports.congress.gov.

Searchable Keyword

Waivers and Ineligibilities. Waiver of Two-Year Home-Country Physical Presence Requirement for J-1 Exchange Visitors. Waiver of Two-Year Home-Country Physical Presence Requirement for J-1 Exchange Visitors, Advisory Opinions. Website Fraud Warning. What is a Visa? William Wilberforce Trafficking Victims, Protection Reauthorization Act.

Work Authorization/Work Authorization Document (EAD): USCIS Website. Workers, Labor Certification: Department of Labor Website. Workers, Employment-based Immigrant. Workers, Temporary Nonimmigrant. World Health Organization (WHO) Website.

What Are Your Reasons for Travelling to the US?

The purpose of your intended travel and other facts will determine what type of visa is required under U.S. immigration laws. As a visa applicant, you will need to establish that you meet all requirements to receive the category of visa for which you are applying. When you apply at a ,U.S. embassy or consulate, a consular officer will determine, based on laws, whether you are eligible to receive a visa and, if so, which visa category is appropriate.

A little-known fact about applying to obtain American, the applicant, visas, either as an immigrant or a nonimmigrant, is that you, the applicant, are presumed guilty until proven innocent. You must prove your innocence.

However, living day-to-day encounters in American society, the opposite is the case: American laws generally assume your innocence until proven guilty. And guess what? The

the arresting/interrogatingThe burden of proof is always on the government or the arresting/interrogating authorities. The precursor to this assumption is the Miranda Warnings, in which you are admonished to remain silent because anything you say can be used against you.

Waiver of Ineligibility: ,the under immigration law; certain foreign nationals are ineligible for visas to enter the U.S. for medical, criminal, security or other conditions and activities. However, some visa applicants can apply for permission to enter the U.S. despite their ineligibility. The applicant must apply for permission to enter the U.S. (waiver). See Classes of Aliens Ineligible to Receive Visas for more information.

Work Authorization: If you are not a citizen or a lawful permanent resident, you may need to apply for an Employment Authorization Document to prove you may work in the U.S. To learn more, visit USCIS's webpage.

X

As of the publication of this dictionary guide, there is no specific "X-visa" type for the United States. U.S. visa categories are typically classified by letters from A to V, based on the purpose of travel and other factors.

The closest equivalent to an "X-visa" would be the Exchange Visitor Visa, which is designated with the letter "J." (Refer to the above sections for further details.

It's also worth noting that the term "X-visa" may be mistakenly associated with the China Student Visa, which is divided into X1 and X2 categories based on the duration of study. However, this visa is intended for foreign students wishing to study in China, not for travel to the U.S.

For more information on visa categories, you can explore the following resources:

- Directory of U.S. Visa Categories
- Exchange Visitor Visa
- China Student Visa (X)
- Department of Homeland Security

Searchable Keyword

X-Visa type is a Chinese government exchange Visa, also known as the Study Visa or Student Visa, which is issued to individuals who come to China for long-term or short-term study and internships. Based on the intended length of stay, the X Visa is categorized into X1 Visa (for stays exceeding 180 days) and X2 Visa (for stays of 180 days or less)

Y

Searching for a US Y-visa type: There is no such thing as a US Y-visa type, at least for now. The US visa types are categorized by letters from A to V, depending on the purpose of travel and other factors. The closest thing to an X-visa type is the exchange visitor visa, which is designated by the letter J. The J-visa is for people who are participating in an approved program for teaching, studying, conducting research, or exchanging skills. Another possible visa type that starts with Y is the Yemen tourist visa, which is required for US citizens who want to visit Yemen for tourism purposes. However, this visa type is only applicable for travel to Yemen, not the US. (Directory of Visa Categories: Exchange Visitor Visa: Yemen Tourist Visa).

Searchable Keyword

Exchange Visitor Visa: Yemen Tourist Visa

Very recently, the Saudi government began issuing visas to Yemenis – Middle East Monitor by Unknown Author. Retrieved on May 18, 2024.

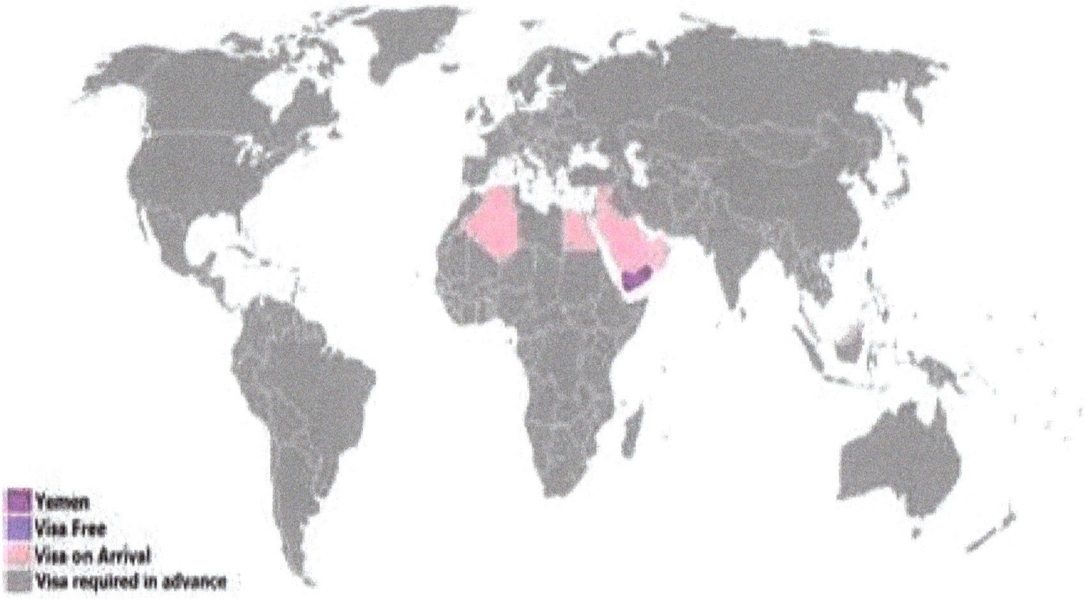

Yemen Travel guide at Wikivoyage by Unknown Author. Retrieved in April 2023.

State Department File: Republic-of-Yemen-passport-non-biometric - Author, unknown.

Z

Searching for a US Z-visa type: There is no such thing as a US Z-visa type; again, as at now. But knowing how the US congress operates, we shall expect to include visa categories, X, Y, and Z during a reprint of this dictionary -guide.

The US visa types as currently exist are categorized by letters from A to V, depending on the purpose of travel and other factors. The closest thing to a Z-visa type is the China work visa, which is divided into Z- 1 and Z - 2 visas, depending on the duration of work. However, this visa type is only applicable to foreign workers who want to work in China, not the US.

See the Directory of Visa Categories: China Work Visa (Z)

Searchable Keyword

Directory of Visa Categories.

SECTION FOUR

A Focus on US Treaty Countries, Classifications, Year treaty entered into Force, Country Specific Footnotes and Fees Charged

Country	Classification	Entered into Force
Albania	E-2	January 4, 1998
Argentina	E-1	December 20, 1854
Argentina	E-2	December 20, 1854
Armenia	E-2	March 29, 1996
Australia	E-1	December 16, 1991
Australia	E-2	December 27, 1991
Australia 12	E-3	September 2, 2005
Austria	E-1	May 27, 1931
Austria	E-2	May 27, 1931
Azerbaijan	E-2	August 2, 2001
Bahrain	E-2	May 30, 2001
Bangladesh	E-2	July 25, 1989

Belgium	E-1	October 3, 1963
Belgium	E-2	October 3, 1963
Bolivia	E-1	November 09, 1862
Bolivia 13	E-2	June 6, 2001
Bosnia and Herzegovina 11	E-1	November 15, 1982
Bosnia and Herzegovina 11	E-2	November 15, 1982
Brunei	E-1	July 11, 1853
Bulgaria	E-2	June 2, 1954
Cameroon	E-2	April 6, 1989
Canada	E-1	January 1, 1994
Canada	E-2	January 1, 1994
Chile	E-1	January 1, 2004
Chile	E-2	January 1, 2004
China (Taiwan) 1	E-1	November 30, 1948
China (Taiwan) 1	E-2	November 30, 1948
Colombia	E-1	June 10, 1948
Colombia	E-2	June 10, 1948
Congo (Brazzaville)	E-2	August 13, 1994
Congo (Kinshasa)	E-2	July 28, 1989
Costa Rica	E-1	May 26, 1852
Costa Rica	E-2	May 26, 1852
Croatia 11	E-1	November 15, 1982
Croatia 11	E-2	November 15, 1982
Czech Republic 2	E-2	January 1, 1993
Denmark 3	E-1	July 30, 1961
Denmark	E-2	December 10, 2008
Ecuador 14	E-2	May 11, 1997
Egypt	E-2	June 27, 1992
Estonia	E-1	May 22, 1926
Estonia	E-2	February 16, 1997
Ethiopia	E-1	October 8, 1953

Ethiopia	E-2	October 8, 1953
Finland	E-1	August 10, 1934
Finland	E-2	December 1, 1992
France 4	E-1	December 21, 1960
France 4	E-2	December 21, 1960
Georgia	E-2	August 17, 1997
Germany	E-1	July 14, 1956
Germany	E-2	July 14, 1956
Greece	E-1	October 13, 1954
Grenada	E-2	March 3, 1989
Honduras	E-1	July 19, 1928
Honduras	E-2	July 19, 1928
Ireland	E-1	September 14, 1950
Ireland	E-2	November 18, 1992
Israel 15	E-1	April 3, 1954
Israel 15	E-2	May 1, 2019
Italy	E-1	July 26, 1949
Italy	E-2	July 26, 1949
Jamaica	E-2	March 7, 1997
Japan 5	E-1	October 30, 1953
Japan 5	E-2	October 30, 1953
Jordan	E-1	December 17, 2001
Jordan	E-2	December 17, 2001
Kazakhstan	E-2	January 12, 1994
Korea (South)	E-1	November 7, 1957
Korea (South)	E-2	November 7, 1957
Kosovo 11	E-1	November 15, 1882
Kosovo 11	E-2	November 15, 1882
Kyrgyzstan	E-2	January 12, 1994
Latvia	E-1	July 25, 1928
Latvia	E-2	December 26, 1996

Liberia	E-1	December 26, 1996
Liberia	E-2	December 26, 1996
Lithuania	E-2	November 22, 2001
Luxembourg	E-1	March 28, 1963
Luxembourg	E-2	March 28, 1963
Macedonia 11	E-1	November 15, 1982
Macedonia 11	E-2	November 15, 1982
Mexico	E-1	January 1, 1994
Mexico	E-2	January 1, 1994
Moldova	E-2	November 25, 1994
Mongolia	E-2	January 1, 1997
Montenegro 11	E-1	November 15, 1882
Montenegro 11	E-2	November 15, 1882
Morocco	E-2	May 29, 1991
Netherlands 6	E-1	December 5, 1957
Netherlands 6	E-2	December 5, 1957
New Zealand 16	E-1	June 10, 2019
New Zealand 16	E-2	June 10, 2019
Norway 7	E-1	January 18, 1928
Norway 7	E-2	January 18, 1928
Oman	E-1	June 11, 1960
Oman	E-2	June 11, 1960
Pakistan	E-1	February 12, 1961
Pakistan	E-2	February 12, 1961
Panama	E-2	May 30, 1991
Paraguay	E-1	March 07, 1860
Paraguay	E-2	March 07, 1860
Philippines	E-1	September 6, 1955
Philippines	E-2	September 6, 1955
Poland	E-1	August 6, 1994
Poland	E-2	August 6, 1994

Romania	E-2	January 15, 1994
Senegal	E-2	October 25, 1990
Serbia 11	E-1	November 15, 1882
Serbia 11	E-2	November 15, 1882
Singapore	E-1	January 1, 2004
Singapore	E-2	January 1, 2004
Slovak Republic 2	E-2	January 1, 1993
Slovenia 11	E-1	November 15, 1982
Slovenia 11	E-2	November 15, 1982
Spain 8	E-1	April 14, 1903
Spain 8	E-2	April 14, 1903
Sri Lanka	E-2	May 1, 1993
Suriname 9	E-1	February 10, 1963
Suriname 9	E-2	February 10, 1963
Sweden	E-1	February 20, 1992
Sweden	E-2	February 20, 1992
Switzerland	E-1	November 08, 1855
Switzerland	E-2	November 08, 1855
Thailand	E-1	June 8, 1968
Thailand	E-2	June 8, 1968
Togo	E-1	February 5, 1967
Togo	E-2	February 5, 1967
Trinidad & Tobago	E-2	February 5, 1967
Tunisia	E-2	February 7, 1993
Turkey	E-1	February 15, 1933
Turkey	E-2	May 18, 1990
Ukraine	E-2	November 16, 1996
United Kingdom 10	E-1	July 03, 1815
United Kingdom 10	E-2	July 03, 1815
Yugoslavia 11	E-1	November 15, 1882
Yugoslavia 11	E-2	November 15, 1882

Country Specific Footnotes

1. **China (Taiwan)** - Pursuant to Section 6 of the Taiwan Relations Act, (TRA) Public Law 96-8, 93 Stat, 14, and Executive Order 12143, 44 F.R. 37191, this agreement which was concluded with the Taiwan authorities prior to January 01, 1979, is administered on a nongovernmental basis by the American Institute in Taiwan, a nonprofit District of Columbia corporation, and constitutes neither recognition of the Taiwan authorities nor the continuation of any official relationship with Taiwan.
2. **Czech Republic and Slovak Republic** - The Treaty with the Czech and Slovak Federal Republic entered into force on December 19, 1992; entered into force for the Czech Republic and Slovak Republic as separate states on January 01, 1993.
3. **Denmark** - The Treaty, which entered into force on July 30, 1961, does not apply to Greenland.
4. **France** - The Treaty, which entered into force on December 21, 1960, applies to the departments of Martinique, Guadeloupe, French Guiana and Reunion.
5. **Japan** - The Treaty, which entered into force on October 30, 1953, was made applicable to the Bonin Islands on June 26, 1968, and to the Ryukyu Islands on May 15, 1972.
6. **Netherlands** - The Treaty which entered into force on December 05, 1957, is applicable to Aruba and Netherlands Antilles.
7. **Norway** - The Treaty, which entered into force on September 13, 1932, does not apply to Svalbard (Spitzbergen and certain lesser islands).
8. **Spain** - The Treaty which entered into force on April 14, 1903, is applicable to all territories.
9. **Suriname** - The Treaty with the Netherlands which entered into force December 05, 1957, was made applicable to Suriname on February 10, 1963.
10. **United Kingdom** - The Convention, which entered into force on July 03, 1815, applies only to British territory in Europe (the British Isles (except the Republic of Ireland), the Channel Islands and Gibraltar) and to "inhabitants" of such territory. This term, as used in the Convention, means "one who resides actually and permanently in a given place, and has his domicile there."

Also, to qualify for treaty trader or treaty investor status under this treaty, the alien must be a national of the United Kingdom. Individuals having the nationality of members of the Commonwealth other than the United Kingdom do not qualify for treaty trader or treaty investor status under this treaty.

11. **Yugoslavia** - The U.S. view is that the Socialist Federal Republic of Yugoslavia (SFRY) has dissolved and that the successors that formerly made up the SFRY - Bosnia and Herzegovina, Croatia,

the Republic of Macedonia, Slovenia, Montenegro, Serbia, and Kosovo a continue to be bound by the treaty in force with the SFRY and the time of dissolution.

12. The E-3 visa is for nationals of the Commonwealth of Australia who wish to enter the United States to perform services in a "specialty occupation." The term "specialty occupation" means an occupation that requires theoretical and practical application of a body of highly specialized knowledge and attainment of a bachelor's or higher degree in the specific specialty (or its equivalent) as a minimum for entry into the occupation in the United States. The definition is the same as the Immigration and Nationality Act definition of an H-1B specialty occupation.

13. **Bolivia** - Bolivian nationals with qualifying investments in place in the United States by June 10, 2012, continue to be entitled to E-2 classification until June 10, 2022. The only nationals of Bolivia (other than those qualifying for derivative status based on a familial relationship to an E-2 principal alien) who may qualify for E-2 visas at this time are those applicants who are coming to the United States to engage in E-2 activity in furtherance of covered investments established or acquired prior to June 10, 2012.

14. Ecuadorian nationals with qualifying investments in place in the United States by May 18, 2018, continue to be entitled to E-2 classification until May 18, 2028. The only nationals of Ecuador (other than those qualifying for derivative status based on a familial relationship to an E-2 principal alien) who may qualify for E-2 visas at this time are those applicants who are coming to the United States to engage in E-2 activity in furtherance of covered investments established or acquired prior to May 18, 2018.

15. Israel: Pursuant to a treaty of friendship, commerce, and navigation between the United States and Israel that entered into force on April 3, 1954, entitled nationals of Israel to E-1 status for treaty trader purposes. Nationals of Israel are not entitled to E-2 classification for treaty investor purposes under that treaty. Public Law 112-130 (June 8, 2012) accords nationals of Israel E-2 status for treaty investor purposes if the Government of Israel provides similar nonimmigrant status to nationals of the United States. The Department has confirmed that Israel offers reciprocal treaty investor treatment to U.S. nationals, and an E-2 visa may be issued to nationals of Israel beginning on May 1, 2019.

16. New Zealand: Public Law 115-226, enacted on August 1, 2018, accorded nationals of New Zealand to E-1 and E-2 status for treaty trader/treaty investor purposes if the Government of New Zealand provides similar nonimmigrant status to nationals of the United States. The Department has confirmed that New Zealand offers similar nonimmigrant status to U.S. nationals and E visas may be

issued to nationals of New Zealand beginning on June 10, 2019.

What Are Your Reasons for Travelling to the US?

The purpose of your intended travel and other facts will determine what type of visa is required under U.S. immigration laws. As a visa applicant, you will need to establish that you meet all requirements to receive the category of visa for which you are applying. When you apply at a ,U.S. embassy or consulate, a consular officer will determine, based on laws, whether you are eligible to receive a visa and, if so, which visa category is appropriate.

A little-known fact about applying to obtain American visas-either as an immigrant or a nonimmigrant is that you the applicant, is presumed guilty until proven innocent. You must prove your innocence. However, living day-to-day encounters in American society, the opposite is the case: American laws generally assume your innocence until proven guilty. And guess what? The burden of proof is always on the government or the arresting/interrogating authorities. The precursor to this assumption is the Miranda Warnings, in which you are admonished to remain silent because anything you say can be used against you.

Immigrant Visa Categories

The chart below contains different purposes for immigrating to the United States, and the related immigrant visa categories for which information is available in this book. Select a visa category below to learn more.

Immediate Relative & Family Sponsored	**Visa Category**
Spouse of a U.S. Citizen	IR1, CR1
Spouse of a U.S. Citizen awaiting approval of an I-130 immigrant petition.	K-3 *
Fiancé(e) to marry U.S. Citizen & live in U.S.	K-1 *
Intercountry Adoption of Orphan Children by U.S. Citizens	IR3, IH3, R4, IH4
Certain Family Members of U.S. Citizens	IR2, CR2, IR5,
Certain Family Members of Lawful Permanent Residents	F1, F3, F4 F2A, F2B
Employment-Based Immigrants, including (preference group):	

• Priority workers [First]	E1
• Professionals Holding Advanced Degrees and Persons of	E2
Exceptional Ability [Second]	E3, EW3
• Professionals and Other Workers [Third] • Employment	C5, T5, R5, I5
Creation/Investors [Fifth]	S (many**)
• Certain Special Immigrants: [Fourth]	
Religious Workers	SD, SR
Iraqi and Afghan Translators/Interpreters	SI
Iraqis Who Worked for/on Behalf of the U.S. Government	SQ
Afghans Who Worked for/on Behalf of the U.S. Government	SQ
Other Immigrants	
Diversity Immigrant Visa	DV
Returning Resident	SB

Important Notes:

***K Visas** – Listed with immigrant visas because they are for immigration related purposes.

About this chart - This chart is a list of many immigrant visa categories, but not every immigrant visa category.

**Refer to the Foreign Affairs Manual, 9 FAM 502.1, for a listing of all immigrant visa categories.

This webpage lists visa application fees and other related visa-related fees collected by the Department of State. Note that many immigration-related forms are submitted to the Department.

Of Homeland Security's United States Citizenship and Immigration Services (USCIS) and not to the Department of State. If the type of information or form you are seeking is not shown here, select USCIS Forms and Fees to go to the USCIS Website to review more.

Coming to the United States Temporarily - Nonimmigrant Visa Services

Nonimmigrant visa application processing fees are tiered, as shown below, based on the visa category for which you are applying.

Notice: Every visa applicant must pay the visa application processing fee for the visa category being applied for unless the application fee is not required, as listed below.

Description of Service and Fee Amount (All fees = $ in US currency)

Nonimmigrant visa application processing fee (non-refundable) for all categories below

□ Non-petition-based nonimmigrant visa (except E): **$185.00**

Includes (but is not limited to) the following visa categories:

B Visitor Visa: Business, Tourism, Medical treatment C-1 Transiting the United States

D Crewmembers - Airline, Ship F Student, Academic

I Media and Journalists J Exchange Visitors

*Applicants for J visas participating in official U.S. Government-sponsored educational and cultural exchanges: **No Fee** (See Exchange Visitor Visas for further detailed fee information.)

M Students, Vocational TN/TD NAFTA Professionals S Witness or Informant*

T Victim of Trafficking in Persons* U Victim of Criminal Activity*

*Though petition-based nonimmigrant visas, the processing fee for these visas is $185.00

□ Petition based visa categories: **$205.00.**

Includes these visa categories:

H Temporary Workers/Employment or Trainees L Intracompany Transferees

O Persons with Extraordinary Ability P Athletes. Artists & Entertainers

Q International Cultural Exchange R Religious Worker

□ E - Treaty Trader/Investor, Australian Professional Specialty category visa: **$315.00**

□ K – Fiancé(e) or Spouse of U.S. citizen category visa: **$265.00**

Border crossing card fees

- Border Crossing Card (Age 15 and Over, Valid for 10 Years): $185.00
- **Border Crossing Card (Under Age 15, Valid for 10 Years or Until Applicant Turns 15, Whichever Comes First):** $15.00

(For Mexican citizens, applicable when a parent or guardian holds or is applying for a border crossing card.)

Other Fees

- L visa fraud prevention and detection fee - for visa applicant included in L blanket petition (principal applicant only): **$500.00**
- The Consolidated Appropriations Act of 2016 (Public Law 114-113) increases fees for certain H-1B and L-1 petitioners. Consular sections collect this fee for blanket L-1 visa applications (principal applicant only) filed by petitioners who employ 50 or more individuals in the United States if more than 50 percent of those individuals are in H-1B or L-1 nonimmigrant status: **$4,500.00.**

When the nonimmigrant visa application processing fee is not required:

- Applicants for A, G, C-2, C-3, NATO, and diplomatic visas (defined in 22 CFR 41.26): **No Fee**
- Applicants for J visas participating in official U.S. Government-sponsored educational and cultural exchanges: **No Fee** (See Exchange Visitor Visas for further detailed fee information.)
- Replacement of machine-readable visa when the original visa was not properly affixed or needs to be reissued through no fault of the applicant: **No Fee**
- Applicants exempted by international agreement as determined by Visa Services, including members and staff of an observer mission to United Nations Headquarters recognized by the UN General Assembly, and their immediate families: **No Fee**
- Applicants travelling travelingtraveling to provide charitable services as determined by Visa Services: **No Fee**
- U.S. government employees traveling on official business: **No Fee**
- A parent, sibling, spouse or child of a U.S. government employee killed in the line of duty who is traveling to attend the employee's funeral and/or burial; or a parent, sibling, spouse, son or daughter of a U.S. government employee critically injured in the line of duty for visitation during emergency treatment and convalescence: **No Fee**

Nonimmigrant visa issuance fee, including border-crossing cards.

- See the Visa Reciprocity Tables to find out the visa issuance fee amount, if applicable: Fee varies (Reciprocal)

When the nonimmigrant visa issuance fee is not required:

- An official representative of a foreign government or an international or regional organization of which the United States is a member; members and staff of an observer mission to United Nations Headquarters recognized by the UN General Assembly; and applicants for diplomatic visas as defined under item 22(a); and their immediate families: **No Fee**
- An applicant transiting to and from the United Nations Headquarters: **No Fee**
- An applicant participating in a U.S. government-sponsored program, which may include the applicant's dependent spouse and children: **No Fee**
- An applicant travellingto provide charitable services as determined by Visa Services: **No Fee**

Other - When a Visa is Not Required - Visa Waiver Program

- Citizens of Visa Waiver Program participating countries and meeting requirements pay a small fee. Select USCIS fees to learn more.

Coming to the United States Permanently - Immigrant Services

Immigrant visa application processing fees are tiered, as shown below, based on the visa category you apply for.

Notice: Every visa applicant must pay the visa application processing fee for the visa category being applied for.

Description of Service and Fee Amount (All fees = $ in US currency)

Filing an Immigrant Visa Petition (When collected by U.S. Embassies and Consulates for USCIS. Fees subject to change.)

Immigrant petition for relative (I-130)	$535.00
Orphan (intercountry adoption) immediate relative petition (I-600, I-800)	$775.00

Immigrant Visa Application Processing Fees (non-refundable per person)

Immediate relative and family preference applications (processed based on an approved I-130, I-600 or I-800 petition)	$325.00
Employment-based applications (processed based on an approved I-140 or I-526 petition)	$345.00
Other immigrant visa applications (including approved I-360 self-petitioners, special immigrant visa applicants, returning resident (SB-1) applicants, and all others, except DV program selectees)	$205.00
Certain Iraqi and Afghan special immigrant visa applications	No Fee

Other Fees

Diversity Visa Lottery fee (per person applying as a DV program selectee for a DV category immigrant visa)	$330.00

Affidavit of Support Review (only when reviewed domestically)	$120.00

Note: Forms and fee amounts are listed for immigration petitions which are submitted to Department of State, either accepted at a U.S. Embassy or Consulate abroad, or within the United States to the National Visa Center or Kentucky Consular Center.

Other immigration related forms can only be approved by the Department of Homeland Security's United States Citizenship and Immigration Services (USCIS). For other fees (relating to forms starting with an "I" select USCIS Forms and Fees for additional information.

Special Visa Services

Description of Service and Fee Amount (All fees = $ in US currency)

Application for Determining Returning Resident Status, Form DS-117	$180.00
Transportation letter for Legal Permanent Residents of the United States	$575.00
Application for Waiver of two-year residency requirement, J Waiver, Form DS-3035	$120.00
Application for Waiver of visa ineligibility, Form I-601 (Collected for USCIS and subject to change)	**$930.00**
Refugee or significant public benefit parole case processing	No Fee

Note: These fee charts are based on the Code of Federal Regulations - Title 22, Part 22, Sections 22.1 through 22.7.).

Intentionally Left Blank

SECTION FIVE

Authentication Certificate Requirements

Before submitting documents for authentication, you must:

1) Notarize each document in front of a notary public.

- Using a notary commissioned by the **county**? Certify your document with the clerk of the court and then the secretary of state.
- Using a notary commissioned by the **state**? Certify your document with the secretary of state.
- If you do not have the correct notarization(s) before you submit your documents, we will not be able to process your request.
- 2) All seals and signatures must be originals
- We cannot accept copies unless they are "true certified copies" from a notary public. Birth, marriage, and death certificates, divorce decrees, court documents, and federally issued documents cannot be certified by a notary public as "true copies." These documents must be certified by the secretary of state.

3) All documents in a foreign language must be translated into English by a certified translator and notarized as a true translation.

Requirements for Each Type of Document

State and Local Documents

Examples of state and local documents include:

- Birth Certificates
- Marriage Certificates
- Death Certificates
- Divorce Decrees
- Probate Wills
- Judgments

Requirements for state and local documents include:

- Original or certified document must include the raised and/or stamped seal of the court or department of vital records.

- Must be certified by the Secretary of State from the state in which the documents were issued. The Secretary of State will certify to the official signing the document under the Seal of the State.

Federally Issued Documents

Examples of federally issued documents include:

- Animal/Plant Certifications (issued by U.S. Department of Agriculture, or USDA)
- Animal Health Certifications (issued by USDA)
- FBI – Background check (issued by U.S. Department of Justice, or DoJ)
    - **Do not notarize FBI background checks.**
- U.S. Federal Court Documents check (issued by DoJ)
- U.S. Bankruptcy Court check (issued by DoJ)
- Immigration Certifications (issued by U.S. Department of Homeland Security)
- Certificate of Foreign Governments (issued by U.S. Department of Health and Human Services, or HHS)
- Certificate of Pharmaceutical/Export (issued by HHS)
- Trademark (Issued by U.S. Patent and Trademark Office)
- Other documents issued by Environmental Protection Agency, Social Security Administration, or Office of Personnel Management

Requirements for federally issued documents include:

- Must be executed by U.S. federal agencies.
- Must include a legible signature of the official's name, printed name and title, and seal of the agency.
- Must be on agency letterhead.
- **Do not notarize FBI background checks.**

Documents Issued by the District of Columbia Superior Court and Court of Appeals

Examples include:

- Marriage Certificates (Issued in the District of Columbia)

Requirements:

- Documents must have the original official signature and the raised seal of the court.

Other Documents

Examples of other documents include:

- Affidavits
- Agreements
- Articles of Incorporation
- Bylaws
- Commercial Invoices
- Copy of a U.S. Passport (identification page only)
- Deeds of Assignment
- Diplomas
- Home Study
- Income Verification
- Powers-of-Attorney
- Single Status
- Transcripts
- Other business documents

Requirements for other documents include:

- Must be certified with a stamp or seal by a notary public.
- Must be certified by the clerk of court from the county in which the notary is commissioned.
- Must be certified by the Secretary of State from the state in which the document was executed.
- Documents from the District of Columbia must be certified by the Government of the District of Columbia Notarial Section.
- **Note:** The document doesn't have to be certified by the clerk of court from the county in which the notary is commissioned if the Secretary of State will certify directly to the notary.

Apostille Requirement

Apostilles authenticate the seals and signatures of officials on public documents such as birth certificates, court orders, or any other document issued by a federal agency or certified by a U.S. or foreign consul. An apostille certifies the document(s), so the document can be recognized in foreign countries that are members of the 1961 Hague Convention Treaty. We only issue apostilles for federal documents to use in countries that **are** members of the 1961 Hague Convention.

Before submitting documents to us, you must:

1. **Notarize each document in front of a notary public:**

- **Using a notary commissioned by the county?** Certify your document at the clerk of court, then the Secretary of State.

- **Using a notary commissioned by the state?** Certify your document at the Secretary of State.

If you do not have the correct notarization(s) before you submit your documents, we will not be able to process your request.

2. **All seals and signatures must be originals**

- We cannot accept copies unless they are "true certified copies" from a notary public. Birth, marriage, and death certificates, divorce decrees, court documents, and federally issued documents cannot be certified by a notary public as "true copies." These documents must be certified by the Secretary of State.

3. **All documents in a foreign language must be translated into English by a certified translator and notarized as a true translation.**

Requirements for Each Type of Document

U.S. Department of State-Issued Documents

Federally issued documents for use in countries that are members of the **1961 Hague Convention** may need to be authenticated with an **apostille** issued by the U.S. Department of State.

Documents signed by the following officials require an apostille issued by the U.S. Department of State:

- U.S. federal official
- U.S. consular officer
- A military notary, judge advocate (10 USC 1044a), or a foreign consul diplomatic official registered with the U.S. Department of State's Office of Protocol

Note: All certifications must include a legible signature of the official's name, title, and seal of the agency.

State-Issued Documents

State-issued documents for use in countries that are members of the **1961 Hague Convention** must be authenticated by the competent authority in the state where the document was executed.

A state-issued document with an **apostille** does not require additional certification by the U.S. Department of State or legalization by a U.S. embassy or consulate overseas to be recognized in a participating country. The U.S. Department of State will not issue an apostille for state-issued documents.

State-issued documents for use in countries that are **not members of the 1961 Hague Convention** may be authenticated with an **authentication certificate** from the U.S. Department of State. For more information, please see **Authentication Certificate Requirements.**

SECTION SIX

Nigeria Proper: The Federal Republic of Nigeria

Reciprocity Schedule: This section showcases how the US applies its immigration policies to Nigeria and other adjacent countries.

Select a visa category below to find the visa issuance fee, number of entries, and validity period for visas issued to applicants from this country*/area of authority.

Explanation of Terms

Visa Classification: The type of nonimmigrant visa you are applying for.

Fee: The reciprocity fee, also known as the visa issuance fee, you must pay. This fee is in addition to the nonimmigrant visa application fee (MRV fee).

Number of Entries: The number of times you may seek entry into the United States with that visa. "M" means multiple times. If there is a number, such as "One", you may apply for entry one time with that visa.

Validity Period: This generally means the visa is valid, or can be used, from the date it is issued until the date it expires, for travel with that visa. If your Validity Period is 60 months, your visa will be valid for 60 months from the date it is issued.

Visa Classification	Fee	Number of Entries
A-1	None	Multiple
A-2	None	Multiple
A-3 1	None	Multiple

Country Specific Footnotes

Although care has been taken to ensure the accuracy, completeness and reliability of the information provided, please contact the U.S. Embassy or Consulate where you plan to apply if you believe this information is in error or if you have further questions.

Visa Category Footnotes

1. The validity of A-3, G-5, and NATO 7 visas may not exceed the validity of the visa issued to the person who is employing the applicant. The "employer" would have one of the following visa

classifications:

- o A-1 A-2
- o G-1 through G-4
- o NATO 1 through NATO 6

2. An E-1 and E-2 visa may be issued only to a principal alien who is a national of a country having a treaty, or its equivalent, with the United States. E-1 and E-2 visas may not be issued to a principal alien if he/she is a stateless resident or national of a country without a treaty.

When the spouse and children of an E-1 or E-2 principal alien are accorded derivative E-1 or E-2 status and are themselves a national of a country that does not have a treaty with the United States – the reciprocity schedule, including any reciprocity fees, of the principal alien's country of nationality should be used. Spouse and children of an E-1 or E-2 visa principal applicant, where the spouse and children are also nationals of a country that has a treaty with the United States – the reciprocity schedule, including any reciprocity fees, of the spouse and children's country of nationality should be used.

*Example 1: Misan Monye is a national of Country A that has an E-1/E-2 treaty with the U.S. however his wife and child are nationals of Country B which has no treaty with the U.S. The wife and child would, therefore, be entitled to derivative status and receive the same reciprocity as John Doe, the principal visa holder.

**Example 2: Echeanu Monye is a national of Country Y that has an E-1/E-2 treaty with the U.S. however his wife and child are nationals of Country Z that also has a treaty with the U.S. The wife and child would, therefore, be entitled to derivative status and receive the reciprocity issued to nationals of Country Z.

3. The validity of H-1 through H-3, O-1 and O-2, P-1 through P-3, and Q visas may not exceed the period of validity of the approved petition, or the number of months shown, whichever is less.

Under 8 CFR §214.2, H-2A and H-2B petitions may generally only be approved for nationals of countries that the Secretary of Homeland Security has designated as participating countries. The current list of eligible countries is available on USCIS's website for both H-2A and H-2B visas. Nationals of countries not on this list may be the beneficiary of an approved H-2A or H2-B petition in limited circumstances at the discretion of the Department of Homeland Security if specifically named on the petition.

Derivative H-4, L-2, O-3, and P-4 visas, issued to accompanying or following-to-join spouses and children, may not exceed the validity of the visa issued to the principal alien.

5. There is no reciprocity fee for the issuance of a J visa if the alien is a United States Government grantee or a participant in an exchange program sponsored by the United States Government.

Also, there is no reciprocity fee for visa issuance to an accompanying or following-to-join spouse or child (J-2) of an exchange visitor grantee or participant.

In addition, an applicant is eligible for an exemption from the MRV fee if he or she is participating in a State Department, USAID, or other federally funded educational and cultural exchange program (program serial numbers G-1, G-2, G-3 and G-7).

However, all other applicants with U.S. Government sponsorships, including other J-visa applicants, are subject to the MRV processing fee.

5. Under the North American Free Trade Agreement (NAFTA), Canadian and Mexican nationals coming to engage in certain types of professional employment in the United States may be admitted in a special nonimmigrant category known as the "trade NAFTA" or "TN" category.

6. Their dependents (spouse and children) accompanying or following to join them may be admitted in the "trade dependent" or "TD" category whether they possess Canadian or Mexican nationality. Except as noted below, the number of entries, fees and validity for non-Canadian or non-Mexican family members of a TN status holder seeking TD visas should be based on the reciprocity schedule of the TN principal alien.

Canadian Nationals

Since Canadian nationals generally are exempt from visa requirement, a Canadian "TN' or "TD" alien does not require a visa to enter the United States. However, the non-Canadian national dependent of a Canadian "TN", unless otherwise exempt from the visa requirement, must obtain a "TD" visa before attempting to enter the United States. The standard reciprocity fee and validity period for all non-Canadian "TD"s is no fee, issued for multiple entries for a period of 36 months, or for the duration of the principal alien's visa and/or authorized period of stay, whichever is less. See 'NOTE' under Canadian reciprocity schedule regarding applicants of Iranian, Iraqi or Libyan nationality.

Mexican Nationals

Mexican nationals are not visa exempt. Therefore, all Mexican "TN"s and both Mexican and non-Mexican national "TD"s accompanying or following to join them who are not otherwise exempt from the visa requirement (e.g., the Canadian spouse of a Mexican national "TN") must obtain nonimmigrant visas.

Applicants of Iranian, Iraqi, Libyan, Somalian, Sudanese, Syrian or Yemeni nationality, who have a permanent resident or refugee status in Canada/Mexico, may not be accorded Canadian/Mexican reciprocity, even when applying in Canada/Mexico. The reciprocity fee and period for "TD" applicants from Libya is $10.00 for one entry over a period of 3 months. The Iranian and Iraqi "TD" is no fee with one entry over a period of 3 months.

7. Q-2 (principal) and Q-3 (dependent) visa categories are in existence because of the 'Irish Peace Process Cultural and Training Program Act of 1998'. However, because the Department anticipates that virtually all applicants for this special program will be either Irish or U.K. nationals, the Q-2 and Q-3 categories have been placed only in the reciprocity schedules for those two countries. Q-2 and Q-3 visas are available only at the Embassy in Dublin and the Consulate General in Belfast.

8. No S visa may be issued without first obtaining the Department's authorization.

9. V-2 and V-3 status is limited to persons who have not yet attained their 21st birthday. Accordingly, the period of validity of a V-2 or V-3 visa must be limited to expire on or before the applicant's twenty-first birthday.

10. Posts may not issue a T-1 visa. A T-1 applicant must be physically present in the United States, American Samoa, the Commonwealth of the Northern Mariana Islands or a U.S. port of entry, where he/she will apply for an adjustment of status to that of a T-1. The following dependents of a T-1 visa holder, however, may be issued a T visa at a U.S. consular office abroad:

- T-2 (spouse)
- T-3 (child)
- T-4 (parent)

11. The validity of NATO-5 visas may not exceed the period of validity of the employment contract or 12 months, whichever is less.

12. The validity of CW-1 and CW-2 visas shall not exceed the maximum initial period of admission allowed by DHS (12 months) or the duration of the transition period ending December 31, 2014, whichever is shortest.

13. The validity of E-2C visas shall not exceed the maximum initial period of admission allowed by DHS (24 months) or the duration of the transition period ending December 31, 2014, whichever is

shortest.

General Documents

General Document Information

The rules and regulations regarding the maintenance of public records and the issuance of certificates in the 36 states of Nigeria are similar; however, those rules and regulations are often ignored. Except for a few federal Government Agencies, no local or federal government body currently has a central database with digitized records. Most records are stored on paper, filed by dates, location, and in regard to divorce cases, presiding court.

- Controls over civil documents are poor to non-existent, such that civil documents generally lack credibility.
- Civil document registrars have been known to issue documents with false information and to certify false documents issued by other registrars.
- False divorce documents and decrees can be filed in the Nigerian court system, backdated, and inserted into older court records.
- Nigerian courts may verify a document as genuine, even if there are no records.

Note: Since fraudulent documents can be easily obtained in Nigeria, the consular officer may wish to consider referring suspect documents to the Fraud Prevention Unit, U.S. Embassy Abuja or U.S. Consulate Lagos, for investigation.

General Issuing Authority Information

In Nigeria the maintenance of public records and the issuance of certificates fall within the jurisdiction of the local governments. Some exceptions apply to civil marriage certificates which are issued under the authority of The Federal Marriage Registry; National Driver's License issued by Federal Road Safety Commission; National Identity Card issued by National Identity Management Commission; Voter's Card issued by Independent National Electoral Commission; birth, attestation of birth and death certificates issued by National Population Commission.

These exceptions fall under the purview of the Federal Government; however, Marriage Registries and the National Population Commission have offices in all the Local Government Secretariats. Civil marriages can only be dissolved by State High Courts, and that Court has exclusive jurisdiction to handle matrimonial causes arising from civil marriages. Customary Marriages and divorces are seldom recorded.

Birth, Death, Burial Certificates

Birth Certificates

Available

Fees: Issuance of birth certificates is free for infants under 2 years of age. Fees may be required for children who are more than 2 years old.

Document Name: Certificate of Birth

Issuing Authority: National Population Commission (NPC)

Special Seal(s) / Color / Format: Multiple versions of this form are issued. They are typically printed on white paper with green background lettering. Seals are inked, most often in blue, black, or purple. Biodata may be typed or handwritten.

Issuing Authority Personnel Title: Registrar

Registration Criteria: The birth of every child born in Nigeria shall be registered by the Registrar of the National Population Commission or any person working under his authority.

Procedure for Obtaining: Visit any National Population Commission office in any of the Local Government Secretariats or designated Primary Health Care Centers, and the birth registration and certificate issuance could be completed within 10 minutes by the Officials. Parents, heads of household or any person who has attained 18 years and present at the birth of a child may visit these centers with or without the child whose birth is to be registered and supply the necessary information to register and obtain a birth certificate on their behalf.

Certified Copies Available: There are no certified copies.

Alternate Documents: For people born prior to 1979 or in some cases prior to 1988, a birth certificate issued by a Local Government Authority or a hospital or a baptismal certificate is acceptable. There is also the National Population Commission Attestation of Birth Certificate

issued to people whose birth occurred before 1979 when the National Population Commission issued birth certificate was first introduced as a pilot program. Any of these is acceptable.

Exceptions: There are no certified copies

Comments: The Compulsory Registration of Birth and death Decree of 1979 was a pilot program involving 4 States only in Nigeria, namely – Anambra (Southeast), Oyo (Southwest), Plateau (Northeast) and Kaduna (Northwest) States. NPC birth and death Certificates were issued under the 1979 Law in these States only. The 1992 Law (Births and Deaths, etc. (Compulsory Registration)

Act, No. 69 of 1992 was made to make the NPC birth and death registration to be of Countrywide application.

Death Certificates

Available

Fees: Registration is free

Document Name: Certificate of Death

Issuing Authority: National Population Commission

Special Seal(s) / Color / Format: Size and format is comparable to birth certificates. Multiple versions of this form are issued. They are typically printed on white paper with green background lettering. Seals are inked, most often in blue, black, or purple. Biodata may be typed or handwritten.

Issuing Authority Personnel Title: The Registrar

Registration Criteria: The death of every person dying in Nigeria as well as the cause of the death thereof shall be registered as from the commencement of the Births and Deaths, etc. (Compulsory Registration) Act, No. 69 of 1992.

Procedure for Obtaining: When the death of any person occurs, information of such a death is given to the Registrar for the area where such a death occurred.

Certified Copies Available: No.

Alternate Documents: Medical Certificate of Death is acceptable for deaths of any person which occurred before the commencement of Births and Deaths, etc. (Compulsory Registration) Act, No. 69 of 1992. Sworn declaration or Affidavit is also acceptable in lieu of a Medical Certificate of Death for cases where the death occurred before the commencement of the Act, and no Medical Certificate was issued, or the issued certificate is lost.

Exceptions: There are no exceptions

Comments: Most recent deaths occur in a hospital and supporting hospital/medical records should also be available. In a case where a death occurs at home, a medical examiner still performs the inspection, and some record of that should exist.

Marriage, Divorce Certificates

Marriage Certificates

Available

Fees: Cost for civil marriage in the Registry would range from Five to Ten Thousand Naira.

Document Name: Certificate of Marriage

Issuing Authority: Marriage Registry

Special Seal(s) / Color / Format: Multiple versions of this form are issued in varying formats. They are typically printed on white or green paper with green background lettering. Seals are inked, most often in blue, black, or purple. Biodata may be typed or handwritten.

Issuing Authority Personnel Title: Registrar or Minister of Religion as the case may be.

Registration Criteria: Must be a marriage celebrated between a man and a woman of consenting age, with no legal incapacity to marry under Native Law and Custom or according to the Marriage Act.

Procedure for Obtaining: For registry marriages, issued by the Marriage Registrar or Minister of Religion upon completion of the marriage process as provided for in the Marriage Act.

Certified Copies Available: There are no exceptions.

Alternate Documents: For marriages under Native Law and Custom, a Registration of Marriage Certificate is sometimes issued by the Local Marriage Registrar after presenting a court affidavit as provided for by the Registration of Customary Marriage bylaws.

Exceptions: Most customary marriages will have no written record.

Comments: Submitted Nigerian marriage certificates will be reviewed by a consular officer at the time of interview

Nigerian law recognizes multiple types of legal marriage, each with their own requirements. The two main types are customary marriages and registry marriages.

(1) Customary Marriages: While customary marriages are legally binding, no registration or written record of the event is required by law. As a result, documentation of customary marriages generally does not exist outside of photographs taken at the ceremony. Individuals will sometimes, when necessary, swear an affidavit in a court that they are married to provide written proof of such a marriage.

(2) Some Local Governments will issue a certificate based on that affidavit by virtue of the Registration of Customary Marriage bylaws. Absence of an affidavit or certificate of this kind cannot be taken as lack of marital status. [Note: The bylaws mentioned vary from state to state and authorize Local Government Authorities (LGAs) to register customary marriages that take place in their jurisdiction. The bylaws do not exist in all states and several states that have them do not make

registration compulsory. There are two types of Customary Marriage: marriage under native law & custom (also known as traditional marriage) and Islamic marriage.

1.) a.) Marriage Under Native Law & Custom: Traditional marriage ceremonies are based on local, unwritten customs. In the case of Lagos residents, the customs of the local area or village where the family originates from (usually outside Lagos State) should also be considered. Cultural context will determine whether a legally binding marriage ceremony took place, versus an introduction or other non-binding ceremony. Some local customs permit proxy marriages, where the groom need not be present at the ceremony.

In nearly all Nigerian cultures, payment of a dowry or bride price is a key component of a traditional marriage ceremony. The dowry may be in the form of money, gifts, or a combination of both. Yams are a typical part of the dowry in many areas within Nigeria. [Note: Modernization has led to some evolution in traditional marriages, and payment of the bride price in some recent marriages is merely symbolic.] Traditional marriage also allows for a man to legally marry more than one wife.

1.) b.) Islamic Marriage: The celebration of Islamic marriage ceremonies (called Nikkai) in Nigeria is governed by the Maliki Law. The marriage must be between a male and a female that have agreed to marry if matured, or consent has been given by their father or male guardian if they are immature. [Note: "Maturity" is not defined by a specific age but is instead determined by the father or male guardian.]

The bride's price, which is a minimum of N5000, is called the sadaq or dower, and is paid to the bride but received by her parents. The ceremony is officiated by a Mallam in the presence of at least three Muslim witnesses. After a celebration of Islamic Marriage, the couple may obtain a certificate from the Local Government Marriage Registry, but this is not required. Islamic law allows a man to marry up to 4 wives.

2.) Registry Marriages: The Marriage Act of 1990 is the primary law governing registry marriages in Nigeria. One notable difference between customary marriages and registry marriages: men who marry at a marriage registry are legally permitted to have only one wife. Therefore, men legally married to multiple wives by way of customary marriages would first need to divorce those wives under native law and custom before completing a registry marriage to a new wife.

Should a man wish to complete a registry marriage with one of his existing wives, he would first need to divorce all other wives under native law and custom. The registry marriage ceremony is conducted by a minister of religion or the marriage registrar in the presence of witnesses. A marriage certificate is issued at the completion of the ceremony. Both federal and local governments perform registry marriages.

2.) a.) Federal Marriage Registry: Nigeria's Federal Marriage Registry currently has offices in only a few states, with plans to expand to include at least one office per state. The office in Abuja has been operating since 2006. The Ikoyi office in Lagos pre-dates the founding of Nigeria and may include records as old as 1802. Note: They are filed by year and place of marriage and can be obtained by writing to the Marriage Registry, 19 Kingsway Road, Ikoyi, Lagos.

In October 2016, additional offices opened in the cities of Owerri (Imo State), Port Harcourt (Rivers State) and Benin City (Edo State). Even when marriages are properly registered at one of these facilities, there is no central database or system; all records are kept in paper files.

2.) b.) Designated churches: Church weddings, or "white weddings" as commonly known in Nigeria, are performed widely. Licensed places of worship can be authorized by the Federal Marriage Registry to perform marriage ceremonies "under the act." The church must create three copies of a marriage certificate using paper stock provided by the Federal Registry: one for the newly wedded couple, one for church records, and one for the Federal Registry. While churches authorized "under the act" are required by law to file a copy of the marriage certificate, often the marriage record is never sent to the Registry.

In addition, many unauthorized churches perform wedding ceremonies that have no legal standing. Marriage certificates issued by churches or other houses of worship not authorized by the Registry are not evidence of a legally binding marriage.

3.) c.) State/Local Registry: The inaccessibility of Nigeria's limited number of Federal Marriage Registry offices has led to the opening of local marriage registry offices by nearly all LGAs. [There are 774 LGAs within Nigeria.] Like the churches described above, some LGAs have been authorized by the Federal Marriage Registry to perform marriage ceremonies "under the act." The vast majority perform marriage ceremonies without any federal authority.

The Federal Marriage Registry has stated that these ceremonies are not legal, however individuals who marry at LGA registries may not know that their marriage is not legally recognized by federal authorities. LGAs authorized by the Federal Marriage Registry are required to use paper stock provided by the Registry for marriage certificates.

Other LGAs who perform civil marriages will issue a certificate titled "Unified Marriage Certificate."

[Note: Many couples perform more than one type of marriage ceremony. For example, couples may choose to have both a traditional and white wedding, or a traditional and registry wedding. When this is the case, the date that the first legally binding ceremony took place serves as the date the marriage began.]

Divorce Certificates

Available

Fees: Varies by location and court.

Document Name: Decree Nisi and Decree Absolute

Issuing Authority: The High Court of Justice

Special Seal(s) / Color / Format: Multiple versions of this form are issued in varying formats. They are typically typed in Times New Roman font and printed on white paper. Seals may be embossed, sometimes over a red sticker, or they may be inked, most often in red or purple.

Issuing Authority Personnel Title: Judge

Registration Criteria: Must be a registry marriage completed according to the Marriage Act.

Procedure for Obtaining: Divorce Proceedings in accordance with The Matrimonial Causes Act of Nigeria.

Certified Copies Available: Certified copies are available.

Alternate Documents: For marriages under Native Law and Custom, a divorce decree may be issued by a Customary Court. For Islamic marriages, a divorce decree may be issued by a Sharia court.

Exceptions: Many divorces for customary marriages will have no written

record. Marriages under native law and custom will also be dissolved by custom; many of these divorces are not recorded while some are recorded by an affidavit after the fact. Islamic marriages may be dissolved in a Sharia Court.

Comments: Documenting a legal divorce is problematic. Each type of marriage listed above has its own legal process for obtaining a divorce, thus it is essential to first understand what type of marriage took place before determining what documentation is acceptable to prove that a divorce is legal.

1.) CUSTOMARY MARRIAGES: There is no legal requirement that a customary marriage should be dissolved by any court, nor any requirement that the divorce be registered or documented.

1.) a.) Marriage Under Native Law and Custom: Traditional marriages are often dissolved without any written record. One legal method of divorce involves the groom or his family returning the bride's prize to the bride or her family. Divorces for some traditional marriages are documented by one or both parties filing an affidavit with a Customary Court.

Finally, traditional marriages may be formally dissolved by a Customary Court and a divorce decree issued by the court. Where there is no Customary Court in the area, a Magistrate Court may dissolve a customary marriage. The courts may dissolve a traditional marriage without one of the spouses being present or even knowing that the divorce took place.

1.) b.) Islamic Marriage: Divorce is most often initiated by the husband. Where a man tells his wife, "I divorce you", that single

pronouncement suspends the marriage. Making this pronouncement 3 times permanently dissolves the marriage. It is not clear if this must be at the same time or different times. However, the most common practice in Nigeria is for the man to write it on paper and give it to the woman. Once this is done, the marriage is technically divorced, and the couple can only remarry if the wife marries another person and divorces. The woman may take the paper her husband has written to the Sharia court to obtain a

Certificate of Divorce. Sharia courts have jurisdiction to dissolve Islamic marriages in many states in northern Nigeria.

In states where there is no Sharia court, the Customary Court may dissolve Islamic Marriages. An Islamic marriage cannot be divorced in a Magistrate court unless there is no Customary Court available. On the other hand, where a woman is dissatisfied with her marriage, she can initiate a divorce herself through a system called Khul, which must be done through a court. The court will then require the woman to prove that she has brought her case under the permissible grounds of divorce in Islam. Most times, Sharia court judges are reluctant to grant these petitions. As in other customary marriages, there is the problem of documentation since the marriage and divorce could be oral.

2.) Registry Marriages: Registry marriages, regardless of whether they are federal or local registry, can only be dissolved through a High Court. Post often sees divorce certificates issued by lower (customary and magistrate) courts purporting to have dissolved a registry marriage; these divorce orders are not legally binding.

There is a strict divorce procedure for marriage contracted under the Marriage Act, as set out in the Matrimonial Causes Act of 1970. One requires the services of an attorney to file a divorce petition and follow through with the legal processes in Court. After filing the necessary papers there is a trial. At the end of the trial, the Court may grant or refuse the Divorce. Where the divorce is granted, the order is temporary and is called a Decree Nisi. There is a three-month period allowed in the event of reconciliation between the couple. At the end of the three months, if the parties have not reconciled, then the divorce decree will automatically become absolute, and a Decree Absolute is issued.

At this point, the legal bonds of marriage are permanently severed unless the couple remarries. However, it is important to know that both parties are free to marry other parties once the Decree Nisi is issued; they need not wait for the Decree Absolute. [Note: As stated above, many couples perform more than one type of marriage ceremony. For divorce proceedings, once a couple has completed a Registry Marriage, the only legal method of divorce is through the High Court process. The High Court process is also the only legal method of divorce for residents of Nigeria who married outside of Nigeria.]

Adoption Certificates

Available

Fees: Stipulated by Court during the adoption process

Document Name: Adoption Order

Issuing Authority: The Family Court or The Chief Magistrate's Court

Special Seal(s) / Color / Format: Multiple versions of this form are issued in varying formats. They are typically typed and printed on white paper. Seals may be embossed, sometimes over a red sticker, or they may be inked, most often in red or purple.

Issuing Authority Personnel Title: Magistrate

Registration Criteria: By order of Court

Procedure for Obtaining

Prospective Adoptive Parent (PAP) to notify The Ministry of Social Welfare of the State where the adoption is to be done, of their intention to adopt. When a child becomes available, and the request is approved, there is a 3 month Fostering Period for the PAP to be in custody of, and bond with the juvenile, thereafter, application is made to the Family Court or the Magistrate Court to approve the adoption through an adoption hearing.

Certified Copies Available: Yes.

Alternate Documents: There are no exceptions.

Exceptions: There are no exceptions

Comments: Only Citizens of Nigeria can adopt under Nigeria's Adoption Laws. The following States do not have Adoption Laws and so cannot issue valid adoption Orders: Sokoto, Katsina, Zamfara, Kebbi, Kaduna, Bauchi, Adamawa, Gombe, Borno, and Yobe States.

Identity Card

National ID Cards

Available

Fees: Free

Document Name: National Identity Card

Issuing Authority: National Identity Management Commission

Special Seal(s) / Color / Format: There are no special seal(s)/color/format.

Issuing Authority Personnel Title: There is no Issuing Authority Personnel Title

Registration Criteria: Must be a Nigerian Citizen of full age.

Procedure for Obtaining: Register at the approved centers set up by the National Identity Management Commission.

Certified Copies Available: No.

Alternate Documents: Nigerian International Passport.

Exceptions: There are no exceptions

Comments: Available, but not widely used. All Nigerians should have a national identification number; however, registration for this number is rarely completed.

Police, Court, Prison Records

Court/Prison Records

Unavailable

Comments: The police record gives all prison sentences, although reliability is questionable.

Police Certificates

Available

Fees: Over the years, applicants are known to have paid five thousand Naira for the Police Character Certificate. The fee should be in the form of a bank draft payable to the Deputy Inspector General of Police, Fingerprint Section, Nigeria Police Force.

Document Name: Police Character Certificate

Issuing Authority: The Nigeria Police

Special Seal(s) / Color / Format: They are typically printed on white paper with red background lettering. Seals are inked, most often in blue, black, or purple. Biodata is typed in Times New Roman font. Fingerprint cards must be submitted along with the police certificate.

Issuing Authority Personnel Title: Central Registrar, Deputy Inspector-General "D" Dept., For Inspector-General of Police

Registration Criteria: N/A

Procedure for Obtaining: Applicants need to contact the Deputy Inspector General, Criminal Investigation Department, Nigeria Police Force, Alagbon Close, Ikoyi, Lagos, Nigeria. The applicant should bring information regarding their full name, place and date of birth, nationality, passport number, date, and place of issuance (for current passport or passport used during applicant's stay in Nigeria), exact periods of residence in Nigeria and addresses where applicant resided.

Certified Copies Available: There are no certified copies.

Alternate Documents: There are no alternate documents.

Exceptions: There are no exceptions

Comments: Applicants outside the country are advised that mailed requests for police certificates are not an effective method of obtaining the records.

It is recommended that applicants outside Nigeria obtain a police certificate upon their next visit or enlist the assistance of a friend or relative able to physically visit the Deputy Inspector General. Note that each applicant 16 years of age and above must also provide (1) a copy of the first three data pages of his or her passport, (2) the pages containing Nigerian visas, entry, and departure stamps and (3) a complete set of fingerprints taken by the police in the district where the applicant resides. The Police Character Certificate is obtained by applying to the relevant Police Department of the Nigeria Police

Military Records:

Passports & Other Travel Documents: **Travel Documents**

Types Available (Regular, Diplomatic, Official, etc.): All are available.

Fees: Diplomatic and Official Passports are Free. Regular Passports when paying in Nigeria cost N8,750 ($65 when paying from abroad) for applicants aged 0 – 17 years, N15,000

($94 when paying from abroad) for applicants aged from 18 – 59 years and N8,750 ($65 when paying from abroad) for applicants aged 60 years and above. These are for the 32 paged passports. For the 64 paged Passports, the fee is N20,000 ($125 when paying from abroad) across the board.

Document Name: Diplomatic Passport, Official Passport, Standard Nigeria Passport, Pilgrims Passport, Seaman's Book

Issuing Government Authority: The Nigeria Immigration Service

Special Seal(s) / Color / Format: There is no special seal(s)/colors/format.

Issuing Authority Personnel Title: There is no issuing authority personnel title.

Registration Criteria: Must be a Citizen of Nigeria.

Procedure for Obtaining: Pay the appropriate fee and provide the following:

- Local Government letter of identification.
- Birth certificate / age declaration.
- 2 recent color passport photographs
- Guarantor's form sworn to before a commissioner of Oaths / Magistrate / High Court Judge
- Parents' letter of consent for minors under 16 years
- Marriage certificate where applicable
- Police report in case of lost passport
- Submit application with supporting documents to passport office / Embassy / High commission

Alternate Documents: Emergency Travel Certificate issued to Nigerians abroad who lose their Passport for the purposes of traveling back to Nigeria. ECOWAS Travel Certificate issued to Citizens of ECOWAS countries for travel within the sub-region.

Exceptions: There are no exceptions

Comments: None

Other Records

Education Credentials

The most reliable education records are national standardized test results. Students generally take standardized tests during both primary and secondary school. Primary school students complete the National Primary School Examination (NPSE). Students in the third year of junior secondary/high school are eligible to register for the Basic Education Certificate Examination (BECE), previously known as the Junior School Certificate Examination. Senior secondary school students complete the

West Africa Secondary School Certificate Examination (WASSCE) or old levels, also known as O levels. The West African Examinations Council (WAEC) records results for the BECE, WASSCE, and WAEC.

Those who successfully complete high school must take the WAEC examination to receive their diplomas. The examinations are scored on a scale of 1 to 9, with 1 being the best and 9 the worst. To enter a university, the applicant must have received credit (a score of 1-6) in five subjects. For diploma programs, he or she must have received 3 or 4 credits. Scores of 7 or 8 are only ordinary passes and give no credit.

A score of P8 or F9 indicates failing. There is a national WAEC office in Lagos where results can be checked to verify educational level. A certified verification may be retrieved one time from the WAEC office and results for recent years are available online with a WAEC-provided scratch card. Colleges and universities will also accept the National Examination Council (NEC) exam, sometimes referred to as NECO. It is administered by the NEC instead of the WAEC. Students can choose to take either exam, but most choose to take the WAEC exam.

The WAEC and NECO exams are not considered sufficient to be admitted to colleges and universities in Nigeria. They only signify the completion of secondary school examinations. The Joint Admission and Matriculation Board (JAMB) examination is required for students attending Nigerian higher institutions and is administered by the Nigerian government. Once students have obtained a score of at least 200 on the JAMB and have gained admittance to an institution, each institution will also administer Post University Matriculation Examinations before accepting students. The score required to accept students depends on the institution and the course of study.

Visa Issuing Posts

Post Contact Information

Post Title: U.S. Embassy Abuja

Address: Plot 1075 Diplomatic Dr, Central Business District, Abuja, FCT, Nigeria

Phone Number: +234 9 461 4000

Visa Services: NIV only

Comments / Additional Information: All applications are reviewed by appointment only. See ng.usembassy.gov for more specifics.

Post Title: U.S. Consulate General Lagos

Address: 2 Walter Carrington Crescent, Victoria Island, Lagos, Nigeria

Phone Number: +234 01 440 6218

Visa Services: NIV and IV

Comments / Additional Information: All applications are reviewed by appointment only. See ng.usembassy.gov for more specifics.

Visa Services

Post Title: U.S. Consulate General Lagos

Address: 2 Walter Carrington Crescent, Victoria Island, Lagos, Nigeria

Phone Number: +234 01 440 6218

Visa Services: NIV and IV

Comments / Additional Information: All applications are reviewed by appointment only. See ng.usembassy.gov for more specifics.

Additional Information for Reciprocity

Although care has been taken to ensure the accuracy, completeness, and reliability of the information provided, please contact the **U.S. Embassy or Consulate** where you plan to apply if you believe this information is in error or if you have further questions.

Resources:

- **Reciprocity: What's New**
- **Temporary Reciprocity Schedule**
- **Country Acronyms**
- **Presidential Proclamations**
- **Terrorist Designation Lists**
- **State Sponsors of Terrorism**
- **Treaty Countries**
- **Visa Issuing Posts**

Diversity Visa Program

Step 1

Submit an entry in a timely manner.

Step 2

The selection of applicants by the Consulate — you may probably have little or no control over their selection criteria.

Step 3

If you are selected, get ready to gather all relevant information and documentation for a cursory interview.

Step 4

You need to confirm your qualification.

Step 5

Submit your immigrant visa and alien registration application, which would be provided to you for completion.

Step 6

Submit your supporting documentation to all department officials requesting them.

Step 7

Awaiting your interview date.

Step 8

Prepare for your interview. If possible, look for, pay for, and attend an **entry reception to the U.S.** You must learn a thing or two about American people, their food, their climate, their culture, and above all, their language.

Step 9

Applicant interview.

Step 10

The interview is over. Now, what next? Attend an **entry orientation** — it might cost you up to **twenty-five dollars an hour!**

Confirm Your Qualifications

The **Diversity Immigrant Visa (DV) Program** requires the principal DV applicant to have:

- A **high school education,** or its equivalent
- **Two years of qualifying work experience** as defined under provisions of U.S. law

If you do not have either the required education or qualifying work experience, you are not eligible for a diversity visa. (Only you, as the principal applicant, must meet this requirement. Your spouse and children do not have to meet this requirement.) You should consider not pursuing a DV application if you do not meet the qualifying education or work experience requirements explained below as you may not be eligible for a diversity visa and any fees you pay for the visa application will not be refunded.

High School Education: A high school education means successful completion of a formal course of elementary and secondary education comparable to a 12-year course in the United States. Only formal courses of study meet this requirement; equivalency certificates (such as the G.E.D.) are not acceptable.

Work Experience: If you are qualifying with work experience, you must have two years of experience in the last five years, in an occupation which, by U.S. Department of Labor definitions, requires at least two years of training or experience that is designated as Job Zone 4 or 5, classified in a Specific Vocational Preparation (SVP) rating of 7.0 or higher.

The U.S. Department of Labor provides information on job duties, knowledge and skills, education and training, and other occupational characteristics on their
website http://www.onetonline.org/. The O*Net online database groups work experience into five "job zones." While many occupations are listed, only two years of experience in certain specified occupations qualify an individual for a Diversity Visa.

How to Find the Qualifying Occupations on the Department of Labor Website

Qualifying **DV Occupations** are shown on the **Department of Labor O*Net Online Database**. Follow these steps when you are in O*Net Online to find out if your occupation may qualify you for a Diversity Visa:

- Under **"Find Occupations"** select **"Job Family"** from the pull-down menu.
- Then **Browse by "Job Family"**. (For example, select **Architecture and Engineering**) and click **"GO"**.
- Then click on the link for your specific occupation.

Example:

Select **Aerospace Engineers**. At the bottom of this **Summary Report for Aerospace Engineers**, under the **Job Zone** section, you will find the designated **Job Zone 4**, **SVP Range, 7.0 to < 8.0**. This means, using this example, **Aerospace Engineering** is a qualifying occupation.

Again, you should consider not pursuing a **DV application** if:

- You do not meet the qualifying education or work experience requirements explained above.
- You provided an invalid passport number with your entry.
- You selected an exemption for which you do not qualify.

Such errors may render you **ineligible** for a diversity visa, and any fees you pay for the visa application will **not be refunded**.

For more information

See the **DV-2024 Instructions** and **DV-2025 Instructions** and **Frequently Asked Questions**.

Photo Examples

Starting **November 1, 2016**, eyeglasses will **no longer be allowed** in new visa photos.

Your photo or digital image is a **vital part** of your visa application. Review the examples below to learn how your photo or digital image should look. We recommend you use a **professional photo service** to ensure your photo meets all the requirements.

The acceptance of your photo or digital image is at the **discretion of the U.S. embassy or consulate** where you apply.

Acceptable Visa Photos

Retrieve detailed examples of **Visa Photos** — Passport photo types on a passport.

Acceptable— Photo is clear and in color, reproduces skin tones accurately, and is properly exposed with no shadows.

Public domain images copied. Publication permission not required as per author. Retrieved on April 24, 2022.

Please review the tabs to the left for examples of both acceptable and unacceptable photos to submit with your visa application. Keep in mind the basics: size, expression, head position, background, print quality, and anything that might obscure the face (hair, shadows).

- Shadows and Lighting
- Glasses
- Size and Position
- Resolution, Print Size, and Quality
- DigitalAlterations and Retouching
- Pose and Expression
- Attire, Hats, and Hair
- Background
- Children

- Online Renewal Application

The principal applicant and all family members applying for a diversity visa program must complete Form DS-260. You will need to enter your DV case number into the online DS-260 form to access and update the information about yourself and your family that you included in your DV entry.

If your family circumstances have changed after you entered the Diversity Visa program, for example, if you have gotten married or had a child, you will need to add your new family members to your case. ("Family member" refers to a spouse and/or unmarried children who had not reached age 21 before you entered the DV program.) When adding family members to your case, you will need to upload a document to prove your relationship to the family member being added.

Important note: If you had a spouse or children prior to submitting your original entry, but you did not include them on your original entry form, such errors may render you, as well as any of your family members, ineligible for a diversity visa. If you listed a spouse or child on your original entry who was not your spouse or child at the time of entry, such errors may render you, as well as any of your family members, ineligible for a diversity visa.

As indicated in the prior paragraph, if your family circumstances have legitimately changed after submitting your original entry, you should add those family members and all family members' applications will be reviewed. For more information, see the DV Instructions.

On the Sign and Submit page of the DS-260, you will need to re-enter your DV case number without the zeros (e.g. if the case number is 2023AF0000012345, enter '2023AF12345'). Entering the full case number with zeros will generate a validation error.

After submitting the Form DS-260 online, print the confirmation page. You must bring the confirmation page to your visa interview.

Please be aware that KCC can only tell you if your form has been processed. KCC cannot tell you whether you or your family members are eligible for diversity visas. Only the consular officer who interviews you can make that decision.

Contacting KCC: If you need to contact the KCC, always include your name, birthdate and case number exactly as they appear in the Entrant Status Check (ESC). Your case number should be clearly written in the upper right-hand corner of your e-mail or in the subject line. KCC only receives inquiries by email.

Do not mail paper documents or correspondence to the Kentucky Consular Center. All paper documents or correspondence received will be destroyed. The KCC e-mail address for Diversity Visa inquiries is KCCDV@state.gov.

Submit Supporting Documents

Notice to DV-2024 Applicants

Until further notice, DV selectees are not required to submit supporting documents to the KCC for fiscal year 2024 (DV-2024) and onward. Selectees are still required to submit the DS-260 application form.

(See Diversity Visa 2024 Update for more information. Retrieved on August 10, 2024 from DOJ Website).

After KCC receives and processes the DS-260 application form for you and your accompanying family members, you will receive instructions for how to submit required supporting documents. Your interview will not be scheduled until you submit scanned copies of all required supporting documents, following the guidelines below.

If you cannot obtain a particular document, send an explanation of why you cannot obtain the document, as an attachment in .jpeg or .pdf format, to KCCDVDocuments@state.gov, with your case number in the subject line. You will bring the original documents to your interview with the consular officer. It is strongly recommended that you begin this process early.

The applicant and each family member who will accompany the applicant to the United States will need to submit scanned copies and any required translations of original documents or certified copies of the documents listed below from an appropriate office, authority, or issuing entity in your country. You will be required to bring the original documents to your visa interview at the U.S. embassy or consulate, along with any translations required.

Documents

Review the information below to determine which documents you will need to obtain. KCC will send instructions explaining how to scan and email the documents and any required translations after you submit a valid DS-260 application for you and all accompanying family members. Your visa interview appointment will not be scheduled until KCC has received and reviewed all required supporting documents. You will take original documents with you to your interview at a U.S. embassy or consulate. Do not mail any of these documents to the Kentucky Consular Center. All paper documents or correspondence mailed to KCC will be destroyed.

Birth Certificates

Court and Prison Records

Military Records

Police Certificates

Photocopy of Valid Passport Biographic Data Page

Additional Embassy or Consulate Instructions

Civil and personal documents may differ from country to country, depending on availability. There may be either additional instructions for obtaining civil documents in a specific country or additional documents required, depending on the U.S. Embassy or Consulate where you will apply. Select the embassy or consulate where you will apply to learn what additional requirements there are, if any.

Note that some of the information included in these instructions may apply to immigrant visa classifications other than diversity visas. If you have questions about the country-specific information included here, please contact the embassy or consulate where you will apply for your visa.

Please visit the List of U.S. Embassies and Consulates to review Embassy/Consulate instructions provided by your city.

The Interview

After the Kentucky Consular Center has reviewed your completed DS-260, you may receive an e-mail from KCC to let you know that an interview has been scheduled at the U.S. Embassy or Consulate you selected on your DS-260 form. The e-mail will instruct you to log into the Entrant Status Check on the Electronic Diversity Visa (E-DV) website, using your DV entry confirmation number, to view the date, time and location of your interview. Print this information to take with you to your interview. You will need to be present at the interview, as well as your spouse and children (as applicable) who are applying for a diversity immigrant visa.

Note: You will only be scheduled for an interview when and if there is a visa number available for you. Visa number allocations are determined by provisions of the Immigration and Nationality Act (INA) which determines the number of diversity immigrant visas available each year. The total number of diversity visas is allocated by visa category and region of the world. The allocations are revised monthly as available visas are issued.

Each month the Department of State publishes the Visa Bulletin which contains important information about updated allocations and the likelihood of a diversity visa number being available. Anyone may view the most recent updated information by clicking Visa Bulletin.

Your completed Form DS-260 will be accessible by the U.S. Embassy or Consulate where you will be interviewed. You do not need to fill out a new application.

Important Applicant Notice:

Based on U.S. law, not everyone who applies for a visa will be found eligible to come to the United States. There are a few possible reasons why someone might not qualify for a visa. The circumstances of each case are different. Approved visas generally are not available on the day of interview.

It is important that you do not decide such as selling your house, car or property, resigning from your job or making non-refundable flight or other travel arrangements until you have received your immigrant visa.

Prepare for the Interview

Important Notice

Presidential Proclamation on Healthcare

All applicants - Read the below information carefully. If you do not bring all the required documents to your appointment, your case will be delayed. You may need to return to the U.S. Embassy or Consulate at another date and your visa may be delayed or denied.

You should prepare for your interview thoroughly and carefully. Failure to be fully prepared for your interview at the U.S. Embassy or Consulate can result in delay or denial of your visa application.

After you have been notified of your scheduled interview, you will need to take the following important steps in advance of the interview date:

1. **Carefully Review** your scheduling information in the Entrant Status Check on the E-DV website, noting the date, time, and location of your immigrant visa interview.

2. Review U.S. Embassy or Consulate Interview Instructions

There may be additional instructions provided by the U.S. Embassy or Consulate where you will be applying and be interviewed, so please review those instructions carefully. To see this information, select below the U.S. Embassy or Consulate where you will be

interviewed. Please note that some of the information included in these instructions may apply to immigrant visa classifications other than diversity visas. If you have questions about the country-specific information included here, please contact the embassy or consulate where you will apply for your visa.

Please visit the List of U.S. Embassies and Consulates to review Embassy/Consulate instructions.

3. Schedule and Complete a Medical Examination

You (and each family member applying for a visa with you) are required to schedule a medical appointment with an authorized physician in the country where you will be interviewed. You must complete your medical examination, along with any required vaccinations, before your scheduled visa interview date. When your medical exam is completed, if you are given a medical exam envelope, you must bring it sealed (not opened) to your visa interview. Some physicians will send the medical exam results directly to the embassy or consulate.

A list of authorized physicians for the U.S. Embassy or Consulate where you will apply is provided in the dropdown list below. You must contact a physician and schedule your medical appointment. The embassy or consulate will not do this for you. Explain that the examination is for an immigrant visa application and give the physician the date of the interview appointment. The physician will tell you the cost of the examination and tests.

Please note that some of the information included in these instructions may apply to immigrant visa classifications other than diversity visas. If you have questions about the country-specific information included here, please contact the embassy or consulate where you will apply for your visa.

Please visit the List of U.S. Embassies and Consulates to review Embassy/Consulate instructions.

4. Gather Photographs and All Remaining Required Documents

Photographs

Each DV applicant will need to bring two (2) identical photos to the interview. Please review the detailed information about photo requirements to ensure that your photos will be acceptable.

Required Documentation

Each applicant will be required to present the following:

- **Appointment information** printed from the **Entrant Status Check** on the **E-DV website**.
- **DS-260 confirmation page** — You can print this from the **Consular Electronic Application Center** any time after you complete your DS-260 application.
- **Passport(s)** valid for **six months beyond** the intended date of entry into the U.S. for you and each family member applying for a visa.
- **Original documents** or **certified copies of civil documents** submitted to **KCC**.

Bring **one photocopy** of any document that you did not submit to **KCC** as part of the interview qualification process.

You should be prepared to present:

Evidence of Required DV Qualifying Education or Work Experience

Deportation Documentation

Marriage Certificate:

Marriage Termination Documentation:

Custody Documentation:

5. Review Additional Information

Visit the U.S. embassy or consulate website where you will be interviewed for any additional information.

Paying Fees

Before the interview, each applicant must pay the Diversity Visa fee. For DV-2022 applicants the fee is $330 per person. This fee is nonrefundable, whether a visa is issued or not. Learn more about Fees. Fee payment procedures vary between different U.S. Embassies and Consulates. At most locations, you should make arrangements to pay your fees before your interview date and time by following the instructions of the U.S. Embassy or Consulate where you will be interviewed. A few U.S. Embassies and Consulates collect fees in the consular section at the time of your interview. Be sure you have looked at the specific instructions for the U.S. Embassy or Consulate where you will be interviewed so that you can follow the appropriate procedures.

Other fees may apply to other parts of the process, such as medical exam fees, or local government fees to obtain certified copies of records.

Applicant Interview

Prior to your interview, ensure you have followed the U.S. Embassy or Consulate interview preparation instructions. On the scheduled date and time of your interview appointment, go to the U.S. Embassy or Consulate. A consular officer will interview you (and accompanying family member beneficiaries) and determine whether you can receive an immigrant visa. As part of the interview process, ink-free, digital fingerprint scans will be taken.

Who Must Attend the Interview?

You, your spouse, and any qualified unmarried children immigrating with you must participate in the interview. If your spouse and/or qualified unmarried children will immigrate later and travel separately from you, they are not required to participate in your interview. They

will be scheduled for a separate interview appointment. You should contact the U.S. Embassy or Consulate directly to arrange separate interviews, if needed.

What to Bring to the Interview

Appointment Letter - Your appointment information from the Entrant Status Check on the Electronic Diversity Visa (E-DV) website.

DS-260 Confirmation Page - You can print this from the Consular Electronic Application Center any time after you complete your DS-260 application.

Passport - For each applicant, an unexpired passport valid for six months beyond the intended date of entry into the United States

Photographs - *Two* identical color photographs for each applicant. Photos must meet the standards explained in the Photograph Requirements.

Medical Exam Results - If the panel physician gave you sealed envelopes containing each applicant's medical examination results, please bring those unopened envelopes. Some physicians send the medical examination results directly to the U.S. Embassy or Consulate. For more information, review Prepare for the Interview.

Original and Supporting Documents - Bring original documents or certified copies of all documents you submitted to KCC for you and each family member applying for a visa (except for your passport). You may also be required to provide evidence of work and education requirements, marriage certificates, marriage termination documentation, and custody documentation. If you have a new document that you did not submit to KCC, bring both the original and one photocopy.

Your original documents will be returned to you when the interview has been completed. The photocopies will be kept. For more information, review Prepare Your Supporting Documents.

English Translations - If documents require English translation, you must obtain certified translations and present them on the day of your interview. For more information, review Prepare Your Supporting Documents.

Visa Fees - If you did not pay your visa fees prior to your interview, you will need to pay them before speaking with a consular officer. For more information, review Prepare for the Interview.

Important Notice

You should not make permanent financial commitments, such as selling your house, car or property, resigning from your job or making non-refundable flight or other travel arrangements until you have received your immigrant visa.

Additional Information

I need to reschedule my appointment - If you cannot appear at your scheduled interview, contact the U.S. Embassy or Consulate as soon as possible. Under U.S. law, all diversity visas for a fiscal year must be issued prior to September 30. Available visas for some countries and regions may be used up prior to that date. If you delay your appointment, you may lose your opportunity to immigrate based on your DV application.

I would like my spouse and/or children to follow me to the United States after I immigrate. Can they do that? - Yes but remember that all diversity visas for a fiscal year must be issued by September 30. Available visas for some countries and regions may be used up prior to that date. If your spouse and children delay obtaining their visas, they may lose their opportunity to immigrate based on their DV applications. If this happens, you will need to file a petition to bring your family to the United States later. If they do not obtain diversity visas prior to September 30, your spouse and/or children may have to wait several years to join you.

Can my spouse or children receive diversity visas, even if they were not on my original entry? – If you were married, or your child was born or adopted after you submitted your entry to the DV program, you can add them to your case, and they may be eligible to receive diversity visas.

If you were married or had children prior to entering the DV program, and you failed to include your family members on your original entry, your case will be disqualified. Neither you nor your family members will receive visas. Your fees will not be refunded.

My child will turn 21 years old soon - Children generally must be unmarried and under age 21 to qualify as derivative applicants. Also, they generally must use their visas to enter the United States while still under age 21.

If you have a child who will be turning 21 soon, you should immediately contact the U.S. Embassy or Consulate where your interview is scheduled. The U.S. Embassy or Consulate will determine whether an earlier appointment is needed. If your child no longer qualifies to immigrate with you based on age, then a separate petition must be filed for the child after you immigrate. There may be a significant delay before your child becomes qualified for a visa.

After the Interview

At the end of your immigrant visa interview at the U.S. Embassy or Consulate, the consular officer will inform you whether your visa application is approved or denied.

Visa approval - When approved, you will be informed how and when your passport and visa will be returned to you.

Visa denial - If denied, you will be informed why you are ineligible to receive a visa. See an example below:

CONSULATE GENERAL OF THE
UNITED STATES OF AMERICA
LAGOS, NIGERIA

Dear Applicant:

This is to inform you that you have been found ineligible for a nonimmigrant visa under Section 214(b) of the U.S. Immigration and Nationality Act. A denial under Section 214(b) means that you were not able to demonstrate that your intended activities in the United States would be consistent with the classification of the nonimmigrant visa for which you applied.

While nonimmigrant visa classifications each have their own unique requirements, one requirement shared by many of the nonimmigrant visa categories is for the applicant to demonstrate that he/she has a residence in a foreign country which he/she has no intention of abandoning. Applicants usually meet this requirement by demonstrating that they have strong ties overseas that indicate that they will return to a foreign country after a temporary visit to the United States. Such ties include professional, work, school, family, or social links to a foreign country. You have not demonstrated that you have the ties that will compel you to return to your home country after your travel to the United States.

Today's decision cannot be appealed. However, you may reapply at any time. If you decide to reapply, you must submit a new application form and photo, pay the visa application fee again, and make a new appointment to be interviewed by a consular officer. If you choose to reapply, you should be prepared to provide information that was not presented in your original application, or to demonstrate that your circumstances have changed since that application.

Sincerely,
Consular Officer
Nonimmigrant Visa Unit

If you would like to report harassment, bribery, fraud or malfeasant behavior to the U.S. Consulate General Lagos, please scan this QR code and complete the form. All submitted information will be kept anonymous.

There is additional information about visa denials at the bottom of this page, and detailed information is available on the Denials webpage.

Note: Some refused visa applications may require further administrative processing. When administrative processing is required, the consular officer will inform the applicant at the end of the interview. The duration of the administrative processing will vary based on the individual circumstances of each case.

Visa Approval - When You Receive Your Visa

Passport with Visa - Your diversity visa will be placed on a page in your passport. Please review the printed information right away to make sure there are no errors. If there are any spelling errors, contact the embassy or consulate promptly.

Sealed Immigrant Packet - You will also receive a sealed packet containing documents that you must present to U.S. Customs and Border Protection (CBP) at a port-of-entry (often an airport) upon your arrival in the United States. You must not open the sealed packet.

When You Should Travel - You must arrive and apply for admission in the United States no later than the visa expiration date printed on your visa. A diversity visa is usually valid for up to six months from the date of issuance unless your medical examination expires sooner, which may make your visa valid for less than six months.

USCIS Immigrant Fee - You must pay the USCIS Immigrant Fee to U.S. Citizenship and Immigration Services (USCIS) after you receive your immigrant visa and before you travel to the United States. Only children who enter the United States under the Orphan or Hague adoption programs, Iraqi and Afghan special immigrants, returning residents (SB-1s), and those issued K visas are exempt from this fee. Select USCIS Immigrant Fee on the USCIS website for more information. Important Notice: USCIS will not issue a Permanent Resident Card (Form I-551 or Green Card) until you have paid the fee.

Vaccination Records - Children are required to have certain vaccinations before they can enroll in school in the United States. Therefore, it is recommended that your child have complete vaccination records before immigrating. Learn about vaccination requirements by state on the Department of Health and Human Services, Centers for Disease Control and Prevention website under State Vaccination Requirements.

X-rays - You must hand-carry your X-rays with you, not pack them in your luggage.

SECTION SEVEN

PREPARE FOR AN ENTRY AND EXIT INTERVIEW

Entering the United States

When traveling to the United States, the primary (or principal) applicant must enter before or at the same time as family members with visas. With your diversity visa (before it expires), and your sealed packet, you will travel to a U.S. port-of-entry (often an airport) and request permission to enter the United States. A visa does not guarantee entry into the United States. The Department of Homeland Security, U.S. Customs and Border Protection (CBP) officials have authority to grant or deny admission. Learn about admission and entry requirements on the CBP website under Travel.

If you are admitted, you will enter as a Lawful Permanent Resident, also called a green card holder, and will be permitted to work and live permanently in the United States.

When You are a Permanent Resident - Coming to the United States to live permanently, you will want to learn more about your status as a Lawful Permanent Resident. See Welcome to the United States: A Guide for New Immigrants to review information on the USCIS website about living in the United States.

Social Security Number - To learn about the U.S. Social Security Administration benefits available to Legal Permanent Residents, and how to apply for a social security number card, visit the Social Security Administration website.

About Visa Denials

- In some situations, the consular officer does not have sufficient information needed to process your application to conclusion, or you may be missing some supporting documentation. The consular officer will inform you if information or documents are missing and how to provide it.
- As noted above, some applications may require additional administrative processing after the interview before the application can be processed to conclusion. The consular officer will inform you if additional administrative processing is necessary.
- Based on U.S. law, not everyone who applies is qualified or eligible for a visa to come to the United States. Under U.S. law, many factors could make an applicant ineligible to receive a visa. See Ineligibilities for U.S. Visas. In some instances, the law might allow you to apply

for a waiver for the ineligibility. If you can apply for such a waiver, the consular officer will advise you on the steps to take.

Ineligibilities and Waivers: Laws

Overview

The Immigration and Nationality Act (INA) establishes the types of visas available for travel to the United States and what conditions must be met before an applicant can be issued a particular type of visa. The situations which make a visa applicant ineligible for a visa, called visa ineligibilities, are found in the INA, and other immigration laws. The INA also contains provisions for certain ineligible applicants to apply for waivers of their ineligibility.

When a visa applicant applies for a visa, a consular officer at a U.S. embassy or consulate outside the United States determines whether the applicant is qualified, under all applicable U.S. laws, to receive the visa applied for. Applicants found qualified are issued visas after all necessary processing is completed. However, when the consular officer determines that the applicant is ineligible to receive a visa, the visa application is denied. The applicant is informed verbally and in writing of the reason for denial based on the applicable section(s) of law.

Review Visa Denials for answers to questions about visa denials, ineligibility, discussion of several ineligibility examples, overcoming visa ineligibility, reapplying for a visa, and waivers of ineligibility.

Below are the sections of the INA for:

- Visa Ineligibilities
- Waivers of Ineligibility

Additionally, to view the INA in its entirety by title, chapter, and section, as well as other immigration-related laws, go to the U.S. Citizenship and Immigration Services (USCIS) website.

Visa Ineligibilities

Section 214(b) of the Immigration and Nationality Act

(b) Every alien (other than a nonimmigrant described in subparagraph (L) or (V) of section 101(a)(15), and other than a nonimmigrant described in any provision of section 101(a)(15)(H)(i) except subclause (b1) of such section) shall be presumed to be an immigrant until he establishes to the satisfaction of the consular officer, at the time of application for a visa, and the immigration officers, at the time of application for admission, that he is entitled to a nonimmigrant status under section 101(a)(15).

An alien who is an officer or employee of any foreign government or of any international organization entitled to enjoy privileges, exemptions, and immunities under the International Organizations Immunities Act, or an alien who is the attendant, servant, employee, or member of the immediate family of any such alien shall not be entitled to apply for or receive an immigrant visa, or to enter the United States as an immigrant unless he executes a written waiver in the same form and substance as is prescribed by section 247(b).

Section 221(g) of the Immigration and Nationality Act

(g) No visa or other documentation shall be issued to an alien if:

1. It appears to the consular officer, from statements in the application, or in the papers submitted therewith, that such alien is ineligible to receive a visa or such other documentation under section 212, or any other provision of law.
2. The application fails to comply with the provisions of this Act, or the regulations issued thereunder.
3. The consular officer knows or has reason to believe that such alien is ineligible to receive a visa or such other documentation under section 212, or any other provision of law.

Provided: A visa or other documentation may be issued to an alien who is within the purview of section 212(a)(4), if such alien is otherwise entitled to receive a visa or other documentation, upon receipt of notice by the consular officer from the Attorney General of the giving of a bond or undertaking providing indemnity as in the case of aliens admitted under section 213.

Further provided: A visa may be issued to an alien defined in section 101(a)(15)(B) or (F), if such alien is otherwise entitled to receive a visa, upon receipt of a notice by the consular officer from the Attorney General of the giving of a bond with sufficient surety in such sum and containing such conditions as the consular officer shall prescribe. This is to ensure that at the expiration of the time for which such alien has been admitted by the Attorney General, as provided in section 214(a), or upon failure to maintain the status under which he was admitted, or to maintain any status subsequently acquired under section 248 of the Act, such alien will depart from the United States.

Section 212(a) of the Immigration and Nationality Act

(a) Classes of Aliens Ineligible for Visas or Admission

Except as otherwise provided in this Act, aliens who are inadmissible under the following paragraphs are ineligible to receive visas and ineligible to be admitted to the United States:

(1) Health-related grounds

(A) In general: Any alien -

1. **Communicable Diseases**:
   - Who is determined (in accordance with regulations prescribed by the Secretary of Health and Human Services) to have a communicable disease of public health significance.
2. **Vaccination Requirements**:
   - Except as provided in subparagraph (C), seeks admission as an immigrant, or who seeks adjustment of status to the status of an alien lawfully admitted for permanent residence, and who has failed to present documentation of having received vaccination against vaccine-preventable diseases, which shall include at least the following:
     - Mumps
     - Measles
     - Rubella
     - Polio
     - Tetanus and diphtheria toxoids
     - Pertussis
     - Influenza type B
     - Hepatitis B
     - Any other vaccinations recommended by the Advisory Committee for Immunization Practices.
3. **Physical or Mental Disorders**:
   - Who is determined (in accordance with regulations prescribed by the Secretary of Health and Human Services in consultation with the Attorney General):
     - **(I)** To have a physical or mental disorder and behavior associated with the disorder that may pose, or has posed, a threat to the property, safety, or welfare of the alien or others.
     - **(II)** To have had a physical or mental disorder and a history of behavior associated with the disorder, which behavior has posed a threat to the property, safety, or welfare of the alien or others and which behavior is likely to recur or to lead to other harmful behavior.
4. **Drug Abuse or Addiction**:

- Who is determined (in accordance with regulations prescribed by the Secretary of Health and Human Services) to be a drug abuser or addict, is inadmissible.

(B) Waiver Authorized

For provisions authorizing the waiver of certain clauses of subparagraph (A), see subsection (g).

(C) Exception From Immunization Requirement for Adopted Children 10 Years of Age or Younger

Clause (ii) of subparagraph (A) shall not apply to a child who:

1. Is **10 years of age or younger**.
2. Is described in **section 101(b)(1)(F)**.
3. Is seeking an immigrant visa as an immediate relative under **section 201(b)** if, prior to the admission of the child, an adoptive parent or prospective adoptive parent of the child (who has sponsored the child for admission as an immediate relative) has executed an affidavit stating:
    - The parent is aware of the provisions of **subparagraph (A)(ii)**.
    - The parent will ensure that, within **30 days of the child's admission**, or at the earliest time that is medically appropriate, the child will receive the vaccinations identified in such subparagraph.

(2) Criminal and related grounds. -

(A) Conviction of Certain Crimes

(i) In General

Except as provided in clause (ii), any alien convicted of, or who admits having committed, or who admits committing acts which constitute the essential elements of:

- **(I)** A crime involving moral turpitude (other than a purely political offense) or an attempt or conspiracy to commit such a crime, or
- **(II)** A violation of (or a conspiracy or attempt to violate) any law or regulation of a State, the United States, or a foreign country relating to a controlled substance (as defined in section 102 of the Controlled Substances Act (21 U.S.C. 802)),

is inadmissible.

(ii) Exception

Clause (i)(I) shall not apply to an alien who committed only one crime if:

- **(I)** The crime was committed when the alien was under **18 years of age**, and the crime was committed (and the alien released from any confinement to a prison or correctional institution imposed for the crime) more than **5 years** before the date of application for a visa or other documentation and the date of application for admission to the United States, or

- **(II)** The maximum penalty possible for the crime of which the alien was convicted (or which the alien admits having committed or of which the acts that the alien admits having committed constituted the essential elements) did not exceed imprisonment for **one year**, and, if the alien was convicted of such crime, the alien was not sentenced to a term of imprisonment in excess of **6 months** (regardless of the extent to which the sentence was ultimately executed).

(B) Multiple Criminal Convictions

Any alien convicted of **2 or more offenses** (other than purely political offenses), regardless of whether the conviction was in a single trial or whether the offenses arose from a single scheme of misconduct and regardless of whether the offenses involved moral turpitude, for which the aggregate sentences to confinement were **5 years or more**, is inadmissible.

(C) Controlled Substance Traffickers

Any alien who the consular officer or the Attorney General knows or has reason to believe:

- **(i)** Is or has been an illicit trafficker in any controlled substance or in any listed chemical (as defined in section 102 of the Controlled Substances Act (21 U.S.C. 802)), or is or has been a knowing aider, abettor, assister, conspirator, or colluder with others in the illicit trafficking in any such controlled or listed substance or chemical, or endeavored to do so; or
- **(ii)** Is the **spouse, son, or daughter** of an alien inadmissible under clause (i), has, within the previous **5 years**, obtained any financial or other benefit from the illicit activity of that alien, and knew or reasonably should have known that the financial or other benefit was the product of such illicit activity,

is inadmissible.

(D) Prostitution and Commercialized Vice

Any alien who:

- **(i)** Is coming to the United States solely, principally, or incidentally to engage in prostitution, or has engaged in prostitution within **10 years** of the date of application for a visa, admission, or adjustment of status,
- **(ii)** Directly or indirectly procures or attempts to procure, or (within **10 years** of the date of application for a visa, admission, or adjustment of status) procured or attempted to procure or

to import, prostitutes or persons for the purpose of prostitution, or receives or (within such **10-year** period) received, in whole or in part, the proceeds of prostitution, or

- **(iii)** Is coming to the United States to engage in any other unlawful commercialized vice, whether related to prostitution,

is inadmissible.

(E) Certain Aliens Involved in Serious Criminal Activity Who Have Asserted Immunity from Prosecution

Any alien:

- **(i)** Who has committed in the United States at any time a **serious criminal offense** (as defined in section 101(h)),
- **(ii)** For whom immunity from criminal jurisdiction was exercised with respect to that offense,
- **(iii)** Who because of the offense and exercise of immunity has departed from the United States, and
- **(iv)** Who has not subsequently submitted fully to the jurisdiction of the court in the United States having jurisdiction with respect to that offense,

is inadmissible.

(F) Waiver Authorized

For provision authorizing waiver of certain subparagraphs of this paragraph, see subsection **(h)**.

(G) Foreign Government Officials Who Have Committed Particularly Severe Violations of Religious Freedom

Any alien who, while serving as a foreign government official, was responsible for or directly carried out, at any time, particularly severe violations of religious freedom, as defined in section 3 of the International Religious Freedom Act of 1998 (22 U.S.C. 6402), is inadmissible.

(H) Significant Traffickers in Persons

(i) In General

Any alien who commits or conspires to commit **human trafficking offenses** in the United States or outside the United States, or who the consular officer, the Secretary of Homeland Security, the Secretary of State, or the Attorney General knows or has reason to believe is or has been a knowing aider, abettor, assister, conspirator, or colluder with such a trafficker in severe forms of trafficking in persons, as defined in section 103 of such Act, is inadmissible.

(ii) Beneficiaries of Trafficking

Except as provided in clause (iii), any alien who the consular officer or the Attorney General knows or has reason to believe is the **spouse, son, or daughter** of an alien inadmissible under clause (i), has, within the previous **5 years**, obtained any financial or other benefit from the illicit activity of that alien, and knew or reasonably should have known that the financial or other benefit was the product of such illicit activity, is inadmissible.

(iii) Exceptions for Certain Sons and Daughters

Clause (ii) shall not apply to a **son or daughter** who was a **child** at the time he or she received the benefit described in such clause.

(I) Money Laundering

Any alien:

- **(i)** Who a consular officer or the Attorney General knows, or has reason to believe, has engaged, is engaging, or seeks to enter the United States to engage, in an offense which is described in section **1956** or **1957** of title 18, United States Code (relating to laundering of monetary instruments); or
- **(ii)** Who a consular officer or the Attorney General knows is, or has been, a knowing aider, abettor, assister, conspirator, or colluder with others in an offense which is described in such section,

is inadmissible.

(3) Security and Related Grounds. -

(A) In general. -Any alien who a consular officer or the Attorney General knows, or has reasonable ground to believe, seeks to enter the United States to engage solely, principally, or incidentally in-

(i) any activity (I) to violate any law of the United States relating to espionage or sabotage or (II) to violate or evade any law prohibiting the export from the United States of goods, technology, or sensitive information,

(ii) any other unlawful activity, or

(iii) any activity a purpose of which is the opposition to, or the control or overthrow of, the Government of the United States by force, violence, or other unlawful means, is inadmissible.

(B) Terrorist Activities-

(i) In general. -Any alien who-

(I) has engaged in a terrorist activity,

(II) a consular officer, the Attorney General, or the Secretary of Homeland Security knows, or has reasonable ground to believe, is engaged in or is likely to engage after entry in any terrorist activity (as defined in clause (iv)).

(III) has, under circumstances indicating an intention to cause death or serious bodily harm, incited terrorist activity.

(IV) is a representative (as defined in clause (v)) of--

(aa) a terrorist organization (as defined in clause (vi)); or

(bb) a political, social, or other group that endorses or espouses terrorist activity.

(V) is a member of a terrorist organization described in subclause (I) or (II) of clause (vi).

(VI) is a member of a terrorist organization described in clause (vi)(III), unless the alien can demonstrate by clear and convincing evidence that the alien did not know, and should not reasonably have known, that the organization was a terrorist organization.

(VII) endorses or espouses terrorist activity or persuades others to endorse or espouse terrorist activity or support a terrorist organization.

(VIII) has received military-type training (as defined in section 2339D(c)(1) of title 18, United States Code) from or on behalf of any organization that, at the time the training was received, was a terrorist organization (as defined in clause (vi)); or

(IX) is the spouse or child of an alien who is inadmissible under this subparagraph, if the activity causing the alien to be found inadmissible occurred within the last 5 years, is inadmissible.

(ii) Exceptions- Subclause (IX) of clause(i) does not apply to a spouse or child—

(I) who did not know or should not reasonably have known of the activity causing the alien to be found inadmissible under this section; or

(II) whom the consular officer or Attorney General has reasonable grounds to believe has renounced the activity causing the alien to be found inadmissible under this section.

(iii) Terrorist activity defined. -As used in this Act, the term terrorist activity means any activity which is unlawful under the laws of the place where it is committed (or which, if it had been committed in the United States, would be unlawful under the laws of the United States or any State) and which involves any of the following:

(I) The high jacking or sabotage of any conveyance (including an aircraft, vessel, or vehicle).

(II) The seizing or detaining, and threatening to kill, injure, or continue to detain, another individual to compel a third person (including a governmental organization) to do or abstain from doing any act as an explicit or implicit condition for the release of the individual seized or detained.

(III) A violent attack upon an internationally protected person (as defined in section 1116(b)(4) of title 18, United States Code) or upon the liberty of such a person.

(IV) An Assassination.

(V) The use of any-

(aa) biological agent, chemical agent, or nuclear weapon or device, or

(bb) explosives, firearms, or other weapons or dangerous device (other than for mere personal monetary gain), with intent to endanger, directly or indirectly, the safety of one or more individuals or to cause substantial damage to property.

(VI) A threat, attempt, or conspiracy to do any of the foregoing.

(iv) Engage In Terrorist activity defined- As used in this chapter, the term "engage in terrorist activity" means, in an individual capacity or as a member of an organization-

(I) to commit or to incite to commit, under circumstances indicating an intention to cause death or serious bodily injury, a terrorist activity.

(II) to prepare or plan a terrorist activity.

(III) to gather information on potential targets for terrorist activity.

(IV) to solicit funds or other things of value for--

(aa) a terrorist activity.

(bb) a terrorist organization described in clause (vi)(I) or (vi)(II); or

(cc) a terrorist organization described in clause (vi)(III), unless the solicitor can demonstrate by clear and convincing evidence that he did not know, and should not reasonably have known, that the organization was a terrorist organization.

(V) to solicit any individual--

(aa) to engage in conduct otherwise described in this subsection.

(bb) for membership in a terrorist organization described in clause (vi)(I) or (vi)(II); or

(cc) for membership in a terrorist organization described in clause (vi)(III) unless the solicitor can demonstrate by clear and convincing evidence that he did not know, and should not reasonably have known, that the organization was a terrorist organization; or

(VI) to commit an act that the actor knows, or reasonably should know, affords material support, including a safe house, transportation, communications, funds, transfer of funds or other material financial benefit, false documentation or identification, weapons (including chemical, biological, or radiological weapons), explosives, or training--

(aa) for the commission of a terrorist activity.

(bb) to any individual who the actor knows, or reasonably should know, has committed, or plans to commit a terrorist activity.

(cc) to a terrorist organization described in subclause (I) or (II) of clause (vi) or to any member of such an organization; or

(dd) to a terrorist organization described in clause (vi)(III), or to any member of such an organization, unless the actor can demonstrate by clear and convincing evidence that the actor did not know, and should not reasonably have known, that the organization was a terrorist organization.

(v) Representative defined. -As used in this paragraph, the term "representative" includes an officer, official, or spokesman of an organization, and any person who directs, counsels, commands, or induces an organization or its members to engage in terrorist activity.

(vi) Terrorist Organizations defined- As used in this section, the term 'terrorist organization' means an organization-

(I) designated under section 219.

(II) otherwise, designated, upon publication in the Federal Register, by the Secretary of State in consultation with or upon the request of the Attorney General or the Secretary of Homeland Security, as a terrorist organization, after finding that the organization engages in the activities described in subclauses (I) through (VI) of clause (iv); or

(III) that is a group of two or more individuals, whether organized or not, which engages in, or has a subgroup which engages in, the activities described in subclauses (I) through (VI) of clause (iv).

(C) Foreign Policy. -

(i) In general. -An alien whose entry or proposed activities in the United States the Secretary of State has reasonable ground to believe would have potentially serious adverse foreign policy consequences for the United States is inadmissible.

(ii) Exception for officials.-An alien who is an official of a foreign government or a purported government, or who is a candidate for election to a foreign government office during the period immediately preceding the election for that office, shall not be excludable or subject to restrictions or conditions on entry into the United States under clause (i) solely because of the alien's past, current, or expected beliefs, statements, or associations, if such beliefs, statements, or associations would be lawful within the United States.

(iii) Exception for other aliens.-An alien, not described in clause (ii), shall not be excludable or subject to restrictions or conditions on entry into the United States under clause (i) because of the alien's past, current, or expected beliefs, statements, or associations, if such beliefs, statements, or associations would be lawful within the United States, unless the Secretary of State personally determines that the alien's admission would compromise a compelling United States foreign policy interest.

(iv) Notification of determinations.-If a determination is made under clause (iii) with respect to an alien, the Secretary of State must notify on a timely basis the chairmen of the Committees on the Judiciary and Foreign Affairs of the House of Representatives and of the Committees on the Judiciary and Foreign Relations of the Senate of the identity of the alien and the reasons for the determination.

(D) Immigrant Membership in a Totalitarian Party. -

(i) In general. -Any immigrant who is or has been a member of or affiliated with the Communist or any other totalitarian party (or subdivision or affiliate thereof), domestic or foreign, is inadmissible.

(ii) Exception for involuntary membership.-Clause (i) shall not apply to an alien because of membership or affiliation if the alien establishes to the satisfaction of the consular officer when applying for a visa (or to the satisfaction of the Attorney General when applying for admission) that the membership or affiliation is or was involuntary, or is or was solely when under 16 years of age, by operation of law, or for purposes of obtaining employment, food rations, or other essentials of living and whether necessary for such purposes.

(iii) Exception for past membership. -Clause (i) shall not apply to an alien because of membership or affiliation if the alien establishes to the satisfaction of the consular officer when applying for a visa (or to the satisfaction of the Attorney General when applying for admission) that:-

(I) the membership or affiliation terminated at least-

(aa) 2 years before the date of such application, or

(bb) 5 years before the date of such application, in the case of an alien whose membership or affiliation was with the party controlling the government of a foreign state that is a totalitarian dictatorship as of such date, and

(II) the alien is not a threat to the security of the United States.

(iv) Exception for close family members.-The Attorney General may, in the Attorney General's discretion, waive the application of clause (i) in the case of an immigrant who is the parent, spouse, son, daughter, brother, or sister of a citizen of the United States or a spouse, son, or daughter of an alien lawfully admitted for permanent residence for humanitarian purposes, to assure family unity, or when it is otherwise in the public interest if the immigrant is not a threat to the security of the United

States.

(E) Participants In Nazi Persecutions, Genocide, Or the Commission of Any Act Of Torture Or Extra Judicial Killings

(i) Participation in nazi persecutions. -Any alien who, during the period beginning on March 23, 1933, and ending on May 8, 1945, under the direction of, or in association with-

(I) the Nazi government of Germany,

(II) any government in any area occupied by the military forces of the Nazi government of Germany,

(III) any government established with the assistance or cooperation of the Nazi government of Germany, or

(IV) any government which was an ally of the Nazi government of Germany, ordered, incited, assisted, or otherwise participated in the persecution of any person because of race, religion, national origin, or political opinion is inadmissible.

(ii) Participation in genocide. -Any alien who ordered, incited, assisted, or otherwise participated in genocide, as defined in section 1091(a) of title 18, United States Code, is inadmissible.

(iii) Commission Of Torture or Extra Judicial Killings- Any alien who, outside the United States, has committed, ordered, incited, assisted, or otherwise participated in the commission of--

(I) any act of torture, as defined in section 2340 of title 18, United States Code; or

(II) under color of law of any foreign nation, any extrajudicial killing, as defined in section 3(a) of the Torture Victim Protection Act of 1991 (28 U.S.C. 1350 note), is inadmissible.

(F) Association With Terrorist Organizations- Any alien who the Secretary of State, after consultation with the Attorney General, or the Attorney General, after consultation with the Secretary of State, determines has been associated with a terrorist organization and intends while in the United States to engage solely, principally, or incidentally in activities that could endanger the welfare, safety, or security of the United States is inadmissible.

(G) Recruitment Or Use of Child Soldiers- Any alien who has engaged in the recruitment or use of child soldiers in violation of section 2442 of title 18, United States Code, is inadmissible.

(4) Public Charge. -

(A) In general. -Any alien who, in the opinion of the consular officer at the time of application for a visa, or in the opinion of the Attorney General at the time of application for admission or adjustment of status, is likely at any time to become a public charge is inadmissible.

(B) Factors to be considered. -

(i) In determining whether an alien is excludable under this paragraph, the consular officer or the Attorney General shall at a minimum consider the alien's-

(I) age.

(II) health.

(III) family status.

(IV) assets, resources, and financial status; and

(V) education and skills

(ii) In addition to the factors under clause (i), the consular officer or the Attorney General may also consider any affidavit of support under section 213A for purposes of exclusion under this paragraph.

(C) Family-Sponsored immigrants. -Any alien who seeks admission or adjustment of status under a visa issued under section 201(b)(2) or 203(a) is excludable under this paragraph unless-

(i) the alien has obtained-

(I) status as a spouse or a child of a United States citizen pursuant to clause (ii), (iii), or (iv) or section 204(a)(1)(A), or

(II) classification pursuant to clause (ii) or (iii) of section 204(a)(1)(B);

(III) classification or status as a VAWA self-petitioner; or

(ii) the person petitioning for the alien's admission (and any additional sponsor required under section 213A(f) or any alternative sponsor permitted under paragraph (5)(B) of such section) has executed an affidavit of support described in section 213A with respect to such alien.

(D) Certain employment-based immigrants. -Any alien who seeks admission or adjustment of status under a visa number issued under section 203(b) by virtue of a classification petition filed by a relative of the alien (or by an entity in which such relative has a significant ownership interest) is excludable under this paragraph unless such relative has executed an affidavit of support described in section 213A with respect to such alien.

(5) Labor Certification and Qualifications for Certain Immigrants. -

A) Labor Certification. -

(i) In general. -Any alien who seeks to enter the United States for the purpose of performing skilled or unskilled labor is inadmissible, unless the Secretary of Labor has determined and certified to the Secretary of State and the Attorney General that-

(I) there are not sufficient workers who are able, willing, qualified (or equally qualified in the case of an alien described in clause (ii)) and available at the time of application for a visa and admission to the United States and at the place where the alien is to perform such skilled or unskilled labor, and (II) the employment of such alien will not adversely affect the wages and working conditions of workers in the United States similarly employed.

(ii) Certain aliens subject to special rule. -For purposes of clause (i)(I), an alien described in this clause is an alien who-

(I) is a member of the teaching profession, or

(II) has exceptional ability in the sciences or the arts.

(iii) Professional Athletes-

(I) In general. -A certification made under clause (i) with respect to a professional athlete shall remain valid with respect to the athlete after the athlete changes employer if the new employer is a team in the same sport as the team which employed the athlete when the athlete first applied for certification.

(II) Definition. -For purposes of subclause (I), the term "professional athlete" means an individual who is employed as an athlete by-

(aa) a team that is a member of an association of 6 or more professional sports teams whose total combined revenues exceed $10,000,000 per year, if the association governs the conduct of its members and regulates the contests and exhibitions in which its member teams regularly engage; or

(bb) any minor league team that is affiliated with such an association.

(iv) Long Delayed Adjustment Applicants- A certification made under clause (i) with respect to an individual whose petition is covered by section 204(j) shall remain valid with respect to a new job accepted by the individual after the individual changes jobs or employers if the new job is in the same or a similar occupational classification as the job for which the certification was issued.

(B) Unqualified Physicians.-An alien who is a graduate of a medical school not accredited by a body or bodies approved for the purpose by the Secretary of Education (regardless of whether such school of medicine is in the United States) and who is coming to the United States principally to perform services as a member of the medical profession is inadmissible, unless the alien (i) has passed parts I and II of the National Board of Medical Examiners Examination (or an equivalent examination as determined by the Secretary of Health and Human Services) and (ii) is competent in oral and written English.

For purposes of the previous sentence, an alien who is a graduate of a medical school shall be considered to have passed parts I and II of the National Board of Medical Examiners if the alien was fully and permanently licensed to practice medicine in a State on January 9, 1978, and was practicing medicine in a State on that date.

(C) Uncertified foreign health-care workers subject to subsection (r), any alien who seeks to enter the United States for the purpose of performing labor as a health-care worker, other than a physician, is excludable unless the alien presents to the consular officer, or, in the case of an adjustment of status, the Attorney General, a certificate from the Commission on Graduates of Foreign Nursing Schools, or a certificate from an equivalent independent credentialing organization approved by the Attorney General in consultation with the Secretary of Health and Human Services, verifying that-

(i) the alien's education, training, license, and experience-

(I) meet all applicable statutory and regulatory requirements for entry into the United States under the classification specified in the application.

(II) are comparable with that required for an American health-care worker of the same type; and

(III) are authentic and, in the case of a license, unencumbered.

(ii) the alien has the level of competence in oral and written English considered by the Secretary of Health and Human Services, in consultation with the Secretary of Education, to be appropriate for health care work of the kind in which the alien will be engaged, as shown by an appropriate score on one or more nationally recognized, commercially available, standardized assessments of the applicant's ability to speak and write; and

(iii) if most States licensing the profession in which the alien intends to work recognize a test predicting the success on the profession's licensing or certification examination, the alien has passed such a test, or has passed such an examination.

For purposes of clause (ii), determination of the standardized tests required and of the minimum scores that are appropriate are within the sole discretion of the Secretary of Health and Human Services and are not subject to further administrative or judicial review.

(D) Application of grounds. -The grounds of inadmissibility of aliens under subparagraphs (A) and (B) shall apply to immigrants seeking admission or adjustment of status under paragraph (2) or (3) of section 203(b).

(6) Illegal Entrants and Immigration Violators. -

(A) Aliens Present Without Admission or Parole. -

(i) In general. -An alien present in the United States without being admitted or paroled, or who arrives in the United States at any time or place other than as designated by the Attorney General, is inadmissible.

(ii) Exception for certain battered women and children. -Clause (i) shall not apply to an alien who demonstrates that-

The alien is a VAWA self-petitioner

What is the Meaning of VAWA? VAWA stands for Violence Against Women's Act. The act explains that if an alien is present in the US although is otherwise inadmissible even though the alien can demonstrate that he or she has been battered can apply for VAWA exemptions. Remember, all allegations are subject to verification through rigorous investigation.

(II)(a) the alien has been battered or subjected to extreme cruelty by a spouse or parent, or by a member of the spouse's or parent's family residing in the same household as the alien and the spouse or parent consented or acquiesced to such battery or cruelty, or (b) the alien's child has been battered or subjected to extreme cruelty by a spouse or parent of the alien (without the active participation of the alien in the battery or cruelty) or by a member of the spouse's or parent's family residing in the same household as the alien when the spouse or parent consented to or acquiesced in such battery or cruelty and the alien did not actively participate in such battery or cruelty, and

(III) there was a substantial connection between the battery or cruelty described in subclause (I) or (II) and the alien's unlawful entry into the United States.

(B) Failure to attend removal proceeding. -Any alien who without reasonable cause fails or refuses to attend or remain in attendance at a proceeding to determine the alien's inadmissibility or deportability and who seeks admission to the United States within 5 years of such alien's subsequent departure or removal is inadmissible.

(C) Misrepresentation. -

(i) In general. -Any alien who, by fraud or willfully misrepresenting a material fact, seeks to procure (or has sought to procure or has procured) a visa, other documentation, or admission into the United States or other benefit provided under this Act is inadmissible.

(ii) Falsely Claiming Citizenship-

(I) In general- Any alien who falsely represents, or has falsely represented, himself or herself to be a citizen of the United States for any purpose or benefit under this Act (including section 274A) or any other Federal or State law is inadmissible.

(II) Exception- In the case of an alien making a representation described in subclause (I), if each natural parent of the alien (or, in the case of an adopted alien, each adoptive parent of the alien) is or was a citizen (whether by birth or naturalization), the alien permanently resided in the United States prior to attaining the age of 16, and the alien reasonably believed at the time of making such representation that he or she was a citizen, the alien shall not be considered to be inadmissible under any provision of this subsection based on such representation.

(iii) Waiver authorized. -For provision authorizing waiver of clause (i), see subsection (I).

(D) Stowaways. -Any alien who is a stowaway is inadmissible.

(E) Smugglers. -

(i) In general. -Any alien who at any time knowingly has encouraged, induced, assisted, abetted, or aided any other alien to enter or to try to enter the United States in violation of law is inadmissible.

(ii) Special rule in the case of family reunification.-Clause (i) shall not apply in the case of alien who is an eligible immigrant (as defined in section 301(b)(1)of the Immigration Act of 1990), was physically present in the United States on May 5, 1988, and is seeking admission as an immediate relative or under section 203(a)(2) (including under section 112 of the Immigration Act of 1990) or benefits under section 301(a) of the Immigration Act of 1990 if the alien, before May 5, 1988, has encouraged, induced, assisted, abetted, or aided only the alien's spouse, parent, son, or daughter (and no other individual) to enter the United States in violation of law.

(iii) Waiver authorized. -For provision authorizing waiver of clause (i), see subsection (d)(11).

(F) Subject of civil penalty. -

(i) In general. -An alien who is the subject of a final order for violation of section 274C is inadmissible.

(ii) Waiver authorized. -For provision authorizing waiver of clause (i), see subsection (d)(12).

(G) Student visa abusers. -An alien who obtains the status of a nonimmigrant under section 101(a)(15)(F)(i) and who violates a term or condition of such status under section 214(l) is excludable until the alien has been outside the United States for a continuous period of 5 years after the date of the violation.

(7) Documentation requirements.

(A) Immigrants. -

(i) In general. -Except as otherwise specifically provided in this Act, any immigrant at the time of application for admission-

(I) who is not in possession of a valid unexpired immigrant visa, reentry permit, border crossing identification card, or other valid entry document required by this Act, and a valid unexpired passport, or other suitable travel document, or document of identity and nationality if such document is required under the regulations issued by the Attorney General under section 211(a), or

(II) whose visa has been issued without compliance with the provisions of section 203, is inadmissible.

(ii) Waiver authorized. -For provision authorizing waiver of clause (i), see subsection (k).

(B) Nonimmigrants

(i) In general. -Any nonimmigrant who-

(I) is not in possession of a passport valid for a minimum of six months from the date of the expiration of the initial period of the alien's admission or contemplated initial period of stay authorizing the alien to return to the country from which the alien came or to proceed to and enter some other country during such period, or

(II) is not in possession of a valid nonimmigrant visa or border crossing identification card at the time of application for admission, is inadmissible.

(ii) General waiver authorized. -For provision authorizing waiver of clause (i), see subsection (d)(4).

(iii)Guam and Northern Mariana Islands Visa Waiver- For provision authorizing waiver of clause (i) in the case of visitors to Guam or the Commonwealth of the Northern Mariana Islands, see subsection (l).

(iv) Visa Waiver Program. -For authority to waive the requirement of clause (i) under a program, see section 217.

(8) Ineligible for citizenship.

(A) In general. -Any immigrant who is permanently ineligible to citizenship is inadmissible.

(B) Draft evaders.-Any person who has departed from or who has remained outside the United States to avoid or evade training or service in the armed forces in time of war or a period declared by the President to be a national emergency is inadmissible, except that this subparagraph shall not apply to an alien who at the time of such departure was a nonimmigrant and who is seeking to reenter the United States as a nonimmigrant.

(9) Aliens Previously Removed

(A) Certain aliens previously removed.

(i) Arriving aliens.-Any alien who has been ordered removed under section 235(b)(1) or at the end of proceedings under section 240 initiated upon the alien's arrival in the United States and who again seeks admission within 5 years of the date of such removal (or within 20 years in the case of a second or subsequent removal or at any time in the case of an alien convicted of an aggravated felony) is inadmissible.

(ii) Other aliens. -Any alien not described in clause (i) who-

(I) has been ordered removed under section 240 or any other provision of law, or

(II) departed the United States while an order of removal was outstanding, and who seeks admission within 10 years of the date of such alien's departure or removal (or within 20 years of such date in the case of a second or subsequent removal or at any time in the case of an alien convicted of an aggravated felony) is inadmissible.

(iii) Exception. -Clauses (i) and (ii) shall not apply to an alien seeking admission within a period if, prior to the date of the alien's re-embarkation at a place outside the United States or attempt to be admitted from foreign contiguous territory, the Attorney General has consented to the alien's reapplying for admission.

(B) Aliens Unlawfully Present.

(i) In general. -Any alien (other than an alien lawfully admitted for permanent residence) who-

(I) was unlawfully present in the United States for a period of more than 180 days but less than 1 year, voluntarily departed the United States

(whether

or not pursuant to section 244(e)) prior to the commencement of proceedings under section 235(b)(1) or section 240, and again seeks admission within 3 years of the date of such alien's departure or removal, or

(II) has been unlawfully present in the United States for one year or more, and who again seeks admission within 10 years of the date of such alien's departure or removal from the United States, is inadmissible.

(ii) Construction of unlawful presence. -For purposes of this paragraph, an alien is deemed to be unlawfully present in the United States if the alien is present in the United States after the expiration of the period of stay authorized by the Attorney General or is present in the United States without being admitted or paroled.

(iii) Exceptions. -

(I) Minors. -No period in which an alien is under 18 years of age shall be considered in determining the period of unlawful presence in the United States under clause (I).

(II) Asylees. -No period in which an alien has a bona fide application for asylum pending under section 208 shall be considered in determining the period of unlawful presence in the United States under clause (i) unless the alien during such period was employed without authorization in the United States.

(III) Family unity. -No period in which the alien is a beneficiary of family unity protection pursuant to section 301 of the Immigration Act of 1990 shall be considered in determining the period of unlawful presence in the United States under clause (I).

(IV) Battered women and children. -Clause (i) shall not apply to an alien who would be described in paragraph (6)(A)(ii) "if violation of the terms of the alien's nonimmigrant visa" were substituted for "unlawful entry into the United States" in subclause (III) of that paragraph.

(V) Victims of a Severe Form of Trafficking in Persons- Clause (i) shall not apply to an alien who demonstrates that the severe form of trafficking (as that term is defined in section 103 of the Trafficking Victims Protection Act of 2000 (22 U.S.C. 7102)) was at least one central reason for the alien's unlawful presence in the United States.

(iv) Tolling for good cause. -In the case of an alien who-

(I) has been lawfully admitted or paroled into the United States,

(II) has filed a nonfrivolous application for a change or extension of status before the date of expiration of the period of stay authorized by the Attorney General, and

(III) has not been employed without authorization in the United States before or during the pendency of such application, the calculation of the period specified in clause (i)(I) shall be tolled during the pendency of such application, but not to exceed 120 days.

(v) Waiver.-The Attorney General has sole discretion to waive clause (i) in the case of an immigrant who is the spouse or son or daughter of a United States citizen or of an alien lawfully admitted for permanent residence, if it is established to the satisfaction of the Attorney General that the refusal of admission to such immigrant alien would result in extreme hardship to the citizen or lawfully resident spouse or parent of such alien.

No court shall have jurisdiction to review a decision or action by the Attorney General regarding a waiver under this clause.

(C) Aliens unlawfully present after previous immigration violations. -

(i) In general. -Any alien who-

(I) has been unlawfully present in the United States for an aggregate period of more than 1 year, or

(II) has been ordered removed under section 235(b)(1), section 240, or any other provision of law, and who enters or attempts to reenter the United States without being admitted is inadmissible.

(ii) Exception. -Clause (i) shall not apply to an alien seeking admission more than 10 years after the date of the alien's last departure from the United States if, prior to the alien's re-embarkation at a place outside the United States or attempt to be readmitted from a foreign contiguous territory, the Secretary of Homeland Security has consented to the alien's reapplying for admission.
(iii) Waiver- The Secretary of Homeland Security may waive the application of clause (i) in the case of an alien who is a VAWA self-petitioner if there is a connection between--
(I) the alien's battering or subjection to extreme cruelty; and
(II) the alien's removal, departure from the United States, reentry, or reentries into the United States; or attempted reentry into the United States.
(10) Miscellaneous
(A) Practicing polygamists. -Any immigrant who is coming to the United States to practice polygamy is inadmissible.
(B) Guardian required to accompany helpless alien. -Any alien-
(i) who is accompanying another alien who is inadmissible and who is certified to be helpless from sickness, mental or physical disability, or infancy pursuant to section 232(c), and
(ii) whose protection or guardianship is determined to be required by the alien described in clause (I), is inadmissible.
(C) International child abduction. -
(i) In general.-Except as provided in clause (ii), any alien who, after entry of an order by a court in the United States granting custody to a person of a United States citizen child who detains or retains the child, or withholds custody of the child, outside the United States from the person granted custody by that order, is inadmissible until the child is surrendered to the person granted custody by that order.
(ii) Aliens Supporting Abductors and Relatives of Abductors. -- Any alien who--
(I) is known by the Secretary of State to have intentionally assisted an alien in the conduct described in clause (i),
(II) is known by the Secretary of State to be intentionally providing material support or haven to an alien described in clause (i), or
(III) is a spouse (other than the spouse who is the parent of the abducted child), child (other than the abducted child), parent, sibling, or agent of an alien described in clause (i), if such person has been designated by the Secretary of State at the Secretary's sole and unreviewable discretion, is inadmissible until the child described in clause (ii) is surrendered to the person granted custody by

the order described in that clause, and such person and child are permitted to return to the United States or such person's place of residence.

(iii) Exceptions. -- Clauses (i) and (ii) shall not apply--

(I) to a government official of the United States who is acting within the scope of his or her official duties.

(II) to a government official of any foreign government if the official has been designated by the Secretary of State at the Secretary's sole and unreviewable discretion; or

(III) so long as the child is in a foreign state that is a party to the Convention on the Civil Aspects of International Child Abduction, done at The Hague on October 25, 1980.

(D) Unlawful Voters-

(i) In General- Any alien who has voted in violation of any Federal, State, or local constitutional provision, statute, ordinance, or regulation is inadmissible.

(ii) Exception- In the case of an alien who voted in a Federal, State, or local election (including an initiative, recall, or referendum) in violation of a lawful restriction of voting to citizens, if each natural parent of the alien (or, in the case of an adopted alien, each adoptive parent of the alien) is or was a citizen (whether by birth or naturalization), the alien permanently resided in the United States prior to attaining the age of 16, and the alien reasonably believed at the time of such violation that he or she was a citizen, the alien shall not be considered to be inadmissible under any provision of this subsection based on such violation.

(E) Former citizens who renounced citizenship to avoid taxation. -Any alien who is a former citizen of the United States who officially renounces United States citizenship and who is determined by the Attorney General to have renounced United States citizenship for the purpose of avoiding taxation by the United States is excludable.

Waivers of Ineligibility

If you are ineligible for a visa based on one or more of the laws listed in Section 212(a) of the Immigration and Nationality Act, you may be able to apply for a waiver. The visa category that you are applying for will determine whether a waiver of ineligibility is available. The consular officer interviewing you will tell you if you may apply for a waiver and will provide detailed instructions for how to apply.

Waivers of Ineligibility are contained in the following sections of law in the Immigration and Nationality Act:

Section 212(d) of the Immigration and Nationality Act

(d)(1) The Attorney General shall determine whether a ground for exclusion exists with respect to a nonimmigrant described in section 101(a)(15)(S). The Attorney General, in the Attorney General's discretion, may waive the application of subsection (a) (other than paragraph (3)(E)) in the case of a nonimmigrant described in section 101(a)(15)(S) if the Attorney General considers it to be in the national interest to do so. Nothing in this section shall be regarded as prohibiting the Immigration Service from instituting removal proceedings against an alien admitted as a nonimmigrant under section 101(a)(15)(S) for conduct committed after the alien's admission into the United States, or for conduct or a condition that was not disclosed to the Attorney General prior to the alien's admission as a nonimmigrant under section 101(a)(15)(S).

(2) repealed.

(3)(A) Except as provided in this subsection, an alien (i) who is applying for a nonimmigrant visa and is known or believed by the consular officer to be ineligible for such visa under subsection (a) (other than paragraphs (3)(A)(i)(I), (3)(A)(ii), (3)(A)(iii), (3)(C), and clauses (i) and (ii) of paragraph (3)(E) of such subsection), may, after approval by the Attorney General of a recommendation by the Secretary of State or by the consular officer that the alien be admitted temporarily despite his inadmissibility, be granted such a visa and may be admitted into the United States temporarily as a nonimmigrant in the discretion of the Attorney General, or (ii) who is inadmissible under subsection (a) (other than paragraphs (3)(A)(i)(I), (3)(A)(ii), (3)(A)(iii), (3)(C), and clauses (i) and (ii) of paragraph (3)(E) of such subsection), but who is in possession of appropriate documents or is granted a waiver thereof and is seeking admission, may be admitted into the United States temporarily as a nonimmigrant in the discretion of the Attorney General.

The Attorney General shall prescribe conditions, including the exaction of such bonds as may be necessary, to control and regulate the admission and return of inadmissible aliens applying for temporary admission under this paragraph.

(B)(i) The Secretary of State, after consultation with the Attorney General and the Secretary of Homeland Security, or the Secretary of Homeland Security, after consultation with the Secretary of State and the Attorney General, may determine in such Secretary's sole unreviewable discretion that subsection (a)(3)(B)

Shall not apply with respect to an alien within the scope of that subsection or that subsection (a)(3)(B)(vi)(III) shall not apply to a group within the scope of that subsection, except that no such waiver may be extended to an alien who is within the scope of subsection (a)(3)(B)(i)(II), no such waiver may be extended to an alien who is a member or representative of, has voluntarily and knowingly engaged in or endorsed or espoused or persuaded others to endorse or espouse or support terrorist activity on behalf of, or has voluntarily and knowingly received military-type training from a terrorist organization that is described in subclause (I) or (II) of subsection (a)(3)(B)(vi), and no such waiver may be extended to a group that has engaged terrorist activity against the United States or another democratic country or that has purposefully engaged in a pattern or practice of terrorist activity that is directed at civilians.

"Such a determination shall neither prejudice the ability of the United States Government to commence criminal or civil proceedings involving a beneficiary of such a determination or any other person, nor create any substantive or procedural right or benefit for a beneficiary of such a determination or any other person". Subsection (a)(3).

Notwithstanding any other provision of law (statutory or non-statutory), including section 2241 of title 28, or any other habeas corpus provision, and sections 1361 and 1651 of such title, no court shall have jurisdiction to review such a determination or revocation except in a proceeding for review of a final order of removal pursuant to section 1252 of this title, and review shall be limited to the extent provided in section 1252(a)(2)(D).

The Secretary of State may not exercise the discretion provided in this clause with respect to an alien at any time during which the alien is the subject of pending removal proceedings under section 1229a of this title.

(ii) Not later than 90 days after the end of each fiscal year, the Secretary of State and the Secretary of Homeland Security shall each provide to the Committees on the Judiciary of the House of Representatives and of the Senate, the Committee on International Relations of the House of Representatives, the Committee on Foreign Relations of the Senate, and the Committee on Homeland Security of the House of Representatives a report on the aliens to whom such Secretary has applied clause (i). Within one week of applying clause (i) to a group, the Secretary of State or the Secretary of Homeland Security shall provide a report to such Committees.

(4) Either or both requirements of paragraph (7)(B)(i) of subsection (a) may be waived by the Attorney General and the Secretary of State acting jointly

(A) Based on unforeseen emergency in individual cases, or

(B) Based on reciprocity with respect to nationals of foreign contiguous territory or of adjacent islands and residents thereof having a common nationality with such nationals, or

(C) in the case of aliens proceeding in immediate and continuous transit through the United States under contracts authorized in section 238(c).

(5)(A) The Attorney General may, except as provided in subparagraph (B) or in section 214(f), in his discretion parole into the United States temporarily under such conditions as he may prescribe only on a case-by-case basis for urgent humanitarian reasons or significant public benefit any alien applying for admission to the United States, but such parole of such alien shall not be regarded as an admission of the alien and when the purposes of such parole shall, in the opinion of the Attorney General, have been served the alien shall forthwith return or be returned to the custody from which he was paroled and thereafter his case shall continue to be dealt with in the same manner as that of any other applicant for admission to the United States.

(B) The Attorney General may not parole into the United States an alien who is a refugee unless the Attorney General determines that compelling reasons in the public interest with respect to that alien require that the alien be paroled into the United States rather than be admitted as a refugee under section 207

.

(6) repealed.

(7) The provisions of subsection (a) (other than paragraph (7)) shall be applicable to any alien who shall leave Guam, the Commonwealth of the Northern Mariana Islands, Puerto Rico, or the Virgin Islands of the United States, and who seeks to enter the continental United States or any other place under the jurisdiction of the United States. Any alien described in this paragraph, who is denied admission to the United States, shall be immediately removed in the manner provided by section 241(c) of this Act.

(8) Upon a basis of reciprocity accredited officials of foreign governments, their immediate families, attendants, servants, and personal employees may be admitted in immediate and continuous transit through the United States without regard to the provisions of this section except paragraphs (3)(A), (3)(B), (3)(C), and (7)(B) of subsection (a) of this section.

(9) repealed.

(10) repealed.

(11) The Attorney General may, in his discretion for humanitarian purposes, to assure family unity, or when it is otherwise in the public interest, waive application of clause (i) of subsection (a)(6)(E) in the case of any alien lawfully admitted for permanent residence who temporarily proceeded abroad voluntarily and not under an order of removal, and who is otherwise admissible to the United States as a returning resident under section 211(b) and in the case of an alien seeking admission or adjustment of status as an immediate relative or immigrant under section 203(a) (other than paragraph (4) thereof), if the alien has encouraged, induced, assisted, abetted, or aided only an individual who at the time of the offense was the alien's spouse, parent, son, or daughter (and no other individual) to enter the United States in violation of law.

(12) The Attorney General may, in the discretion of the Attorney General for humanitarian purposes or to assure family unity, waive application of clause (i) of subsection (a)(6)(F)-

(A) in the case of an alien lawfully admitted for permanent residence who temporarily proceeded abroad voluntarily and not under an order of deportation or removal and who is otherwise admissible to the United States as a returning resident under section 211(b), and

(B) in the case of an alien seeking admission or adjustment of status under section 201(b)(2)(A) or under section 203(a), if no previous civil money penalty was imposed against the alien under section 274C and the offense was committed solely to assist, aid, or support the alien's spouse or child (and not another individual). No court shall have jurisdiction to review a decision of the Attorney General to grant or deny a waiver under this paragraph.

(13)(A) The Secretary of Homeland Security shall determine whether a ground for inadmissibility exists with respect to a nonimmigrant described in section 101(a)(15)(T), except

that the ground for inadmissibility described in subsection (a)(4) shall not apply with respect to such a nonimmigrant.

(B) In addition to any other waiver that may be available under this section, in the case of a nonimmigrant described in section 101(a)(15)(T), if the Secretary of Homeland Security considers it to be in the national interest to do so, the Secretary of Homeland Security, in the Secretary of Homeland Security's discretion, may waive the application of--

(i) subsection (a)(1); and

(ii) any other provision of subsection (a) (excluding paragraphs (3), (4), (10)(C), and (10(E)) if the activities rendering the alien inadmissible under the provision were caused by, or were incident to, the victimization described in section 101(a)(15)(T)(i)(I).

(14) The Secretary of Homeland Security shall determine whether a ground of inadmissibility exists with respect to a nonimmigrant described in section 101(a)(15)(U). The Secretary of Homeland

Security, in the Secretary of Homeland Security's discretion, may waive the application of subsection (a) (other than paragraph (3)(E)) in the case of a nonimmigrant described in section 101(a)(15)(U), if the Secretary of Homeland Security considers it to be in the public or national interest to do so.

Section 212(g) of the Immigration and Nationality Act

(g) The Attorney General may waive the application of-

(1) subsection (a)(1)(A)(i) in the case of any alien who-

(A) is the spouse or the unmarried son or daughter, or the minor unmarried lawfully adopted child, of a United States citizen, or of an alien lawfully admitted for permanent residence, or of an alien who has been issued an immigrant visa,

(B) has a son or daughter who is a United States citizen, or an alien lawfully admitted for permanent residence, or an alien who has been issued an immigrant visa; in accordance with such terms, conditions, and controls, if any, including the giving of bond, as the Attorney General, in the discretion of the Attorney General after consultation with the Secretary of Health and Human Services, may by regulation prescribe; or

(C) is a VAWA self-petitioner,

(2) subsection (a)(1)(A)(ii) in the case of any alien-

(A) who receives vaccination against the vaccine-preventable disease or diseases for which the alien has failed to present documentation of previous vaccination,

(B) for whom a civil surgeon, medical officer, or panel physician (as those terms are defined by section 34.2 of title 42 of the Code of Federal Regulations) certifies according to such regulations as the Secretary of Health and Human Services may prescribe, that such vaccination would not be medically appropriate, or

(C) under such circumstances as the Attorney General provides by regulation, with respect to whom the requirement of such a vaccination would be contrary to the alien's religious beliefs or moral convictions; or

(3) subsection (a)(1)(A)(iii) in the case of any alien, in accordance with such terms, conditions, and controls, if any, including the giving of bond, as the Attorney General, in the discretion of the Attorney General after consultation with the Secretary of Health and Human Services, may by regulation prescribe.

Section 212(h) of the Immigration and Nationality Act

(h) The Attorney General may, in his discretion, waive the application of subparagraphs (A)(i)(I),

(B), (D), and (E) of subsection (a)(2) and subparagraph (A)(i)(II) of such subsection insofar as it relates to a single offense of simple possession of 30 grams or less of marijuana if-

(1)(A) in the case of any immigrant it is established to the satisfaction of the Attorney General that-

(i) the alien is inadmissible only under subparagraph (D)(i) or (D)(ii) of such subsection or the activities for which the alien is inadmissible occurred more than 15 years before the date of the alien's application for a visa, admission, or adjustment of status.

(ii) the admission to the United States of such alien would not be contrary to the national welfare, safety, or security of the United States, and

(iii) the alien has been rehabilitated; or

(B) in the case of an immigrant who is the spouse, parent, son, or daughter of a citizen of the United States, or an alien lawfully admitted for permanent residence if it is established to the satisfaction of the Attorney General that the alien's denial of admission would result in extreme hardship to the United States citizen or lawfully resident spouse, parent, son, or daughter of such alien; or

(C) the alien is a VAWA self-petitioner; and

(2) the Attorney General, in his discretion, and pursuant to such terms, conditions and procedures as he may by regulations prescribe, has consented to the alien's applying or reapplying for a visa, for admission to the United States, or adjustment of status.

No waiver shall be provided under this subsection in the case of an alien who has been convicted of (or who has admitted committing acts that constitute) murder or criminal acts involving torture, or an attempt or conspiracy to commit murder or a criminal act involving torture.

No waiver shall be granted under this subsection in the case of an alien who has previously been admitted to the United States as an alien lawfully admitted for permanent residence if either since the date of such admission the alien has been convicted of an aggravated felony or the alien has not lawfully resided continuously in the United States for a period of not less than 7 years immediately preceding the date of initiation of proceedings to remove the alien from the United States. No court shall have jurisdiction to review a decision of the Attorney General to grant or deny a waiver under this subsection.

Section 212(i) of the Immigration and Nationality Act

(i)(1) The Attorney General may, in the discretion of the Attorney General, waive the application of clause (i) of subsection (a)(6)(C) in the case of an immigrant who is the spouse, son, or daughter of a United States citizen or of an alien lawfully admitted for permanent residence, if it is established to the satisfaction of the Attorney General that the refusal of admission to the United States of such immigrant alien would result in extreme hardship to the citizen or lawfully resident spouse or parent of such an alien or, in the case of a VAWA self-petitioner, the alien demonstrates extreme hardship to the alien or the alien's United States citizen, lawful permanent resident, or qualified alien parent or child.

(2) No court shall have jurisdiction to review a decision or action of the Attorney General regarding a waiver under paragraph (1).

Fraud Warning

Diversity Visa

Program Scammers Sending Fraudulent Emails and Letters

The Department of State, Office of Visa Services, advises the public of a notable increase in fraudulent emails and letters sent to Diversity Visa (DV) program (Visa Lottery) applicants. The scammers behind these fraudulent emails and letters are posing as the U.S. government to extract payment from DV applicants. All applicants should be familiar with information about DV scams provided by the Federal Trade Commission. Applicants are encouraged to review the rules and procedures for the DV program so that you know what to expect, when to expect it, and from whom.

While DV applicants may receive an email from the U.S. government reminding them to check their status online through DV Entrant Status Check, they will not receive a notification letter or email informing them that they are a successful DV entrant. Applicants can only find out if they were selected to continue with DV processing by checking their status online through the DV Entrant Status Check at https://dvprogram.state.gov.

Finally, remember that fees for the DV application process are paid to the U.S. Embassy or consulate cashier at the time of your scheduled appointment. The U.S. government will never ask you to send payment in advance by check, money order, or wire transfer.

Anti-Fraud Tips for Applicants

When entering the U.S. Diversity Visa Lottery, the most basic way to ensure you are not scammed or your entry is not disqualified is to read and follow the instructions at the Diversity Visa Program page on travel.state.gov. Just as important is to be honest! Entering fake information or submitting fake documents may disqualify your entry or even keep you from ever going to the United States.

If possible, fill out the form yourself. If you need help, make sure the person helping you is entering your true information. Avoid visa consultants who offer to improve your chances by adding false information to your application. False information can disqualify you. Also avoid visa consultants who charge upfront money because they claim they can improve your chances of winning. The facts are that consultants of any stripe may or may not improve your chances of being selected for interview; but at least, you may learn a thing or two from their professional experiences. Obtaining a visa is entirely up to you and the work you put into achieving your goals.

When entering, use your own e-mail address and make sure you keep the entry confirmation number. You will need the entry confirmation number to check the results to see if you have been selected. If someone is helping you to apply, make sure they give you the entry confirmation number. A free email account can be set up from a computer or smartphone if you don't have one.

Only submit one entry per eligible person. If you are entered more than once, you will be disqualified.

Make sure your photo was taken in the last six months. Photos more than six months old will be disqualified.

If you are selected to apply for a visa, do not add any person who is not legally your spouse or child to your visa application. Doing so may disqualify you and may keep you from ever going to the United States. If you are selected and have been pressured by a visa consultant

to add people to your application who are not your legal family members, immediately inform the Consular Officer at your interview.

Visa Related Fraud Information - Refer to these frequently asked questions.

Some Questions you might prefer some answers to may be:

How do I know if a website or email is from the U.S government?

Internet sites ending in the ".gov" top-level domain suffix are official government websites. To link directly to the more than 200 U.S. Embassy and Consulate websites,

visit www.usembassy.gov. Visa information on official U.S. government websites ending in ".gov" is official and correct. Official U.S. government email addresses also end in ".gov," and any visa-related correspondence coming from an address that does not end with ".gov" should be considered suspect. Always cross-check with the United States' government websites for credible information.

To avoid running afoul of the US immigration systems and laws-even if you are already in the US, please, consult an attorney. Below are a few helpful websites to gather more information.

The main U.S. government websites containing official visa and immigration information, including free information and forms, are:

U.S. Embassy and Consulate websites:
Department of State, Consular Affairs travel website:
Department of State, Diversity Visa Program website:
Department of Homeland Security (DHS):
DHS, U.S. Citizenship, and Immigration Services:
DHS, U.S. Customs and Border Protection:
DHS, Immigration and Customs Enforcement:
Department of Labor:
http://www.usembassy.gov/
http://travel.state.gov
https://dvprogram.state.gov
http://www.dhs.gov
http://www.uscis.gov
http://www.cbp.gov
http://www.ice.gov
http://www.doleta.gov

Is Immigration Information on Other Websites Official?

Many other non-governmental websites (e.g., addresses ending with ".com," ".org" or ".net") provide legitimate and useful immigration and visa-related information and services. Regardless of the content of other websites, the Department of State does not endorse, recommend, or sponsor any information or material shown on these other websites.

The information provided may not be correct or up to date, so should always be verified by consulting an official U.S. government source. Visa applicants are advised to be cautious in all dealings with companies that claim to offer any assistance in obtaining U.S. visas.

How Do I Recognize Fraudulent Websites and Emails?

Some websites and emails try to mislead customers and members of the public into thinking they are official U.S. government websites. These websites are designed to appear official, and often have images of the U.S. flag, U.S. Capitol, White House, or Statue of Liberty. What these websites and emails are missing is the **".gov"** suffix on their addresses.

Remember that anything that does not end with **".gov"** should be considered suspect.

What is the Purpose of These Fraudulent Websites and Emails?

Some of these fraudulent organizations may require payment for immigration and visa services. Note, if payment is made to a non-governmental source, this payment is not received by the U.S. government and does not apply toward visa processing.

Sometimes these costs are for information or forms that are otherwise available for **free** on official U.S. government websites. Additionally, these imposter websites and emails cannot provide the services they advertise and for which they require payment. For example, many fraudulent emails promise U.S. visas or **"green cards"** in return for a large fee.

These non-governmental, unofficial organizations are not able to provide these services. These services can only be obtained from official U.S. government entities, such as:

- The Department of State
- A U.S. embassy or consulate
- The Department of Homeland Security

Finally, be wary of providing any **personal information** through these fraudulent websites and emails, since such action could result in **identity fraud** or **theft**. Visa applicants are strongly advised to be cautious in all dealings with non-governmental companies that claim to offer any assistance in obtaining U.S. visas.

Where Do I Get Official Information on the Diversity Visa Program and How Do I Check My Status?

The only official information about the DV program is found on U.S. government websites ending in **".gov"**, such as:

- http://travel.state.gov
- https://dvprogram.state.gov

The only official way to apply for the DV program is directly through the **official U.S. Department of State website** during the specified and limited registration period.

DV program entrants must check the status of their DV lottery entry online at:

☞ https://dvprogram.state.gov

to find out if they were selected or not. The U.S. Department of State Kentucky Consular Center does not mail or email notifications to DV entrants informing them of their winning entries.

For more information about the Diversity Visa program and the process, review the **Department of State Diversity Visa Program** webpage.

No other organization or private company is authorized to notify DV applicants of their winning entries or the next steps in the process. Imposters frequently contact DV applicants to extract money or personal information through websites, emails, and letters.

Entrants should only refer to:

- The online status check at https://dvprogram.state.gov
- Instructions on the Diversity Visa Program webpage

for **official information** about the DV process.

Where Can I Find Information on International Financial Scams?

For more information about international scams involving:

- Internet dating
- Inheritance
- Work permits
- Overpayment
- Money laundering

please visit the **International Financial Scams** page.

How Do I Report Internet Fraud or Unsolicited Email?

If you wish to file a complaint about **internet fraud**, please visit:

- econsumer.gov — a joint effort of consumer protection agencies from **17 nations**, hosted by the Federal Trade Commission.
- The **Federal Bureau of Investigation (FBI)** Internet Crime Complaint Center (**IC3**) website.

To file a complaint about **unsolicited email**, contact the **Department of Justice**.

Visa Types

What Types of Visas Are Available for People to Come to the United States?

According to the **U.S. government's websites**, there are more than **20 nonimmigrant visa types** for people traveling to the United States temporarily. There are many more types of **immigrant visas** for those coming to live permanently in the United States.

However, for the sake of clarity in preparing this guide, we have grouped all the various visa types into a manageable number—**26**, following the **26 letters of the English alphabet**.

The type of visa you need is determined by the **purpose of your intended travel**.

For an overview of visa types, please see:

- **Types of Visas for Temporary Visitors**

- **Visa Types for Immigrants**

After Visa Issuance, What Next?

How Do I Read and Understand My Visa?

Please use the illustrated guide below to learn how to read your new **nonimmigrant visa** (for travel to the U.S. as a temporary visitor).

In addition, as soon as you receive it, check to make sure the information printed on the visa is **correct** (see below).

If any of the information on your visa does not match the information in your **passport** or is **incorrect**, please contact the **nonimmigrant visa section** at the embassy or consulate that issued your visa.

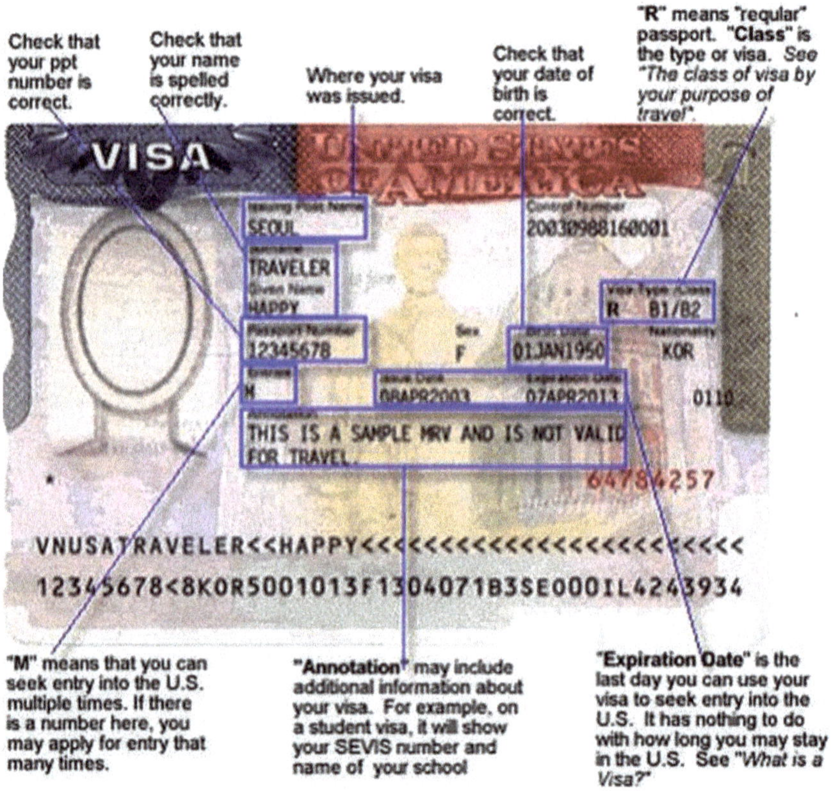

Persons holding visas valid for multiple entries may make repeated trips to the United States, for travel for the same purpose, if the visa has not expired, and the traveler has done nothing to become ineligible to enter the United States, at port-of-entry.

Visa Validity

My old passport has already expired. My visa to travel to the United States is still valid but in my expired passport. Do I need to apply for a new visa with my new passport?

No. If your visa is still valid you can travel to the United States with your two passports, if the visa is valid, not damaged, and is the appropriate type of visa required for your principal purpose of travel.

(Example: tourist visa when your principal purpose of travel is tourism).

Both passports (the valid and the expired one with the visa) should be from the same country and type (Example: both Uruguayan regular passports, both official passports, etc.). When you arrive at the U.S. port-of-entry (POE, generally an airport or land border) the Customs and Border Protection Immigration Officer will check your visa in the old passport and if s/he decides to admit you into the United States they will stamp your new passport with an admission stamp along with the annotation "VIOPP" (visa in another passport).

Do not try to remove the visa from your old passport and stick it into the new valid passport. If you do so, your visa will no longer be valid. This act may be interpreted as forgery.

My visa will expire while I am in the United States. Is there a problem with that?

No. If the Department of Homeland Security, Customs and Border Protection Immigration Officer at the port-of-entry admitted you into the United States for a specific period, s/he will note your authorized period of stay on your admission stamp or paper Form I-94, called an Arrival/Departure Record.

You will be able to remain in the United States during your authorized period of stay, even if your visa expires during the time, you are in the United States. Since your admission stamp or paper Form I-94 documents your authorized stay and is the official record of your permission to be in the United States, it is very important to keep inside your passport.

What are indefinite validity visas (Burroughs visas) and are they still valid?

Indefinite validity visas (Burroughs Visas) are tourist/business visas manually stamped into a traveler's passport which were valid for ten years. Effective April 1, 2004, all indefinite validity Burroughs

visas became void. Therefore, if you have an indefinite validity visa you must apply for a new visa for travel to the U.S.

Administrative Processing

What is Administrative Processing?

Some visa applications require further administrative processing, which takes additional time after the visa applicant's interview by a consular officer. Applicants are advised of this requirement when they apply.

Visa Denials

My visa application has been refused. Why can't I get my money back?

The fee that you paid is an application fee. Everyone who applies for a U.S. visa anywhere in the world must pay this fee, which covers the cost of processing your application. This fee is non-refundable regardless of whether you are issued a visa or not since your application was processed to conclusion.

As one example, if your application was refused under Section 214(b) and you choose to reapply for a visa, whether applying at the same embassy or elsewhere, you will be required to pay the visa application processing fee. See the Fees for Visa Services page for a list of fees.

Renewals

I have a nonimmigrant visa that will expire soon, and I would like to renew it. Do I need go through the whole visa application process again?

Yes, you will have to go through the whole visa application process each time you want to apply for a visa, even if your visa is still valid. There are some situations where a visa applicant may not need to be interviewed when renewing his/her visa. See the U.S. Embassy or Consulate website for more information.

My immigrant visa expired before I was able to travel to the United States. What should I do?

You should contact the Immigrant Visa Unit of the U.S. Embassy or Consulate that issued your visa. You do not need to file a new petition with USCIS, but you may need to submit a new application (DS-260) and pay another immigrant visa application processing fee. In addition, you may need to submit new supporting documents, such as a new medical examination and

police certificate. Please be prepared to return your unused, expired visa and visa package (if applicable).

Requests to reissue or replace visas are considered on a case-by-case basis, and all applicants are required to re-establish their eligibility; there is no guarantee that you will receive a new visa.

Entering and Departing the United States

After I have my visa, I will be able to enter the U.S., correct?

Not correct. A visa does not guarantee entry into the United States. A visa allows a foreign citizen to travel to the U.S. port-of-entry, and the Department of Homeland Security U.S. Customs and Border Protection (CBP) immigration inspector authorizes or denies admission to the United States. See Admissions on the CBP website.

How can I find out how long I am authorized to stay in the United States?

A visa does not guarantee entry into the United States, but allows a foreign citizen coming from abroad, to travel to the United States port-of entry (generally an airport or land border) and request permission to enter the United States. The Department of Homeland Security, U.S. Customs and Border Protection (CBP) officials have authority to permit or deny admission to the United States and determine how long a traveler may stay.

At the port of entry, upon granting entry to the United States, the Department of Homeland Security, U.S. immigration inspector, provides you an admission stamp or paper Form I-94, Arrival/Departure Record in your passport. On this admission stamp or paper Form I-94, the U.S. immigration inspector records either a date or "D/S" (duration of status).

If your admission stamp or paper Form I-94 contains a specific date, then that is the date by which you must leave the United States. Your admission stamp or paper Form I-94 is very important to keep in your passport, since it shows your permission to be in the United States. Review information about Admission on the CBP Website. Also, see Duration of Stay.

I did not turn in my paper Form I-94 when I left the United States, what should I do?

If you failed to turn in your paper Form I-94 Departure Record, see Department of Homeland Security, Customs and Border Protection website for more information.

Lost and Stolen Visas

My passport with my visa was stolen, what should I do?

If your passport with your admission stamp or paper Form I-94 is lost or stolen, you must get them replaced immediately. There are a number of steps you need to take, learn more,

see Lost and Stolen Passports, Visas, and Form I-94s.

My visa was damaged. What should I do?

If your visa has been damaged in any way, you will need to reapply for a new visa at a U.S. Embassy or Consulate abroad.

U.S. Citizens

I may have a claim to U.S. citizenship. Can I apply for a U.S. visa?

With few exceptions, a person born in the United States acquires U.S. citizenship at birth. A state-issued birth certificate serves as evidence of citizenship. Review the Apply for a

Passport webpage to learn more.

Persons born in countries other than the United States may have a claim to U.S. citizenship if either parent is a U.S. citizen under U.S. law. Learn more on the Birth of U.S. Citizens Abroad webpage.

If a person is a U.S. citizen, he or she is not eligible for a visa. Any prospective applicant believing he or she may have a claim to U.S. citizenship should have his or her citizenship claim adjudicated (officially determined) by a consular officer at a U.S. Embassy or Consulate before applying for a U.S. visa.

I have dual citizenship. Which passport should I use to travel to the United States?

All U.S. citizens, even dual citizens/nationals, must enter and depart the United States using his/her U.S. passport.

Further Questions

How do I know whether to contact the Department of State or Department of Homeland Security about my issue?

Contact the Department of State, U.S. Embassy or Consulate abroad with questions about U.S. visas, including application, the status of visa processing, and for inquiries relating to visa denial. Once in the United States, the traveler falls under the authority (jurisdiction) of Department of Homeland Security.

The Department of Homeland Security, U.S. Citizenship and Immigration Services (USCIS) is responsible for the approval of all petitions, the authorization of permission to work in the United States, the issuance of extensions of stay, and change or adjustment of an applicant's status while the applicant is in the United States.

I would like to know if my friend has applied for a visa and what the status is. Who should I contact?

You may contact your friend, the visa applicant. Under U.S. law, specifically the Immigration and Nationality Act (INA) 222(f), visa records are confidential. Therefore, the visa applicant should inquire at the U.S. Embassy or Consulate abroad where he/she applied regarding necessary information about visa application status. Because of confidentiality of visa records, you'll need to ask your friend, the visa applicant your questions about whether a visa application was made, or a visa was issued or denied.

Visa Applicants from State Sponsors of Terrorism Countries

To find information regarding FAQs from visa applicants from state sponsors of terrorism countries please, go to the State Department's website.

How can you overcome a denial under US Immigration rule, Section 214 (b)?

Section 214(b) of the Immigration and Nationality Act (INA) establishes a presumption that every alien applying for a visa is an intending immigrant unless they can demonstrate otherwise. In other words, you are guilty until proven innocent, and the burden of proof is on you the applicant! So, the burden falls on the visa applicant to prove that they do not intend to stay permanently in the United States and meet the requirements for a nonimmigrant visa.

Steps to Overcome a 214(b)-Visa Denial

1. **Strong Ties to Your Home Country:** The primary consideration for consular officers is whether you have **strong ties** to your country of residence. These ties can include:
   - Career
   - Family responsibilities
   - Real estate ownership
   - Educational plans
   - Other commitments

Demonstrating these ties can help establish that you **do not intend to abandon your home country** and stay in the U.S. permanently.

2. **Evidence of Ties:** Compile evidence that supports your strong ties. For example:
   - **Employment:** If you have a job or a promising career in your home country, provide documentation.
   - **Family:** If you have family members (spouse, children, parents) in your home country, emphasize these relationships.
   - **Property Ownership:** If you own property, provide relevant documents.
   - **Educational Plans:** If you're pursuing education or have educational commitments, highlight them.
   - **Financial Ties:** Show financial stability and ongoing financial responsibilities.
3. **Reapply with New Evidence:** Although there is no **official appeal process** for a 214(b) denial, you can reapply with **credible, new, and compelling evidence** that demonstrates your strong ties outside the U.S. and aligns with the terms of the visa you are seeking.
4. **Consult an Immigration Attorney:** Seek advice from an **experienced immigration attorney**. They can:
   - Guide you through the process
   - Help identify the specific reason for your denial
   - Assist in building a **stronger case** for your next application

How Long Does It Take to Overcome a 214(b) Refusal?

Overcoming a 214(b) refusal can vary significantly based on individual circumstances, the specific visa category, and the steps taken. However, here are some general considerations:

1. **Reapplication Timing:** After receiving a 214(b) denial, you can **reapply immediately**. There is no mandatory waiting period. However, it's essential to address the reasons for the initial denial and gather additional evidence before reapplying.
2. **Evidence Preparation:** The time required to gather **strong evidence** depends on your situation. You'll need to demonstrate substantial ties to your home country. This process may involve collecting documents related to:
    - Employment
    - Family
    - Property ownership
    - Educational plans
    - Financial stability
3. **Consular Processing Time:** Once you submit your new application, the **consular processing time** varies. It can take **several weeks to a few months**. Factors affecting processing time include:
    - Specific U.S. embassy or consulate
    - Their workload
    - The visa category
4. **Interview Scheduling:** After submitting your application, you'll be scheduled for an **interview**. The wait time for an interview appointment can also vary. Some consulates have **longer wait times** due to high demand.
5. **Interview Outcome:** During the interview, consular officers will assess your case. If they are satisfied with your evidence and find that you meet the nonimmigrant visa requirements, they may **approve your visa**. If not, you'll receive another refusal.
6. **Multiple Attempts:** Overcoming a 214(b) refusal may require **multiple attempts**. Each time you reapply, ensure that you've addressed the previous concerns and strengthened your case.

Common Reasons for a 214(b) Denial

A 214(b)-visa denial occurs when the consular officer believes that you intend to stay permanently in the United States, rather than temporarily as a nonimmigrant. Here are some common reasons for such denials:

- **Limited Ties to Your Home Country:** Lack of strong connections (such as a job, family, or assets) in your home country.

- **Extended Stays in the U.S.:** Prolonged visits to the U.S. may raise concerns about your genuine residency in your home country.
- **Vague or Unconvincing Purpose of Travel:** An unclear or weak purpose of travel.
- **Prior Visa Overstays or Immigration Violations:** Past violations can affect your eligibility for a new visa.
- **Country Conditions:** High visa denial rates from your country of origin can impact your application.
- **Inability to Demonstrate Sufficient Funds:** Failure to prove your financial ability to fund your trip.

Reapplying After a Visa Denial

Yes, you can **reapply** after a visa denial. There is no mandatory waiting period. However:

- If your refusal was due to a **simple error or missing document**, you can typically reapply immediately.
- If the refusal was due to **fraud or misrepresentation**, you may face a **reentry bar** (a waiting period) based on the severity of the offense.

When Reapplying:

- **Analyze the Refusal Letter:** Carefully review the reasons for your visa refusal. Understand what needs correction or improvement.
- **Gather Additional Information or Documentation:** Collect any additional evidence that strengthens your case.
- **Ensure that your new application addresses the issues identified** in the previous refusal.

Strengthening Your Case:

Consider the following strategies:

Strong Ties to Your Home Country: Emphasize your connections (job, family, property) in your home country.

Clear Purpose of Travel: Provide a well-defined and convincing reason for your U.S. visit.

Updated Documentation: Include updated bank statements, employment letters, educational certificates, or any relevant supporting documents.

Address Previous Concerns: If your prior application had weaknesses, ensure your new application resolves them.

Consult an Immigration Attorney: Seek professional guidance to build a stronger case.

How to Overcome Section 214(b) of the Immigration and Nationality Act.

According to some records, on average, more than a million visa applicants are rejected every year under Section 214(b) of the Immigration and Nationality Act.

Nonimmigrant visa applicants, excluding H-1B and L-1 visa holders, bear the responsibility of demonstrating their non-immigrant intent. Under 214(b), applicants must not only qualify for the visa but also agree to adhere to its terms upon entering the US. For B visa applicants, proof of a foreign residence and temporary visit intentions for business or pleasure is necessary.

The F visa applicants additionally need to demonstrate both qualifications for studies and the intent to return home after completion. Employment visa seekers must exhibit qualifications relevant to their visa type. Notably, there's no time restriction on invoking 214(b); for instance, prolonged previous stays in the US leading to suspected employment violations more than 10 years ago can prompt its application.

Consular officers commonly resort to visa revocation. This affects thousands annually due to "new information that came to light after visa issuance" that raises doubts about the applicant's qualification for the visa, potentially invoking 214(b) or other ineligibility

clauses. Consular staff regularly conduct B visa validation studies on applicants who received visas: they check to see whether the visa was used, and if so, whether the person returned in a timely fashion.

Rejected nonimmigrant visa applicants receive standard letters citing reasons such as insufficient ties to their home countries or failure to meet the requirements of the visa category, although the actual grounds for denial vary significantly. Often, the actual reason might not be legitimate or valid. Some common reasons might be limited ties to home country, interview problems, inaccurate consular understanding of facts or law, among others.

A 214(b) can be among the hardest refusals to overcome because of the broad consular discretion. An analysis of the underlying reason for the denial is imperative. For example, an individual came to us after his ESTA had been revoked and visa denied under Section

214(b). We did a deep dive into his situation. We learned that having spent substantial time in the US and being young, unmarried, and lacking permanent employment in his home country, CBP revoked his ESTA and refused his entry under Section 212(a)(7)(A)(i).

This incident can leave a black mark on his record, triggering a subsequent visa denial under Section

214(b). He then settled in a third country, had a serious American girlfriend, set up a small business, and established himself. He wanted to travel to the US to visit his girlfriend's family. Initially, we examined his CBP Record of Sworn Statement (I-877) and collaborated with him to devise a strategy: when would be the best time to apply; how could he strengthen his ties; how can he present his case after the incident with CBP? We assisted him in completing his DS-160 form and prepared him for the interview. After a brief interview, he was granted the B-2 visa.

As can be seen, every denial is different depending on one's circumstances. To see how we have helped individuals avoid 214(b) refusals or overcome 214(b) denials, please contact an Attorney to discuss your situation.

SECTION EIGHT

EXIT AND ENTRY INTERVIEWS

US Immigration Requirements for Entry and Exit Interviews

Entry Requirements

1. **Valid Passport:** Ensure your passport is valid for at least six months beyond your intended stay.
2. **Visa:** Depending on your nationality, you may need a visa. This could be a tourist visa (B-2), business visa (B-1), or other types of visas.
3. **ESTA:** Citizens of Visa Waiver Program countries must obtain an Electronic System for Travel Authorization (ESTA) before traveling.
4. **Customs Declaration:** Complete a customs declaration form, declaring any goods you are bringing into the country.
5. **Inspection by CBP Officers:** Upon arrival, you will be inspected by Customs and Border Protection (CBP) officers. They will verify your documents and may ask questions about your trip.

Exit Requirements

1. **Departure Record:** Ensure your departure is recorded. If you entered on a visa, you might need to submit an I-94 departure record.
2. **Visa Compliance:** Ensure you have not overstayed your visa. Overstaying can lead to penalties and future entry bans.
3. **Customs Declaration:** Declare any goods you are taking out of the country, especially if they exceed the duty-free allowance.

Tips for Entry and Exit Interviews

1. **Be Honest:** Answer all questions truthfully. Providing false information can lead to denial of entry or other penalties.
2. **Have Documentation Ready:** Keep all necessary documents, such as your passport, visa, and customs declaration, easily accessible.
3. **Know Your Itinerary:** Be prepared to explain the purpose of your visit, your travel plans, and where you will be staying.
4. **Stay Calm:** Remain calm and polite during the interview. Nervousness can sometimes be

misinterpreted.

Would you like more detailed information on any specific aspect of the entry or exit process?

Common Mistakes Travelers Make

1. **Overpacking:** Bringing too much can lead to heavy luggage and extra fees. Pack light and focus on versatile items.
2. **Not Checking Passport Validity:** Ensure your passport is valid for at least six months beyond your travel dates.
3. **Ignoring Travel Insurance:** Travel insurance can save you from unexpected expenses due to cancellations, medical emergencies, or lost luggage.
4. **Not Researching Destinations:** Learn about local customs, attractions, and weather to avoid cultural misunderstandings and make the most of your trip.
5. **Forgetting to Notify Your Bank:** Inform your bank about your travel plans to avoid having your cards blocked for suspicious activity.
6. **Miscalculating Connection Times:** Allow enough time between connecting flights to avoid missing your next flight.
7. **Not Checking Visa Requirements:** Ensure you have the necessary visas for your destination.
8. **Overplanning:** Leave some flexibility in your itinerary to enjoy spontaneous experiences.
9. **Showing Valuables:** Keep valuables out of sight to avoid attracting thieves.
10. **Not Checking the Weather Forecast:** Pack appropriate clothing for the weather at your destination.

How to Avoid Issues When Departing from the US

1. **Check Travel Advisories:** Stay informed about any travel advisories for your destination by visiting the U.S. Department of State's travel advisory page.
2. **Arrive Early:** Arrive at the airport at least 2-3 hours before your flight to allow time for check-in, security, and any unexpected delays.
3. **Have All Documents Ready:** Ensure you have your passport, visa, boarding pass, and any other required documents easily accessible.
4. **Declare Goods:** If you are carrying goods that need to be declared, make sure to do so to avoid fines.
5. **Enroll in STEP:** Enroll in the Smart Traveler Enrollment Program (STEP) to receive updates and alerts about your destination.

6. **Check Customs Regulations:** Be aware of what you can and cannot bring back into the U.S. to avoid issues with customs.
7. **Stay Informed:** Keep an eye on flight status updates and any changes to your travel plans.

How Can I Avoid Issues with Customs When Returning to the US?

To avoid issues with customs when returning to the US, follow these tips:

1. **Declare All Items**
    - **Honesty is Key:** Declare all items you are bringing back, including gifts, souvenirs, and any food products. If in doubt, declare it.
    - **Customs Declaration Form:** Complete the CBP Declaration Form 6059B accurately. You can do this on the plane, at a Global Entry kiosk, or an Automated Passport Control kiosk.
2. **Know What You Can and Cannot Bring**
    - **Prohibited Items:** Familiarize yourself with items that are prohibited or restricted, such as certain fruits, vegetables, plants, seeds, meats, and animal products.
    - **Duty-Free Limits:** Be aware of duty-free exemptions, which vary depending on the countries you visited and the length of your stay.
3. **Keep Receipts**
    - **Proof of Purchase:** Keep all receipts for items you purchased abroad. This helps in accurately declaring the value of goods and avoiding disputes.
4. **Pack Smart**
    - **Separate Items:** Pack items that need to be declared in an easily accessible part of your luggage. This makes the inspection process smoother.
    - **Avoid Overpacking:** Overpacking can lead to delays during inspection. Pack only what you need and keep your luggage organized.
5. **Be Prepared for Inspection**
    - **Cooperate with Officers:** Be polite and cooperative with Customs and Border Protection (CBP) officers. Answer their questions truthfully and provide any requested documentation.
    - **Random Checks:** Be aware that random checks can occur. Even if you have nothing to declare, you may still be selected for a secondary inspection.
6. **Stay Informed**

- **Check Regulations:** Before you travel, check the latest customs regulations and guidelines on the CBP website.
- **Travel Advisories:** Stay updated on any travel advisories or changes in customs regulations that might affect your return.

By following these tips, you can minimize the risk of issues when going through US customs and ensure a smooth return from your travels.

Would you like to know more about **Global Entry** and **Automated Passport Control kiosks**?

Global Entry

Global Entry is a program by U.S. Customs and Border Protection (CBP) that allows expedited clearance for pre-approved, low-risk travelers upon arrival in the United States.

Key Points:

1. **Eligibility:**
    - U.S. citizens, U.S. lawful permanent residents, and citizens of certain other countries can apply.
    - Applicants undergo a rigorous background check and an in-person interview.
2. **Benefits:**
    - Expedited processing through automatic kiosks at select airports.
    - No processing lines or paperwork.
    - Reduced wait times.
3. **Application Process:**
    - Complete an online application and pay a non-refundable fee.
    - Schedule an interview at a Global Entry Enrollment Center.
    - If approved, you will receive a Global Entry card.
4. **Using Global Entry:**
    - Upon arrival, proceed to the Global Entry kiosks.
    - Scan your passport or U.S. permanent resident card.
    - Place your fingerprints on the scanner for verification.
    - Complete the customs declaration.
    - Receive a transaction receipt and proceed to baggage claim and exit.

Automated Passport Control (APC) Kiosks

Automated Passport Control (APC) kiosks are self-service kiosks that expedite the entry process for

U.S. and Canadian citizens, as well as eligible Visa Waiver Program travelers.

Key Points:

1. **Eligibility:**
    - U.S. citizens, U.S. lawful permanent residents, Canadian citizens, and certain Visa Waiver Program travelers.
2. **Benefits:**
    - No pre-registration or membership required.
    - Reduces wait times by allowing travelers to submit their customs declaration and biographic information electronically.
3. **Using APC Kiosks:**
    - Scan your passport.
    - Take a photograph using the kiosk.
    - Answer customs declaration and biographic questions.
    - For Visa Waiver Program travelers, scan your fingerprints.
    - Receive a receipt confirming your information.
    - Proceed to a CBP officer for final verification.

Both **Global Entry** and **APC kiosks** aim to streamline the entry process, making it faster and more efficient for travelers.

SECTION NINE

Epilogue

In the beginning, all was darkness and void, and the spirit of God moved (migrated) over the face of the chaos **(Genesis 1:1).** To move is to migrate. The biblical story is a migration story. The Bible begins with God's spirit migrating over the face of the water, followed by God, who, after creating the birds, fish, and animals (all of which migrate), moved throughout creation looking for a caretaker for this world. Not finding one, God said, "Let us create humankind, male and female, in our own image..." **(Genesis 1:26).**

God did just that and created Adam and Eve in God's own image and gave them dominion over all the earth and told them to multiply and fill the earth. To do that, it was necessary for them to begin the human migration story. That story is told throughout the Bible and continues to this day in the movement of the migrating pilgrim people of God, who continue to move, to multiply, and to maintain and nourish the earth.

We are all part of God's great plan of migration. The great majority of people have either lived out the migration story or can trace their roots back to ancestors traveling from one land to another. In fact, if we embrace Adam and Eve as our original ancestors, we are all migrants in a strange land and very far from home. Take a moment and consider your personal migration. Are you where you were born? Have you moved, and, if so, for what reason? How many times have you moved? Many of us move by choice, others by necessity, and yet others by
force. Humankind's story is a story of migration.

We all are, or have been migrants, immigrants, refugees, or asylum seekers. As believers in the God of Abraham, we trace our roots back to the Garden of Eden located around four rivers: Pishon, Gihon, Tigris, and Euphrates. Although the exact location of the garden is not known geographically, we can surmise the location from the full text which says the Gihon flows around the land of ancient kingdom of Cush or around ancient Sudan, (which is now known as modern day Ethiopia) and the Tigris River is east of Assyria and the other is the Euphrates.

Therefore, using biblical data, the Garden of Eden can be surmised to be in either Ethiopia or modern-day Iraq, just like the Mississippi River can be said to have sourced from Lake Itasca, Minnesota to New Orleans, Louisiana, (nearly 2,500 miles apart). Those of us who live in the Western World are a long way from home and living in lands that were not even known to have existed in biblical times.

Adam and Eve had to emigrate a very long way.

The Creator God brought Adam and Eve into being. According to Maruskin, there are two creation stories in the Bible. The first is the full chapter of **Genesis 1-2:3,** in which God creates the world and all things in it in six days. God states that it is very good and rests on the seventh day. In **Genesis 2:4-25,** God first created Adam and then Eve and gives instructions on living in the Garden, and how to live off the land. Adam and Eve do not follow God's directions, and, because of their disobedience, they are eventually exiled (Genesis 3:22-24), but not before God sews skins together to cover them and protect them from the elements.

God's concern for the strangers moving throughout the world begins at this point and continues throughout the Bible.

Welcoming the stranger is the central theme of biblical hospitality. Africans are known to be very welcoming to strangers. This concept is an inclusive hospitality that always makes room for strangers. It also shows that no person is to be excluded. The first example of inclusive hospitality is seen when Adam and Eve's son Cain kills his brother, Abel **(Genesis 4:8-16).** As punishment, God makes him a wanderer on the earth. But before sending him away, God puts a mark of protection on Cain – so that no one will kill him. The criminal migrant was protected so he would not be harmed in his wanderings. Earlier European migrants to the new world were Europe's rejected bunch, even including the Vikings! Yes, it would behoove you to know, that White settlers of the antebellum South were Europe's cultural rejects, who fought wars against the Indian Natives-who happened to be their benefactors. In fact, ancient White American immigrants to the new world had come to bastardize the ideas of Christianity to create a superiority complex amongst people: Read, Luke 22 verse 25.

(Today very few migrants [criminals or not] are protected. If they are undocumented, they are arrested and deported. Asylum seekers, who have been persecuted in their homelands, are routinely placed in immigration detention in American ports, and must defend themselves or seek legal help from behind bars.)

According to Maruskin, as humans multiplied, the population of the earth continued to increase until it became corrupt and filled with violence. God's plan included a great flood that would wipe out all of humanity except for one small remnant. At over five hundred years of age, according to the bible, Noah was chosen to continue humanity. With the help of his wife, sons, and their wives, he built the ark and filled it with two of each kind of living creature as attested to in (**Genesis 6:5–8:22).**

The "Noahs" were forced to flee their land because of the great flood, which was probably the greatest natural disaster in the course of human history, perhaps even greater than the tsunami in 2004 and the hurricanes of 2005. These events are considered to have been of biblical proportions and to have happened in areas with much denser populations than those of ancient biblical history, when the world was still being populated, and therefore may have resulted in much higher loss of life.

Noah and his family according to Maruskin, became migrants without a known destination. Eventually their ark landed several thousand miles from Ellis Island, in New York, and the inhabitants were blessed by God and were told, "Be fruitful and multiply, and fill the earth" **(Genesis 9:1b).** Later, scripture tells us that from the three sons of Noah – Shem, Ham, and Japheth – and their wives, the whole earth was populated **(Genesis 9:19).**

"It is important to note that, in today's world, victims of a natural disaster are not considered eligible for refugee resettlement. Many of them spend the rest of their lives stranded in a strange country or displaced in their homelands. This happened to thousands of displaced persons from the Gulf Coast of the United States and to the victims of the earthquake in Pakistan in 2005). Victims of natural disasters generally need food, water, medicines, and shelter, to include psychological counselling for their daily survival"**.** Retrieved December 9, 2023. Source unknown.

Genesis 10 gives an accounting of the migration of Noah's sons and their descendants as "from these the nations spread abroad on the earth after the flood." Note that there was freedom of movement. As the Church of the brethren teaches: "God made people – people made borders."

"It is theorized that if people were free to migrate anywhere in the world, the world's population would balance out and everyone would be able to meet their physical needs in God's economy. Much of the world is starving; however, the world would be able to sustain us all if the products and produce of the world were shared more equitably. Or, if arable lands were harvested more evenly. Part of inclusive hospitality is being willing to share what we have with those who do not have it." Retrieved December 9, 2023. Source unknown.

The whole earth spoke one language as the family of Noah migrated **(Genesis 11).** As they had a common language, they built a tower to the heavens. This did not please God, who "scattered them abroad from there over the face of all the earth…Therefore it was called Babel." The migration story continued with multiple languages developing as people moved from one location to another and cultures were created to complement each migration.

"It also causes one to wonder about the wisdom of those calling for English only in the United States.

The first explorers brought Spanish into the New World, which was already inhabited by indigenous Native Americans with many languages". Retrieved December 9, 2023. Source unknown.

In addition, the US Southwestern states were originally part of Mexico, in which Spanish was the first language of those states. English is the second western language that is spoken in the US and although the primary language, it is enhanced by numerous other languages, which further improves the linguistic traditions of the US.).

The generations continued to populate the earth, and the biblical story picked up with Terah (the father of Abram), Abram, his wife Sarai, and his brother's son Lot settling in Haran-present day Turkey, bordering North of Syria by 12 miles. It is there that God spoke to Abram and said, "Go from your country and your kindred and your father's house to the land that I will show you" **(Genesis 12:1).**

Abram, Sarai, and Lot became migrants going into and out of Canaan, to the hill country on the east of Bethel. They then journeyed toward the Negreb and because of famine went down to Egypt to reside there as aliens – strangers! (**Genesis 12:10).** They came out of Egypt and eventually separated, with Lot settling near Sodom on the plain of the Jordan and Abram settling by the oaks of Mamre in Hebron (Genesis 13).

"The God of Abram instructed him to migrate just as today, the voice of God continues to direct people to paths of migration and immigration. Within any faith-based group, many people can be found who have embarked on a faith journey taking them to strange lands because they heard God calling them to migrate to a new land, job, or specific ministry." Retrieved December 9, 2023. Source unknown.

In **Genesis 14**, we see the first of very many biblical battles. In the war, Lot is first taken captive and forced to leave his land. Eventually, Abram rescued him, and he was able to return.

It is important to remember that whenever and wherever there was war, there was always people who are being uprooted and there are migration stories, refugee stories, and asylum stories along the way. Note that, in biblical times, as in previous centuries before now, most victims of wars were the warriors themselves. But, in the 20th and 21st century, most victims are civilians, and most civilians are women and children. Eighty 80 percent of the world's refugees are women and children, as are those being killed. They are often referred to as collateral damage.

In **Genesis 15**, God told Abram of his role in the migration story. It is stated, "Know this for certain, that your offspring shall be aliens in a land that is not theirs, and shall be slaves there, and they shall be oppressed for four hundred years" **(Genesis 15:13).** God continued by telling Abram that his offspring would come back to the land of Abram in four generations.

The story continues as Abram and Sarai exercise their desire for children. At Sarai's insistence, Hagar, the Egyptian slave-girl, the foreigner, bears Abram a child,

Ishmael. Eventually they were exiled into the wilderness and God promises to make Ishmael a great nation – the same promise given later to Isaac in **(Genesis 21).**

Ishmael's offspring become the Muslims and populate much of the Middle East, Africa, and Asia, and spread across the world. It is important to remember the geographical location of biblical history and to look at the ethnicity of the patriarchs and matriarchs, who are the foundation of the Christian faith. They were Africans but are mistakenly referred to today as middle easterners-why? because there is no such location as the west easterners, and their descendants are presently being targeted and imprisoned because of their ethnicity.

After the birth of Ishmael and prior to the birth of Isaac, God renames Abram and calls him Abraham and Sarai become Sarah. We are then exposed to the biblical mandate to care for the stranger, as one never knows when the stranger might be God. In **Genesis 18:1-8**, God appears to Abraham as three strangers near the oaks at Mamre. He offers the three men – the strangers – hospitality. He refers to them as "my Lord" and offers them the best of what he has. This is the first biblical description of ideal inclusive hospitality – of giving the very best to strangers – who in this case turned out to be God.

The biblical concept of hospitality is based on offering hospitality to the stranger, the sojourner, the alien, the migrant, and the foreigner. It can be verified in **Deuteronomy 6,** which speaks of being brought into a new land by the Lord. This, and many other passages in Deuteronomy, which will be included later, stress the importance of being one with the strangers in the land.

The importance of this concept of hospitality is seen in the story of Sodom and Gomorrah. Lot welcomed the angels, but the townspeople did not. Their lack of hospitality to the stranger brought about their destruction. "Behold, this was the guilt of your sister Sodom: She and her daughters had arrogance, abundant food and careless ease, but she did not help the poor and needy" **(Ezekiel 16:49).** This story not only points to **Matthew 25** in the New Testament but also shows the importance of listening to God and moving when told to move – without looking back. Lot's wife looked back and became a pillar of salt.

The refugee story is one of not being able to look back, because there is often only death and destruction behind. The refugee seeks refuge and safety and sanctuary. You cannot move forward if you continue to look backwards. Those of us in safer lands are mandated and blessed to welcome immigrants with open arms. Welcoming refugees, migrants, immigrants, and/or asylum seekers is an example of inclusive hospitality.

Building a fence around the borders of the US borders to keep out strangers in need has not, and neither will that stop migration to the US. Instead, the fence has kept out Jesus Christ and the blessings Americans would receive by welcoming the strangers.

The biblical migration story continued with famine, causing Isaac to settle in the land of Gerar as an alien **(Genesis 26:2).** Then it picked up with Jacob traveling to another land for a wife. Later he was forced to flee because of his brother's violence. God directed him to Bethel. We eventually learn that Jacob settled in "the land where his father had lived as an alien, the land of Canaan" **(Genesis 37:1).** Slavery and trafficking are experienced when Joseph was sold into slavery by his brothers and was transported to Egypt.

Again, Maruskin (2005) hinted that slavery continues to this day under the guise of trafficking. Men, women, and children are trafficked and brought into the U.S. and countries around the world, and forced into hard labor, domestic service, and sexual slavery.

Joseph overcame the circumstances that forced him into slavery. The captive slave rose to power as an integral part of the Egyptian government. He had an opportunity to retaliate for having been sold into slavery, when famine caused mass hunger in his homeland and his brothers came to Egypt seeking grain. Instead of striking back, Joseph followed God's mandate to care for strangers by offering inclusive hospitality and welcomed them, as though they were strangers (in fact, he pretended that they were strangers), gave them grain, and sent them back.

The circle was eventually completed when Joseph's father and brothers, their families, flocks, and all they possessed left Canaan and migrated to Goshen, where there was food and Joseph welcomed them **(Genesis 37-47)**

Neither famine nor starvation are grounds for asylum, refugee status, or immigration. United States immigration laws do not allow persons to enter this country simply because they are starving and need to feed their families. This economy needs the migrant workers, who come to feed their families, but it forces them to live undocumented lives, and to work in substandard conditions.

The book of **Exodus**, the story of the Exodus – is the story of the movement of the people of God away from slavery and injustice to freedom and a new life. It is perhaps the world's greatest and best-known migration story. Exodus began with the Hebrews being oppressed by their taskmasters. Their persecution was increased with the orders of the King of Egypt to have all newborn Hebrew boys killed.

However, one was protected and hidden until he was three months old, at which time he was placed in a basket in the river. In today's language he would be referred to as an "Unaccompanied Alien Child." The child was rescued from the river by Pharaoh's daughter, who chose to ignore her father's orders to kill all male infants. She named him Moses and raised him in Pharaoh's palace.

Unaccompanied children picked up at a U.S. border, unless immediately returned to their country of origin, are placed in juvenile detention facilities. If they are very lucky, they are placed in foster care until a decision about their immigration status is reached. Many such children have been found to die.

Moses grew up to witness the oppressive treatment of the Hebrews by the Egyptians. In response to this injustice, he killed an Egyptian, and became a criminal alien, who fled for his life to a strange land. He was taken in and given sanctuary in Midian.

Today, in the U.S., he would be put in prison, serve his sentence, and eventually be deported back to Egypt, to be imprisoned there if that country would accept him. If it would not, he would spend the rest of his life in prison in the United States.

In Midian, Moses married Zipporah and was eventually called by God to return to Egypt because, in God's words, "The cry of the Israelites has now come to me; I have also seen how the Egyptians oppress them. So come, I will send you to bring my people, the Israelites, out of Egypt." Moses wonders how he could possibly do this, and God replied, "I will be with you" **(Exodus 3:1- 3:12).** The key phrase was "I will be with you." In the Exodus story, God migrated with the Hebrews.

If you have been reading this book with all seriousness, have you come to notice that God himself is a migrant moving with the people? Throughout the Book of Exodus, God traveled with the people and continues to travel with the migrants till today. Yet, in America of today, many old immigrants rail against new immigrants forgetting that they themselves were once migrants in a strange world.

Moses returned to Egypt and facilitated the Hebrew Exodus through a series of plagues and dialogues with Pharaoh meant to bring about the release of his people. When the Hebrews were finally permitted to leave, they left as most refugees leave, with not enough time to pack, but with God leading them. As with all refugees, the Hebrews had to leave abruptly and leave forever, heading to an unknown but promised land.

In **Exodus 14:7** we read, "When Pharaoh let the people go, God did not lead them by way of the land of the Philistines...God led the people by the roundabout way of the wilderness toward the Red Sea..."

"The Lord went in front of them in a pillar of cloud by day.... and a pillar of fire by night, to give them light, that they might travel by day and night. Neither ...left its place in front of the people." God migrated with the people. God was, is, and always will be a migrant, migrating with the migrants of the world, seeking to protect them and find haven for them. And it is important to remember that this migration pattern also included care of the refugees. God provided manna and water and all they needed to survive.

Eventually the Hebrews reached Canaan and prepared to enter the Promised Land. According to Maruskin, a compass might have taken a few years off the 40-year journey, which if done today using a map is an 11-day walk. They entered the Promised Land, and the Canaanites had their land taken away from them, became refugees and

internally displaced persons, and were made to do forced labor. Thus, the joy of the Hebrews resulted from the destruction and displacement of the Canaanites. There cannot be victors without victims.

Details can be found in Exodus, Numbers, Deuteronomy. An example that is even closer to home is the knowledge that the indigenous people of North America, the Native Americans, were decimated from disease and violence and placed on reservations. Their homeland was taken away from them, so others could claim it as their promised land. Along with the details of entering the Promised Land, the Bible also contains advice on how the people are to act once they are in that land, and one of the first instructions is found in **Deuteronomy 10:17-19**, "For the Lord your God is God of gods and Lord of lords, the great God, mighty and awesome, who is not partial and takes no bribe, who executes justice for the orphan and the widow, and who love the strangers, providing them food and clothing. You shall also love the stranger, for you were strangers in the land of Egypt."

Deuteronomy includes numerous statements of how God's people are to care for the aliens in the land. In **Deuteronomy 14:19,** we read, "The Levite, because he has no portion of inheritance among you, and the alien, the orphan and the widow who are in your town, shall come and eat and be satisfied, in order that the Lord your God may bless you in all the work of your hand which you do."

Believe it or not, many of us in today's America, do not relate our blessings from God as directly dependent on our welcoming the stranger among us. God blesses us with grace and God expects us to respond to the blessings we are given by blessing others.

Additional passages in **Deuteronomy** are: " **23:7,** "You shall not detest an Edomite, for he is your brother; you shall not detest an Egyptian, because you were an alien in his land." " **24:17**, "You shall not pervert the justice due an alien or an orphan, nor take a widow's garment in pledge." " **25:19**, "When you reap your harvest in your field and have forgotten a sheaf in the field, you shall not go back to get it; it shall be for the alien, for the orphan, and for the widow, in order that the Lord your God may bless you in all the work of your hands." (The Bible, NKJV).

All of **Deuteronomy 26** is important, as it shows the relationship between each person's ancestry and the responsibility that is placed on the people of God to care for the alien. One example is **Deuteronomy 26:5b**, which reads, "A wandering Aramean was my ancestor**;** he went down into Egypt and lived there as an alien…." We are reminded that we all spring from wanderers on this earth.

In fact, care of the alien is so important that **Deuteronomy 27:19** states, "Cursed is he who distorts the justice due an alien, orphan, and widow. And all the people shall say Amen.

Along with Genesis, Exodus, Leviticus, and Deuteronomy in the Hebrew Bible giving guidance for treating refugees, we also find advice in Psalms. It is important to note that refugees will often refer to the Psalms that they read and recited to themselves as they were fleeing and seeking a haven. Why is that?

One that is used very often is Psalm **91**, which begins: "You who live in the shelter of the Most High, who abide in the shadow of the Almighty, will say to the Lord, "My refuge and my fortress; my God, in whom I trust." For God will deliver you from the snare of the fowler and from the deadly pestilence; he will cover you with his pinions, and under his wings you will find refuge…." Amen.

As well as giving hope to the uprooted people of the world since biblical times, the Psalms also define the refugee experience. This is best seen in **Psalm 137**: "By the rivers of Babylon – we sat down there, and we wept when we remembered Zion. On the willows there we hung up our harps. For there our captors asked us for songs, and our tormentors asked for mirth, saying, 'Sing us one of the songs of Zion!' How could we sing the Lord's song in a foreign land?"

The story of uprooted people continues throughout the Hebrew Bible as the Hebrews claim the Promised Land and are eventually sent into exile and later return. This pattern can be followed in Kings, Chronicles, Esther, Jeremiah, Isaiah, Ezekiel, and Amos.

In 605 BC, Daniel and his three friends were captured by Nebuchadnezzar and taken to Babylon. Eventually the prophets Ezekiel and Isaiah were also in exile. It is while in exile that Isaiah prophesies the coming of Christ. See **Isaiah 40-55.**

In Isaiah **40:3** we read, “A voice cries out: "In the wilderness prepare the way of the Lord, make straight in the desert a highway for our God.” In addition, in **Isaiah 61: 1- 2a** we read the words that are on the scroll that Jesus reads when he first stands up to read in the synagogue to formally begin his ministry. They are: “The Spirit of the Lord God is upon me, because the Lord has anointed me; he has sent me to bring good news to the oppressed, to bind up the brokenhearted, to proclaim liberty to the captives, and release to the prisoners; to proclaim the year of the Lord’s favor….” The time of exile was a time of prophecy preparing the way of the Lord.

In Amos 5:24, the prophet calls for justice to roll down like water and righteous like an ever-flowing stream. In God’s economy, all people are sisters and brothers and share equally and are welcomed. The stranger is cherished and welcomed.

Literally everyone was on the move and most went into exile at some time. This includes the prophets, the priests, and the people. Exile shows no mercy; however, there are persons who did not and do not go into exile. **2 Kings 24:14** explains, “Then he led away into exile all Jerusalem and all the captains and all the mighty men of valor, ten thousand captives, and all the craftsmen and the smiths. None remained except the poorest people of the land.”

The migration story is key to understanding biblical ancestry. In the book of **Ruth**, one family is the focal point. It began with Elimelech, his wife Naomi, and their two sons, who took Moabite wives, having to leave Judah and move to Moab because of a famine. Eventually all the men died, and the women were left alone. Naomi was a stranger in a strange land. She learned that there was no longer famine in Judah, so she exercised her right to return. However, she did not go alone. Ruth, her Moabite daughter-in-law, said, in **Ruth 1:16**, “Do not press me to leave you or to turn back from following you! Where you go, I will go; where you lodge, I will lodge; your people shall be my people and your God my God!”

The rest of the story is the story of Boaz adhering closely to God’s requirement to offer hospitality to the stranger. He permitted Ruth to glean, protected her, and eventually married her bringing the undocumented sojourner into the fold, making her part of the family.

Job also knew the importance of caring for strangers. In **Job 31:32**, he states, “The alien has not lodged outside, (for) I have opened my doors to the traveler”.

The Hebrew Bible closes with an admonition from God through the prophet Malachi, who, in **Malachi 3:5,** repeats the words of the Lord of Hosts, “Then I will draw near to you for judgment; and I will be a swift witness against the sorcerers and against the adulterers and against those who swear falsely, and against those who oppress the hired workers in their wages, the widow and the orphan, against those who thrust aside the alien, and do not fear me, says the Lord of hosts."

The New Testament begins with a migration story, and perhaps the only documented, recorded "alien" story. Alien is a term that is offensive to many, as it suggests a vision of someone from outer space. Looking at it in that manner, one might say that perhaps Jesus was truly an "alien." He came from heaven (the outer limits of space – although he did tell us the kingdom is within and took the form of a human being to become for us the Refugee Christ. The reality is that all Christians owe their salvation to a refugee, Jesus.

Jesus was born in Bethlehem, to which his parents had traveled because of the taxation decree. Tradition says the Christ Child was born in a manger, a stable, a shed like the children of many of today's migrants, who are born along the road as their parents seek work and a place to call home. The news of his birth was given first to the shepherds, the group of people lowest on the social scale at that time. They were also a group of migrants, who moved and lived with their flocks doing seasonal work.

Also, at the birth of Jesus, "Magi" from the east, who were probably astrological magicians or sorcerers from Persia, Babylon, or Arabia, come to Jerusalem seeking the "child who has been born King of the Jews." The Bible does not indicate that there were three Magi or that they were kings. In fact, a distinction of "king" and "Magi" is made in **Matthew 2:1.**

The term "Magi" comes from the same root as "magic" and "magicians." Such people (Dan. 2:2) watched the stars, and were able to predict solar and lunar eclipses, and attempted to predict events to come. Thus, strangers/foreigners from afar read the stars and identified the Messiah.

According to Luke, Jesus, Mary, and Joseph stayed in Bethlehem until they took Jesus to the temple in Jerusalem to be dedicated and then returned to Nazareth. But, according to Matthew, they stayed in Bethlehem until the visit of the Magi.

It is estimated that Jesus was about two years old at the time. Once the Magi left, an angel appeared to Joseph in a dream and said, "Get up, take the child and his mother, and flee to Egypt, and remain there until I tell you; for Herod is about to search for the child, to destroy him. Then Joseph got up, took the child and his mother by night, and went to Egypt and remained there until the death of Herod. This was to fulfill what had been spoken by the Lord through the prophet, "Out of Egypt I have called my son" **(Matthew 2:13-15).**

Jesus, Mary, and Joseph became asylum seekers in Egypt. Without travel documents, they crossed the border, looking for safety and sanctuary. Although they were strangers, someone took them in. Someone welcomed them and protected them. Keep ethnicity in mind, to be able to hide in Egypt, the Holy Family would have had to look very much like the people of that land, which would be very different from the modern-day images of them.

Meanwhile, in Bethlehem, Herod had plans to find and kill Jesus. When he discovered the Magi had left without telling him the location of the Child, he ordered the killing of all the children in and around Bethlehem who were two years old and under.

Jesus and his family fled political and religious persecution. These conditions are both warranted present day grounds to seek asylum and refugee status.

However, were the Holy Family to arrive at a U.S. border today, it is most likely that Jesus would be sent to a children's detention center, Mary to a women's detention center, and Joseph to a men's detention center. Each would be required to secure their own legal help, or plead their case, on their own, for asylum. Asylum seekers do not receive legal help from the government, and although there are a few family shelters in the US, most families are separated on arrival at the border.

After the death of Herod, the family was able to return to their home, in the district of Galilee, in a town called Nazareth. That was not Jesus' last move. **Matthew 4:12 explains** that eventually he left Nazareth and made his home in Capernaum by the sea. It was from there that he began to call his disciples to follow him. Later in **Luke 9:58**, Jesus says, "The foxes have holes and the birds of the air have nests, but the son of man has nowhere to lay His head."

This is the migrant's story. Like Jesus, who had a home in Capernaum, but often no place to lay his head because of his travels, today's migrants, too, have homes in their countries, but no place to lay their heads in the country to which they have migrated.

Throughout his life, Jesus moved around. He called his disciples to leave what they were doing and to follow him. In fact, if Jesus and the twelve disciples tried to enter the United States today, they would either be the victims of expedited removal, which means they would be immediately returned to their point of origin, or they would, most probably, be put in immigration detention.

Jesus was quite active in supporting the people most in need. He readily saw the plight of the day laborers and resonated with their desire to make a living. Most notable is **Matthew 20:1-16**. In it, he likens the kingdom of heaven to a landowner who hires laborers for his vineyard. He hires people throughout the day and pays them all equally, finally summarizing what he does with "the last will be first and the first will be last." Jesus understood the plight of the workers and resonated with the Hebrew Bible mandate to treat the workers fairly.

This importance of just wages is seen in **Malachi 3:5,** when God says, "... I will be swift to bear witness against.... those who oppress the hired workers in their wages, the widow, and the orphan, against those who thrust aside the alien, and do not fear me, says the Lord of Hosts." The fair treatment of day laborers is seen in **Leviticus 19:13,** "You shall not defraud your neighbor; you shall not steal; and you shall not keep for yourself the wages of a day-laborer until morning."

The most compelling argument Christ gave for caring for the stranger can be found in **Matthew 25:35-41**. In it he gives the inheritance of the kingdom to those who cared for him by stating, "...for I was hungry and you gave me food, I was thirsty and you gave me something to drink, I was a stranger and you welcomed me, I was naked and you gave me clothing, I was sick and you took care of me, I was in prison and you visited me.... Truly I tell you, just as you did it to one of the least of these who are members of my family, you did it to me."

Persons working with immigrant, migrant, refugee, and asylum populations are often heard wondering how to convince more churchgoers to help these members of Christ's family. Jesus was very clear in his message: Help them and you go to heaven. Don't help them and you go to hell. Jesus came to bring a new commandment, a commandment of love of all people.

He taught love of God, neighbor, and yourself; and he added a completely new thought – a completely new teaching – love your enemy. With that he commanded us to love all people. There is no room in Christ's teachings for "them and us" mentality. Yet, in **Matthew 25:40**, he clearly states that all, including people who might be seen as the "least of these," are members of his family.

When Jesus is asked by the young man, "Who is my neighbor?", Jesus answers through the parable of the Good Samaritan in **Luke 10:33,** who was on a journey, came upon a man – not a Samaritan, most probably someone who would not have spoken to the Samaritan. However, the man had been badly beaten and needed help. When the Samaritan saw him, he felt compassion, and cared for him. The Samaritan would have been considered the stranger in the land, the outsider, not a citizen of the land. His presence was not wanted by the people of the land, and yet he, the outsider, is the one who helps the man who has been robbed. He shows compassion and responds by showing love to the person who would consider him an enemy. For this act he became known throughout history as "The Good Samaritan."

Jesus' life was a life of service to others, without regard for their national origin. His service to strangers can be seen in **Luke 17:1-19** with the healing of the lepers. Ten are made clean, but only one returns. In verse **17-18**, when only the foreigner returns, Jesus asked, "But the other nine, where are they? Were we not ten made clean? Was none of them found to return and give praise to God except this foreigner?" Jesus offered his healing love to all. Americans are called to do the same, but do they?

Jesus was not only a refugee and a migrant. He was also undocumented both as a child and at the end of his life. We know that Jesus was crucified "outside the gates" of the city because he was not a citizen **(Hebrews 13:12).** As Christians, we know that he died for the sins of the world, but at that time the theological implications of his death were not considered in handing down his sentence. Jesus was crucified because he was one with the oppressed and marginalized people of that time, and the religious and political powers feared he was instigating an uprising of the poor.

The Romans thought Jesus was planning to overthrow those Romans, who were in power. He was one with the stranger, the sojourner, the migrant, the day laborer, the least, the last, and the lost. He did not have the rights of a citizen. In fact, he was one with each undocumented migrant in the world. Because he did not have these rights, his crucifixion had to be outside the gates, and it was in the garbage dump of the city. He suffered, so others would not have to do the same.

The next time you hear of the death of an undocumented person, stop a moment, and think of the undocumented Christ and remember we never know when the person we are looking at is Christ in one of his disguises. Since 1995, over 3,000 migrants have died crossing the U.S./Mexico border in their search for work and survival. American evangelical Christianity is simply at odds with these Christian mandates.

By reinforcing biblical hospitality, the New Testament urges validation of each person. **Hebrews 13:1-3** urges, "Let mutual love continue. Do not neglect to show hospitality to strangers, for by doing that some have entertained angels without knowing it. Remember those who are in prison, as though you were in prison with them, those who are being tortured, as though you yourselves were being tortured." The Greek word for hospitality is "philoxenos." It means love for the stranger and was recognized as a primary characteristic of the early followers of Christ.

The mandate was, is, and remains clear: to live lives of inclusive hospitality, to recognize that Christ comes to us in the form of the stranger, and to be one with the prisoners, the persecuted, the undocumented, the refugee, the migrant, the immigrant, the stranger. Throughout the New Testament, we see people moving freely, without borders, and we see new life, as their lives are changed through contact with Christ and/or his disciples. Paul reinforces this teaching in **Romans 12:13**, with, "Contribute to the needs of the saints; and extend hospitality to strangers."

Jesus' last message to his disciples was a migration/immigration message. It is a statement that not only calls for migration, but also insists on it. **Matthew 28:18-19 is** the great commission, in which Jesus says, "All authority in heaven and on earth has been given to me. Go therefore, and make disciples of all nations, baptizing them in the name of the Father and of the Son and of the Holy Spirit, and teaching them to obey everything that I have commanded you. And remember I am with you always, to the end of the age."

But the story was not over at that point. It continued, as followers of Christ became migrant messengers, taking his teachings throughout the known world. They recognize that divisions between all of humankind have been dismantled. **Galatians 3:29-29** states, "There is no longer Jew or Greek; there is no longer slave or free; there is no longer male or female; for all of you are one in Christ Jesus." They took this message and belief with them, and they traveled as immigrants, as refugees, and as migrants. They were and are imprisoned, they were and are persecuted, and they were and are exiled. Religious persecution is still grounds for asylum.

The early disciples believed they were strangers in this life moving on to the heavenly kingdom. In **I Peter 2:11-13,** they are reminded that they are aliens and exiles in this world. They are the beginning of a long line of pilgrim people and a part of the continuing biblical migratory cycle following the mandates of God, the teachings of Christ and the guidance of the Holy Spirit.

The New Testament ends with John's writings in the Book of Revelation, in exile, on the Isle of Patmos. The biblical story that began with migration ends with migration and exile and continues as the migrant God accompanies every migrant on his or her journey of hope. And it extends far, far, into the future, with the new Jerusalem, the city of God, on the move, coming from heaven to earth. When that happens, the circle of migration would have been completed, and the world made new.

THE END

www.ingramcontent.com/pod-product-compliance
Lightning Source LLC
LaVergne TN
LVHW070851210926
848482LV00016B/914
* 9 7 9 8 3 4 9 2 7 4 8 1 7 *